Obama Talks Back

Global Lessons—A Dialogue with America's Young Leaders

Obama Talks Back

Global Lessons—A Dialogue with America's Young Leaders

GREGORY J. REED, Esq

Foreword by William Alexander Haley

Amber Books

Phoenix   New York   Los Angeles

Obama Talks Back
Global Lessons—A Dialogue with America's Young Leaders
Published by Amber Books
An Imprint of Amber Communications Group, Inc
1334 East Chandler Boulevard, Suite 5-D67
Phoenix, AZ 85048
E-mail: AMBERBK@aol.com
WWW.AMBERBOOKS.COM

Tony Rose, Publisher/Editorial Director
Yvonne Rose, Associate Publisher, Senior Editor
Caitlin Buchanan, Editor
The Printed Page, Interior and Cover Design

Amber Books are available at special discounts for bulk purchases, sales promotions, fund raising or educational purposes. For details, contact: Special Sales Department, Amber Books, 1334 E. Chandler Boulevard, Suite 5-D67, Phoenix, AZ 85048, USA. Phone: 602-743-7211 or fax: 480-283-0991.

Paperback ISBN # 978-1-937269-38-8
Ebook ISBN # 978-1-937269-39-5

Library of Congress Cataloging-in-Publication Data

Obama, Barack.
[Correspondence. Selections.]
Obama talks back : global lessons : a dialogue with America's young leaders / Gregory J. Reed ; foreword by William Alexander Haley.
     pages cm
Includes bibliographical references and index.
ISBN 978-1-937269-38-8 (alk. paper)
1. Obama, Barack--Correspondence. 2. Presidents--United States--Correspondence.
3. Youth--United States--Correspondence. 4. Children--United States--Correspondence.
5. American letters. I. Reed, Gregory J., editor. II. Title.
E908.A4 2012
973.932092--dc23
                    2012040437

Dedicated

To those who have given themselves selflessly to humanity in the face of immeasurable odds and unknown forces:

Mother, Ghandi, Carter G. Woodson, Robert Green, Clifton Wharton, Jr., Jack Boland, Johnnie Cochran, Jr., Madame C.J. Walker, Robert Millender, Coleman A. Young, Malik Shabazz, Rosa Parks, Martin Luther King, Jr., Nelson Mandela, CL. Franklin, Oprah Winfrey, Deepak Chopra, Barack, Michelle, Malia and Sasha Obama…and countless others…for their courage and bravery.

We Shall Overcome

*Relationships are immeasurable resources
to have that can exceed wealth....nourish them well*

Acknowledgement

I thank each student, school, and teacher who, at this historic moment in time, contributed to *Obama Talks Back-Global Lessons—A Dialogue with America's Young Leaders* —a movement that is greater than anyone of us alone. I thank the volunteers who helped directly and indirectly and shared in the collective efforts and results in immeasurable ways:

Otis Stanley, Patrice Wilson, Monika Christian, Caitlin Buchanan, Paula Willuweit, Sharon Lawson, ReeJade Richmond, Justin Heiman, Bill Hunter, Hon. Kwame Kenyatta, Hon. JoAnn Watson, Hon. John Conyers, Jr., O'Neil Swanson, Don Davis, Hon. Brenda Jones, Richard Manson, and Candace Cox-Wimberley

I am deeply grateful for the spiritual support of Bertha Montgomery, Zemine Wourman, Pon Phounsavath, Arian Simone, Ashley Sierra, Narraine Reed, Jame Reed Bey, Alma Whitley, William Alexander Haley, Maurita Coley, Maureen Pearson, Kenneth Watson, Herb Boyd, Stan Gundrie, Renaissance Unity, Charles H. Brown, Betty Shabazz, Antoinette Wright, Linda Bernard, Elbert Hatchett, Jack Martin, June Baldwin, Solomon Ennis, Linda Lott, Marie Christmon, Aretha Franklin, Nicholas Hood II, James Perkins, Bobbie Wourman, Dorthy Wourman, Sarah Blessman , Robert Wourman, Bessie Wourman, Nancy Wourman, Patricia Taylor, Reuben Cannon, Larkin Arnold, Vickie Browne, Lou Ann Simon, Mildred Gaddis, Greg Dunmore, Jeff Gerritt, Dave Ashenfelder, Brian Cox, Rod Spencer...and many others.

A special thanks to Amber Communications Group, Inc. on this historic occasion.

Critical Acclaim for Obama Talks Back
Global Lessons—A Dialogue with America's Young Leaders

Collective Thoughts:

Obama Talks Back *is an eye opener and an essential piece of reading for both America's families and America's leaders. It connects us to where we are in terms of values and lessons in the 21ˢᵗ century.*

Open Magnet Charter School   Cass Technical High School
Los Angeles, CA   Detroit, MI

The letters provide profound insight from our young people who are both children of Republicans and supporters of Obama.

Hill Gaston Middle   Medrano Elementary
Campus of Arts and Science   Dallas, TX
Denver, CO

Obama Talks Back *provides endless possibilities for our young people, enabling them to see through the 44th president into what America can be if we work together with shared responsibilities.*

Ballou S.T.A.Y. H.S.   William J. Beckham Academy   Louis Pasteur School
Washington, D.C.   Detroit, MI   Detroit, MI

Obama Talks Back *provides a rare glimpse into the private letters sent to the President and his accompanied remarks to our young people and Americans.*

Carmel Middle School	Northeast Academy	New Orleans College Prep
Charlotte, NC	Denver, CO	Charter School
		New Orleans, LA

Obama Talks Back *offers us all a sense of hope, understanding, and peace. We should embrace change and not go backwards. A new world order is evolving around our young people and we must work with them.*

Bates Academy	Boston Public School	Boston Latin School
Detroit, MI	Jamaica Plan, MA	Boston, MA
Swift School	Theodore Roosevelt	Highline Academy
Chicago, IL	Washington, D.C.	Denver, CO

Obama Talks Back *offers us all shared opportunities to move forward based on this dialogued exchanged. We are grateful to contribute to a worthy project that can be used as a guide for each elected official and leaders in the 21ˢᵗ century.*

Paul Robeson Academy	Northland High School	Belle Chase Academy
Detroit, MI	Columbus, OH	Belle Chase, LA
John C. Conley	MacArthur University	Merrill Middle School
Chicago, IL	Southfield, MI	Des Moines, IA
Coral School for Science & Math	Thurgood Marshall, ES	Down Town School
Alexander, VA	Chesapeake, VA	Des Moines, IA

Table of Contents

Preface

"The Concept"

Obama Talks Back: Global Lessons—A Dialogue with America's Young Leaders focuses on values, lessons of life, and truths that we have coined as "Global Lessons" from America's Young Leaders. The concept was inspired from the multi-award winning and NAACP book *Dear Mrs. Parks: A Dialogue with Today's Youth* and the Keeper of the Word Foundation's exhibit entitled, "Dear Mr. Mandela...Dear Mrs. Parks: Children's Letters, Global Lessons," presented in South Africa and at Michigan State University. The Obama conversation with today's young leaders is an extension of the book *Dear Mrs. Parks.* Many young leaders across the globe with inquiring minds and thoughts sent letters to Mrs. Parks in search of guidance. Likewise, thousands of Young Leaders in *Obama Talks Back: Global Lessons*—are in search for a better America and the book was conceived to share their ideas and thoughts with America and future generations.

Barack Obama achieved a landslide victory in 2008 and touched the lives of young people more so than any previous president. During his presidency, he has sought to continue that inspiration by maintaining an engaged relationship with the nation's youth. While the president was able to enroll young people of voting age to be a part of the democratic process, what has not been examined are the thousands of thoughts, ideas, and contributions from young people aged four to twenty who were not able to vote in the 2008 election, or who have never voted.

Obama Talks Back's letters mirror those of *Dear Mrs. Parks* readers and reflect each generation's fears and needs for emotional guidance and support.

President Obama's campaign inspired a new 21st century generation of future voters to be involved in the democratic process as digitally oriented and globally minded American citizens. Their interest in domestic and international issues paired with their adeptness with new technologies and social media in this digital age cannot be overlooked. This generation is extremely valuable and has gradually changed the landscape of America's future.

Thousands of young people of America began speaking up by writing the president with their concerns during his first twenty days in office and President Obama is talking back with responses from his days as President-Elect and with responses from today, at the end of his first term as president. Their collection of letters demonstrate their continued demands for changes in the economy, their schools, and their communities. These young people feel that change has already started to take place within themselves, and they are participating in the process of changing their country regardless of their legal inability to vote. This was made evident by *Ty'Sheoma Bethea*, the young girl from South Carolina who appeared at Obama's 1st joint session speech to Congress asking her government to use stimulus funds to make repairs to her dilapidated school, and by the several thousand letters received by the Keeper of the Word Foundation.

The Foundation as an advocate for the young people received 2,000 letters in eight days from young people demanding "the change we can believe in" promised by their new president. One of the first two letters we received was from the first public school founded in America, Boston Latin School of Boston, Massachusetts. Boston Latin school's motto is "we are first," *as it* was *established in 1635, fifteen years after the Pilgrims settled Plymouth Rock (1620) and 141 years before the signing of the Declaration of Independence (1776). Five of the fifty-six signers of the Declaration of Independence were pupils at Boston Latin school: John Hancock, Samuel Adams, Benjamin Franklin, Robert Treat Paine, and William Hooper.* The first was a well-written letter from Daniel Whitelock, a student who acknowledged he had supported Republican

Senator McCain, but after the 2008 election he decided "we, the young people must unite and unify our nation" now that Senator Barack Obama is the president. The second young activist's letter was from *Maya Feagin*, who attended one of Michigan's outstanding schools, Cass Technical High School of Detroit.

Both young leaders' letters revealed that President Obama's talks empowered them to seek a "new beginning" and a "change Americans can believe in." President Obama gave them hope. In the past, many young people in America ignored the creed "We the People" as a mantra for the political process. They have lost faith in our system because of wars, an economy in recession, a health care system in need of reform, a failing education system, and corporate greed. Our leaders have failed them in numerous ways: the government failing to stand up for Hurricane Katrina victims, the collapse of the mortgage and banking industry, rising unemployment, and other system defects. President Obama's election restored dignity and a sense of empowerment in the majority of young people to do great things in their lifetimes-to change our nation's failures into the nation's successes.

The young people began to understand that they have choices so they are not limited by their previous mindsets and the matrix conditions as they were during the years prior to Obama's election. President Obama demonstrated that the ability to transform their circumstances lies within them. Before his campaign, many of the young people could not grasp this idea of self-empowerment or shared opportunities. Now, more than ever before, most young people believe in the power of the words "yes we can," and that anything is possible in America, regardless of race, creed, or religion.

In some of President Obama's remarks, he talks of global lessons or universal lessons of change taught to him by his mother and discoveries from prior leaders like Abraham Lincoln, Mahatma Gandhi, Franklin Roosevelt, Rosa Parks, Malcolm X, Martin Luther King Jr., and Nelson Mandela. He speaks as to how these lessons can transform the lives of our youth by adopting the values of *perseverance, power of one, confidence, purpose, sacrifice, patience, unity, integrity, courage, dignity, selflessness, and commitment* among other values, global lessons, and truths. These values and lessons are not new, but have been misplaced by adults and parents, and now have been renewed as a result of Barack Obama's engaging philosophy with the youth of America.

The central focus of the young leaders' letters is change, and each young author of these letters believes he or she can change this nation so it shines as a beacon of light in every American's heart. It is the light that illuminated in Barack Obama's heart as he became the 44th president of the United States of America in 2008, and it is the same light that continues to guide him as he seeks re-election in 2012.

Foreword by

William Alexander Haley

"This New World"

Finding one's way in this global world is a challenge for today's young people and adults alike, and will be for future generations as well. The American people and today's young people in their quest to confront the challenges of today declared, **"Yes, we can 'Change' the challenges we are faced with in America today!"**

In recent years, we have seen the growing breakdown of families, community values, and urban infrastructures. Thus, our youths are growing up morally confused. President Obama's speeches, action, and engagement provided the young people and the rest of America with a renewed sense of hope and purpose with an intellectual GPS to navigate the roadblocks. His words encourage and empower them to confront this new, 21st century frontier facing them and the rest our global society.

Young people and their families are confronted with complex challenges of change more so today than in previous years as different nations and peoples of diverse cultures become more interactively involved with each other through the use of new technologies. Parents and family members of older generations are sometimes discouraged and concerned for their young loved ones because of these rapid changes and need support in addressing *this new world*. Despite concerns, we trust the young people's honestly given words in these letters, and know that the responses in *Obama Talks Back* will aid readers and these writers in their journey to adulthood and responsible citizenship.

A 21st century social movement and dialogue has been launched with the nation's youth via the internet, digital media, and online social networking devices. In this digital age, knowledge has become the *"digital currency"* and is empowering the sharing of information. Today's youth have grown up in this digital age and are well versed in the art of gathering online information, but they have extended their search for answers and support to other areas. Many of our young citizens are now considering the relevance and wisdom of not only President Obama, but also their predecessors Abraham Lincoln, Franklin D. Roosevelt, Rosa Parks, Dr. Martin Luther King Jr., Malcolm X, John F. Kennedy, and Nelson Mandela. Their predecessors' words and wisdom play a part in these young leaders' letters and are featured in this rare anthology of letters received from schools across the nation by mail and digital technology. President Obama has nurtured a grass-roots power of the Web movement and a dialogue with the young citizens of America.

Their letters and the responses in *Obama Talks Back: Global Lessons—A Dialogue with America's Young Leaders* reflect that each one of us counts, and that each of us can make a difference through voting and involvement in our communities. Their realization features President Obama as symbol of change, a symbol of **"Yes, we can,"** and a symbol of **"Yes, we did."** The young leaders' letters provide insight and proof of the individual's growth that is happening among young people today. This digital generation is exercising their voice as they are beckoned to meet the current challenges confronting this nation and the world.

Americans, as a people, recognized after eight years under the Bush Administration that we must return to the basic, self-evident truth that all people are created equal with the inalienable rights of life, liberty, and the pursuit of happiness. We need to reaffirm the Declaration of Independence for all Americans and for our young people. During his campaign and throughout his presidency, President Obama's inspiring messages to our youth and our nation translate many of the Declaration of Independence's values into *global lessons of transparency, honesty, integrity, responsibility, commitment, courage, hope, faith, and service to others.* Whatever has been lacking in the young generation, many are seeking to correct the dialogue within themselves. They desire to better themselves as a generation and better America by facing the challenges in their lives, homes, and communities.

The letters of these young citizens reinforce who we are in relation to change, and can fortify older generations in realigning them with the following global lessons: education, commitment to this great nation, and government transparency. President Obama visually narrated the course for America to change during his campaign, and is now seeking to lead America to a greater and a brighter future provided we unite and support the president's mission. God Bless America!

William Alexander Haley
CEO, Alex Haley Foundation

Introduction

"The Digital Age"

In navigating our way in this global world and digital age, one needs currency. Digital technology and information have become the new exchange medium of digital currency. Digital currency is the information of the 21st century, and it is the new challenge for younger and older generations alike. The young people of today are no different than those of yesterday in seeking guidance, support, and understanding when it comes to the challenges of today's world. It is our moral obligation to help our young people to move their generation forward with the help of our president.

The letters authored by the young people presented in this anthology show great insight and thoughtfulness. Their letters are insightful, truthful, painful, humorous, serious, and honest. These young people showed great courage to stand up for America and have America hear their voices; their intention is to communicate directly with President Barack Obama, they voiced their concerns and hopes for their country. Their dreams for America were their inspiration to write President Obama before and during his presidency, and to use the Keeper of the Word Foundation, an activist organization, to communicate their thoughts and ideas to the nation and to the world.

Their letters, including those of the Boston Latin School of Massachusetts are priceless, timeless, and powerful as were the ones sent to Mrs. Rosa Parks for her book and to Nelson Mandela's during his imprisonment.

This collection of students' letters accompanied with President Obama's responses, speeches, public statements, and quotations during his campaign, tenure as President-Elect, and his presidency is the most comprehensive collections of letters and responses ever assembled as a book in the history of our nation for a sitting president. This collection of letters featuring the voices of today's young leaders and their mission to be heard is a rarity. Letters *addressed to the President of the United States are kept sealed by the government office for up to twelve years after the president has left office.*

The personal thoughts of the writers are a rare and private glimpse into the dialogue between our nation's youth and their sitting president in office.

The inspiration for this project was launched in 2008 when Michigan State University arranged to take a conceptual exhibit, "Dear Mrs. Parks," to South Africa. Based on the "Dear Mrs. Parks" letters, the staff of former South African President Nelson Mandela discerned that the themes and lessons addressed to Mrs. Parks were similar to those of South African students. The letters addressed to President Mandela were merged with the letters to Mrs. Parks and created the first international, collaborative exhibit to move our young generations forward between two continents, America and Africa.

President-Elect Barack Obama provided the opening remarks for the unveiling of the Parks/Mandela exhibit event during Mandela's 90th birthday (the events can be viewed on Youtube.com). The young people's values articulated in their letters to President Obama are an extension of the Parks'/Mandela's letters that show there is a universal desire for global and positive change in our society and government. *Obama Talks Back* highlights the global lessons to be learned from all young people whenever and wherever they are located.

The young people's letters cover a wide range of human emotions, fears, and concerns and echo President Obama's message for change as these young people make their spiritual and intellectual pilgrimage into adult citizenship.

Their letters reveal they have concerns *for peace, healthcare, freedom, education, poverty, religious tolerance, love, materialism, and equality in America. Their letters address our nation's unattended concerns like immigration issues, crime, poverty, global climate change, economic issues, racism, war, religion, same-sex marriage, discrimination, and many more.* They recognize that President Obama shares their creativity, concerns, and supports their mission with his words and actions.

From these letters, we learn that these young citizens are committed to their country. They are not quitters. From President Obama we learn the importance of listening to one another, and of perseverance. We learn in desperate times, we must have faith and know we are empowered to change the circumstances and conditions of our lives and the destiny of America for the better.

Digital Currency

We are in the age of social transformation. Young persons ages 11 to 13 years are using the internet more and more frequently. This is the first generation to grow up in an age, digitally referred to as the Net Generation, which uses the internet far differently than any other generation in the past. The Net Generation of multi-taskers are able do many things at once, such as texting friends, downloading music, uploading videos, watching movies, tweeting, using Facebook, etc.

The internet, as a tool, provides and exchanges information globally as a means for the 21st Century. Some refer to it as digital currency and that *currency is information.* This generation of young people in this 21st Century uses digital currency as their voice of empowerment. The young people's letters in this anthology, and some written via email have created a social movement and an internet community for networking with the President. President Obama harnessed the grass-roots power of the Web to relate and develop an army of young activists to involve themselves in democracy and take America's and his message to the "streets" via digital technology.

The young people's letters demonstrate that they know they are a part of change and a "social movement." Even though some of them cannot vote, they believe that their letters can change America and affect democracy for the better.

Digital currency has enhanced government transparency and created an open system for sharing information with blogs, Twitter, Facebook, emails, texts, YouTube, etc., as a means for the young people's voices, opinions, concerns and feelings to be expressed. The digital system has led to more discussions that produce changes, and has led to people making more informed decisions. Today's community of young people are expressing themselves freely as a collective force of individuals unlike any other generation in America. Their letters herein indicate the young people's social movement is here to stay, and they will be heard. They are the voices at the far end of a long table declaring, "We are the future, and we will be heard at this moment, at this hour, at this time, and we have currency to spend on the Web." Obama hears them and talks back with the same digital currency in their language. Obama recognizes that this is the moment and it is urgent!

Who Is

Barack Obama and Why Do People Honor Him?

BARACK HUSSEIN OBAMA (August 4, 1961-) is known as the voice of change. He is the first of African-American descent to be elected the 44th President of the United States of America. The son of a father from Kenya and a mother from Kansas; raised in Hawaii and Indonesia, educated at Columbia University and Harvard Law School. He was the first African-American President of Harvard Law Review and he became a United States Senator in 2004 from Illinois. For many he represents the symbol of hope for the new America in the 21st Century. As America embarks on its new mission President Obama said, "This is our Moment. This is our Time." And, the journey has just begun.

Questions For Our Young People:

- Why do Americans like President Obama?
- Why did people around the world celebrate his election to the presidential office?
- Why does he represent change or hope?
- What positive changes can you make in your life, community or family?

Answers:

The students' letters herein answer the questions above across the United States without the questions actually being presented to them. They intuitively felt what many thought and the need to express themselves. The young people trust you will discern President Obama is a visionary planner and equipped to lead us through these challenging times.

The Commonly Asked Questions About President Barack Obama

Where was he born?

He was born in Honolulu, Hawaii on August 4, 1961.

How did he get his name?

He was named after his father, Barack Obama Sr., who was born in Nyanza Province in Kenya. His father moved to the United States and attended the University of Hawaii and later Harvard University. He married

President Obama's mother on February 2, 1961. They were divorced when Barack was still a young child.

Is he married?

Yes, he married Michelle Robinson on October 3, 1992 in Chicago, Illinois.

Does he have children?

Yes, their names are Sasha and Malia. Malia was born in 1998, and Sasha was born in 2001.

Does he have any siblings?

Yes, he has one half-sister, Maya Soetoro-Ng, born to his mother and stepfather in 1970. She holds Indonesian and American citizenship and urrently lives in Honolulu, Hawaii.

What schools did he attend?

While living with his grandparents in Hawaii, Obama enrolled Punahou Academy and graduated with honors. After high school Obama studied at Occidental College in Los Angeles, California and then transferred to Columbia University in New York where he graduated in 1983 with a degree in Political Science. In 1988 he was accepted into Harvard Law School.

How well did he do in school?

He graduated with honors from his high school in Hawaii and received numerous scholarships throughout his college career. He was elected as the first African American President of the Harvard Law Review and graduated magna cum laude from Harvard Law School.

What did he do before being elected to the office of the President?

After his undergraduate work at Columbia, he was a Community Organizer for low-income residents on the South Side of Chicago. After law school he returned to Chicago and worked as a civil rights attorney, taught at the University of Chicago Law School, and worked as an organizer for Bill Clinton's 1992 presidential campaign. President Obama authored two books, Dreams of My Father and The Audacity of Hope. He was elected to the United States Senate, representing the state of Illinois, in 2004.

Was he always successful in his career choices?

No, he lost an election to be the United States Senator for Illinois in 2000.

What are his favorite foods?

Chili and pizza from an Italian Fiesta Pizzeria in Hyde Park, Chicago.

What were his presidential campaign slogans?

"Change," "Yes we can," "Change we can believe in."

Does he like music or the arts?

Yes, he likes live jazz, classic rock, Motown, and classical music among other genres.

Did he play any sports while growing up?

Yes, he played basketball in high school.

Did he always want to be a president?

No, he had other desires such as becoming an architect.

The Global Lessons

Perseverance

Power of One

Confidence

Purpose

Unity

Integrity

Courage

Dignity

Selflessness

Commitment

Honesty

Responsibility

Hope

Faith

Honor

Service to Others

Equality...

To Malia & Sasha

What I Want for you and Every Child

Dear Malia and Sasha,

I know that you've both had a lot of fun these last two years on the campaign trail, going to picnics and parades and state fairs, eating all sorts of junk food your mother and I probably shouldn't have let you have. But, I also know that it hasn't always been easy for you and Mom, and that as excited as you both are about that new puppy, it doesn't make up for all the time we've been apart. I know how much I've missed these past two years, and today I want to tell you a little more about why I decided to take our family on this journey.

When I was a young man, I thought life was all about me-about how I'd make my way in the world, become successful, and get things I want. But then the two of you came into my world with all your curiosity and mischief and those smiles that never fail to fill my heart and light up my day. And suddenly, all my big plans for myself didn't seem so important anymore. I soon found that the greatest joy in my life was the joy I saw in yours. And I realized that my own life wouldn't count for much unless I was able to ensure that you had every opportunity for happiness and fulfillment in yours. In the end, girls, that's why I ran for President:; because of what I want for you and for every child in this nation.

I want all our children to go to schools worthy of their potential-schools that challenge them, inspire them, and instill in them a sense of wonder about the world around them. I want them to have the chances to go to college even if their parents aren't rich. And I want them to get good jobs: jobs that pay well and give them benefits like health care, jobs that let them spend time with their own kids and retire with dignity.

I want us to push the boundaries of discovery so that you'll live to see new technologies and inventions that improve our lives and make our planet cleaner and safer. And I want us to push our own human boundaries to

12

reach beyond the divides of race and region, gender and religion that keep us from seeing the best in each other.

Sometimes we have to send our young men and women into war and other dangerous situations to protect our county-but when we do, I want to make sure that it is only for a very good reason that we try our best to settle our differences with others peacefully, and that we do everything possible to keep our servicemen and women safe. And I want every child to understand that the blessings these brave Americans fight for are not free that with the great privilege of being a citizen of this nation comes great responsibility.

That was the lesson your grandmother tried to teach me when I was your age, reading me the opening lines of the **Declaration of Independence** *and telling me about the men and women who marched for equality because they believed those words put to paper two centuries ago should mean something.*

She helped me understand that America is great not because it is perfect but because it can always be made better and that the unfinished work of perfecting our union falls to each of us. It's a charge we pass on to our children, coming closer with each generation to what we know America should be.

I hope both of you will take up that work, righting the wrongs that you see and working to give others the chances you've had. Not just because you have an obligation to give something back to this country that has given our family so much-although you do not have that obligation. *But because you have an obligation to yourself. Because it is only when you hitch your wagon to something larger than yourself that you will realize your true potential.*

These are the things I want for you-to grow up in a world with no limits on your dreams and no achievements beyond your reach, and to grow into compassionate, committed women who will help build that world. *And I want every child to have the same chances to learn and dream and grow and thrive that you girls have. That's why I've taken our family on this great adventure.*

I am so proud of both of you. I love you more than you can ever know. And I am grateful everyday for your patience, poise, grace, and humor as we prepare to start our new life together in the White House.

Love,
Dad

The Letters

My Message To Young People

Obama Talks Back

Dear Young People:

Let me begin by saying thanks to all of you.

You believe in justice and what this country can be. In the face of war, you believe there can be peace. In the face of despair, you believe there can be hope. In the face of politics that's shut you out, that's told you to settle, that's divided us for too long, you believe we can be one people, reaching for what's possible, building that more perfect union.

That's the journey we're on today.

I understand your concerns. In my experience, I saw that the problems people faced weren't simply local in nature—that the decision to close a steel mill was made by distant executives; that the lack of textbooks and computers in your schools could be traced to the skewed priorities of politicians a thousand miles away; and that when a child turns to violence, there's a hole in his heart no government alone can fill. It was in Chicago neighborhoods that I received the best education I ever had, and where I learned the true meaning of my Christian faith.

I came to understand that our cherished rights of liberty and equality depend on the active participation of an awakened voter. Each and every time, a new generation has risen up and done what's needed to be done. Today we are called once more—and it is time for our generation to answer that call.

All of us know what those challenges are today—a war with no end, a dependence on oil that threatens our future, schools where too many of you aren't learning, and families struggling paycheck to paycheck despite working as hard as they can. We know the challenge. We've heard them.

The special interests who've turned our government into a game only they can afford to play. *They write the checks and you get stuck with the bills, they get the access while you get to write a letter, they think they own this government, but we're here today to take it back.*

We'll have to make hard choices. And although government will play a crucial role in bringing about the changes we need, more money and programs alone will not get us where we need to go. ***Each of us, in our own lives, will have to accept responsibility—for instilling an ethic of achievement in each one of you***, for adapting to a more competitive economy, for strengthening our communities, and sharing some measure of sacrifice. So let us begin. ***Let us begin this hard work together. Let us transform this nation.***

We always knew our climb would be steep. But with a million voices, you came to Washington, D.C. on January 20, 2009. And with your voices and your letters and emails, you made it clear that at this moment—there is something happening in America.

There is something happening when Americans who are young in age and in spirit—who have never before participated in politics and want to be involved. You know in your hearts that this time must be different. That is what's happening in America right now. Change is what's happening in America. And we challenge ourselves to reach for something better, there's no problem we can't solve—no destiny we cannot fulfill. We can stop sending our young ones like some of you to schools with corridors of shame and start putting you on a pathway to success. We can stop talking about how great teachers are and start rewarding them for their greatness. We can do this with our new majority. That's why this moment belongs to you. We know the battle ahead will be long, but always remember that no matter what obstacles stand in our way, nothing can withstand the power of millions of voices calling for change.

Yes We Can,
President Obama

I.

Education / Digital Currency

"There is no future without an education."
—Rosa Parks

Sacrifice

Dear President Obama,

The statement that you wrote, "Today we begin in earnest work of making sure that the world we leave our children is just a little bit better than the one we inhabit today." means that you, Mr. Obama, do not want to do the same things as President Bush did during the past four years. I believe you want to help children and families make sure that every child gets an education.

I believe you want to make sure that our children all get put in school first by investing in early childhood education. You will make sure that all schools are adequately funded and led by high quality teachers. I feel you will reform "No Child Left Behind" and set high standards for schools to give them the resources they need to succeed and make college more affordable.

One thing I will do to help leave the world better for the future generations is to donate money to children who are less fortunate. I want to see less fortunate children be able to go to schools like kids who are more fortunate. Mr. Obama, if you can do all this for me, you will make me the happiest girl alive.

Nafisat
Swift School
Chicago, IL

Opportunity

Dear Nafisat,

Your letter caused me to reflect on the letter I presented to Sasha and Malia, my daughters. I realized that my own life wouldn't count for much unless I was able to ensure that Malia and Sasha had every opportunity for happiness and fulfillment in their lives. That is what I want for them, for you and every child in this nation.

I want all our children to go to schools worthy of their potential— schools that challenge them, inspire them, and instill in them a sense of wonder about the world around them. I want them to have the chance to go to college even if their parents aren't rich. I want them to get good jobs; jobs that pay well and give them benefits like health care, and jobs that let them spend time with their own kids and retire with dignity. I want us to push the boundaries of discovery so that you'll live to see new technologies and inventions that improve our lives and make our planet cleaner and safer. And I want us to push our own human boundaries to reach beyond the divides of race and region, gender and religion that keep us from seeing the best in each other.

Barack Obama

Appreciation

Dear President Obama,

Today's youth can be inspired to make the world a better place. But before we even get to that, I must offer you my congratulations on becoming the first African-American President of the United States. This mere feat alone is enough for a lifetime of praise. I hope you understand the significance of your victory in breaking down the color barrier.

Many children, myself included, do not understand the luxuries that we have today in the United States. Most of us always have something to eat, have heat during the winter, and television to watch when we get home from school.

And then there is school. Most children in the U.S. think that school itself is a given, when, in fact, it is a luxury that we do not cherish. Many children see school as an obstacle that they must get over by the time they are 18. But, then comes college, yet another luxury. Children in the third world countries would love to have school for 6 hours a day and to get off the streets where there is no disease and war.

Mr. President, I feel that the students of this country and the future leaders of tomorrow, should be taught the values of life. I feel that, in extreme cases, punishment can be severe. Children should know the extent of what is going on in third world countries, even if it means getting sent to one themselves.

I know, it sounds harsh, but in reality, this will create well-rounded citizens of the future. Many families coddle their young so that all there is left is a lop-sided person. They would have never learned how to be self-sufficient. They would have never learned how to be a true American and appreciate each and every single commodity that we get every day. By teaching our students, we would have ensured that the people of tomorrow will strive their hardest to give back to the poorest parts of the globe. By doing this, we will have ensured a better tomorrow.

Sincerely yours,
Michael
Boston Latin School
Boston, MA

Responsibility

Dear Michael,

I couldn't agree with you more that the future of America's children and their education is invaluable. At this defining moment in our history, America faces few more urgent challenges than preparing our children to compete in the global economy. The decisions our leaders make about education in the coming years will shape our future for generations to come. It will help determine not only whether our children have the chance to fulfill their God-given potential or whether our workers have a chance to build a better life for their families, but whether we as a nation will remain in the 21st century the kind of global economic leader that we were in the 20th century. The rising importance of education reflects the new demands of our new world.

The responsibility for education must be shared between government, parents, and the students themselves in order to make it work. As a nation, we have an obligation to make sure that all children have the resources they need to learn: quality schools, good teachers, the latest textbooks, and the right technology. Parents must be willing to do what's necessary to give every child a chance to succeed.

That responsibility begins not in our classrooms, but in our homes and communities. It's family that first instills the love of learning in a child. Only parents can make sure the TV is turned off and homework gets done. We have to tell our children that their education is not a passive activity, you have to be actively engaged in it. If we encourage that attitude and our community is enforcing it, I have no doubt we can compete with our global neighbors.

Our schools share this responsibility. When a child walks into a classroom, it should be a place of high expectations and high performance. And America's students must be willing to work hard to meet those high expectations. The first step is making the decision to put yourself on the right path. And, I can guarantee you this: if you put yourself on the right path and you're willing to keep walking, eventually you'll make progress. So Michael, I hope you will continue to work with me, Congress, and the students of your generation to put yourselves on that right path.

Barack Obama

Power of Choice

Dear President Barack Obama,

We need to inform the youth about the dangers of the outside world. I think the most important thing we need to inform them about are gang bangers. Gangs are no joke. They can be very dangerous. If you are even near a gang you can get hurt, raped or even worse… killed. If we encourage the youth to stay away, it can prevent future tragedies.

The next important thing is drugs. Drugs will affect you physical, mental, and social health. There is all kinds of side effects that drugs have, like getting high or drunk. Drugs can even kill you. Also, other people stop trusting you. They'll even try to avoid you. Drugs can even make you commit suicide. Drugs are very dangerous. I know that if we encourage the youth to not be influenced by others, they'll most likely stay away from drugs and people who do them.

The third thing we need to inform them about is diversity. The youth today need to know that it's not what color you are, but what counts inside [mindset]. There are a variety of people out there who are trying to bring us down. We need to inform the youth of today that we can do whatever you can do as long as you put your mind to it.

The fourth thing is dropping out of school. I think we need to prevent the youth from dropping out. They need to know that dropping out affects your future. We need to encourage them to finish school so they can reach their dream. These are all things I think we should inform our youth about. Thank you most sincerely for your time and consideration.

Sincerely,
Alex
Chesapeake Alternative
Chesapeake, VA

Safety

Dear Alex,

Thank you for your poignant letter. During my time as president, I, like you and millions of other Americans, want to address and find resolutions to each of the issues you mentioned: violence in our communities, drugs, racism, and the failures of our education system, as they are great challenges that average Americans face everyday.

No child should have to walk to school every morning in fear for their safety because of the presence of gang members and drug dealers in their neighborhoods. We must do more to address this issue than passing harsher punishments for drug use and distribution and enforcing stricter gun laws. We must get to the root of the problem.

For example, I believe in keeping guns out of our inner cities, and that our leaders must say so in the face of the gun manufacturer's lobby. But I also believe that when a gangbanger shoots indiscriminately into a crowd because he feels someone disrespected him, we have a problem of morality. Not only do we need to punish that man for his crime, but we need to acknowledge that there's a hole in his heart, one that government programs alone may not be able to repair.

When a young man or woman turns to drugs because they are having problems at home or they feel rejected by their peers, it's not enough to send them to jail for possession of an illegal substance. We need to have an approach that emphasizes prevention and treatment; a public health model for reducing drug use in our country. Part of our challenge is getting into schools early and making sure that young people recognize the perils of drug use.

And I believe the best place to start in solving these issues is in our education system. At a time when other countries are doubling down on education, tight budgets have forced States to lay off thousands of teachers. A great teacher can offer an escape from poverty to the child who dreams beyond his circumstance. Every person in the Capitol Building can point to a teacher who changed the trajectory of their lives. Most teachers work tirelessly, with modest pay, sometimes digging into their own pocket for school supplies, just to make a difference. Teachers matter. So instead of bashing them or defending the status quo, let's offer schools a deal. Give them the resources to keep good teachers on the job and reward the best ones. And in return, grant schools flexibility to teach with creativity and passion, to stop teaching to the test, and to replace teachers who just aren't helping kids learn. That's a bargain worth making.

Barack Obama

Need vs. Want

Dear Mr. President,

Congratulations! I bet you are very proud to be the next president and America is proud of you too. Now that you are president I'm sure you have a lot of big things to deal with, but I hope that you will also help Americans make some small changes as well.

The change I would like to see is in the food that schools serve in the cafeteria. Sometimes it is not only unhealthy but its tastes bad too. My parents always make sure that I eat healthy foods like fruits and vegetables and that I don't eat foods that are bad for me like fast food and chips and soda. But then when I go to school, they serve food like pizza and French fries in the cafeteria. And kids can get candy and chips out of the vending machine if they want a snack. How are us kids supposed to stay healthy when our schools don't try to help?

Kids need to eat good, health, nutritious foods in order to grow up strong and do well in school. I know you have a lot of things to do deal with President Obama like the war in Iraq and Afghanistan and the economy, but I think the health of us kids is important too.

I'm going to help deal with this problem by encouraging my friends to eat healthy foods and stay away from fast food and junk food. I will pack my lunch so I don't have to eat the food in the cafeteria. Also, I will start a petition for my school to serve better, healthy food.

Sincerely,
Shelby
New Orleans College Prep Charter School
New Orleans, LA

Balance

Dear Shelby,

Thank you for your congratulations and your letter that addresses an issue that is of great concern for both myself and my wife, Michelle Obama. America is experiencing an obesity epidemic and your generation is facing it as well. As parents and teachers, as neighbors and citizens, we have to face this issue. We all know the numbers. One in three kids are overweight or obese, and Americans are spending $150 billion a year treating obesity-related illnesses. So we know this is a problem, and there's a lot at stake.

That's why my wife, Michelle has launched a campaign called "Let's Move" that targets four key pillars: getting parents informed about nutrition and exercise, making healthy foods more affordable and accessible for families, focusing more on physical education, and improving the quality of food in schools. I believe that "Let's Move" has enormous promise in improving the health of our children, and in giving support to parents to make the kinds of healthy choices that oftentimes are very difficult in this kind of environment.

Now I love burgers and fries, and I love ice cream and cake. So do most kids. We're not talking about a lifestyle that excludes all that. That's the fun of being a kid. But, what we need is balance. We have to balance these things with healthy, nutritious foods and exercise. I know that government is going to be a very minor player in this very big approach. Kids and parents are going to have to be the ones to make healthy decisions for themselves, but as president, I can help.

I have set a goal to solve the problem of childhood obesity within a generation so that children born today will reach adulthood at a healthy weight. The first lady will lead a national public awareness effort to tackle the epidemic of childhood obesity. She will encourage involvement by actors from every sector—the public, nonprofits, and private sectors, as well as parents and youth—to help support and amplify the work of the federal government in improving the health of our children.

I am proud of the first lady for her outstanding work, and I am proud of you Shelby for doing your part in ensuring your health and the health of your classmates.

Barack Obama

Inspiration

Dear President Barack Obama,

Congratulations on the election! I grew up with George Bush as my president, and it is a relief to see a new, intelligent, young man to be elected for the highest office in this country.

I would like to talk with you about education, which is so vital to a child's life. I attend the Open Magnet Public School in Los Angeles, CA. I feel very lucky to be a student here. Every morning I am glad to go to school. However, it bothers me that some children might try to think of any excuse not to go because they are scared of being bullied or called names by other kids, or are simply bored in the classroom. Also there is the issue of bad school materials and teachers who are not interested in putting their all into teaching. I cannot stand the fact that children might grow up to make wrong decision, and might even break the law, due to the lack of a good education.

We need to act now! Not next year. Not in a month. We need to install computers in classrooms, get quality books and materials, and, most importantly, we need to employ experienced teachers who really love to teach and are enthusiastic and inspiring.

Making the schools safer, getting better materials and teachers, however, is not enough. The real commitment begins at home with parents. Parents need to make sure that kids not only study, but do their homework instead of playing video games and read books instead of watching television. My parents help me with my homework as soon as I get home. They provide me with wonderful books because they know I love to read. I am worth the time and effort and love. So are all the other kids out there! We need to stand up for all children! We need to act now!

Please give my best to your beautiful wife, Michelle, and your adorable daughters, Malia and Sasha.

Sincerely,
Maegan
Open Magnet Charter School
Los Angeles, CA

Excellence

Dear Maegan,

There is no excuse for inaction when it comes to the education of our children, and I'm glad you share the same sense of urgency that I do when it comes to this matter.

As a nation, we have an obligation to make sure that all children have the resources they need to learn: quality schools, good teachers, the latest textbooks, and the right technology. When a child walks into a classroom, it should be a place of high expectations and high performance.

But too many schools don't meet this standard. That's why instead of just pouring money into a system that's not working, we launched a competition called Race to the Top. To all 50 states, we said, 'If you show us the most innovative plans to improve teacher quality and student achievement, we'll show you the money.' Race to the Top is the most meaningful reform of our public schools in a generation. For less than 1 percent of what we spend on education each year, it has led over 40 states to raise their standards for teaching and learning.

In 2009 and in 2010, we provided aid to States to keep hundreds of thousands of teachers in the classroom, but we need to do more.

That's why a critical part of the jobs bill that I sent to Congress back in September of 2011 was to help States prevent even more layoffs and rehire even more teachers who had lost their jobs. And so, when I sent the American Jobs Act to Congress back in 2011, it was to put tens of thousands of teachers back to work across the country and modernize at least 35,000 schools. That's why I have so urgently pressed Congress to pass that bill. Our children need the nation's support.

But there are still many more steps to be taken to improve the education of our young people. Putting teachers back in our kids' classrooms is one of those steps. You work hard in school, Maegan. Your parents work hard at their jobs. Your leaders should work hard too, especially at this make-or-break moment for the middle class. I know this year, 2012, is an election year. But some things are bigger than an election. Some things are bigger than politics. So I hope you'll join me in telling Congress to do the right thing, to get to work, and to help our teachers in the classroom. We can't afford to wait any longer. Now is the time.

Barack Obama

II.

Courage & Hope

"Courage faces fear and thereby masters it."
—Martin Luther King, Jr.

"Today we begin in earnest the work of making sure that the world we leave our children is just a little better than the one we inhabit today."

Commitment

Dear President Obama,

What this means to me is that all people should try to make the world a better place for all of us, young and old, rich and poor, big and small, especially the small. Until now, too many children did not dare to dream that they too could achieve great things such as becoming president of the United States, but now we know that there is nothing in the world that we can't do and it has given us something that too many of us have never known: Hope. Making the world a better place than the one we inhabit today means that all children should be able to hope and dream and be given the chance to do the same great things as others. We should also remember that young people need to be surrounded by a supportive community that sets good examples, a community that is going to treat them well and be respectful of them.

One thing I will commit to in helping to make our world better for the future generations, is that I will encourage others to believe in what they can do and help give them a better community by setting an example with my own actions. I will encourage others to be kinder and take care of others around them. It is the least that any of us can do, and hopefully, we will do much, much more.

Sincerely,
Zoe
Hyde Elementary School
Washington, D.C.

Choice

Dear Zoe,

In no other country could a story like mine be possible. I did not come from a rich family or a family with strong political influence. I am the son of a man from Kenya and a woman from Kansas who held fast to the belief that in America, you can be anything. And today, I am the President of the United States. If my dreams can be a reality, yours can too, Zoe.

But to achieve our dreams we must choose hope over fear. If we want to make our dreams for this nation we must choose unity over division and send a powerful message that change is coming to America.

The time has come for a President who will be honest about the choices and the challenges we face; who will listen to you and learn from you even when we disagree; who won't just tell you what you want to hear, but what you need to know.

Barack Obama

Respect

Dear President Obama,

I was one of the millions of young people who were newly registered to vote for the 2008 Presidential Election, and one of the fifty-seven million Americans who cast their vote for Senator John McCain. I am a conservative who has a hard time embracing the liberal ideology. However, I accept the results of the election, and hope that America can be restored to her stature of the greatest country on earth. We all take for granted the peaceful transition of power we, in the free world, enjoy. The next four years counts on conservatives, as well as liberals, to get together and be able to compromise.

I defined "justice" as living by the Golden Rule—to do unto others as you'd like done to you. Government only exists because of our failures as a society to live up to those ideals. If Americans wanted to create a society with minimal government intervention, the people must embrace that idea. There would be less crime, we would take part in not harming our environment, all impoverished families would be taken care of, no CEO would be making gaudy wages, and no politician taking bribes. The main focus of society would be the supreme human dignity of each and every person. In that state, government would intrude minimally, because there is no need for it. It is time for someone to inspire that mentality into Americans, so we can foster American creativity to come up with new ideas to solve all problems-both new and old. President

Obama, you have learned that words carry weight through your own rise to the presidency. Harness that power; help bring the real "change" America needs. I hope you realize that "change" is more than just a meaningless word.

President Obama, you said, "Today, we begin in earnest the work of making sure that the world we leave our children is just a little bit better than the one we inhabit today." This sounds an awful like Ronald Reagan's remarks at the 1992 Republican National Convention. My goal in life is to live up to that idea, and to make the world a little better for me having been here. That idea has inspired me to be a leader of this great country I love with all my heart. We need a president who respects the supreme dignity of every man, woman, and child on this earth. If that means leading America into war to free those oppressed and to secure the "unalienable" rights we take for granted—so be it.

Every martyr who dies for the advancement of this cause is a martyr to those rights granted to us by God. We need a President who will promote the idea of respect and love among Americans, and not division, hate, and violence. The task at hand as been passed down by every leader our nation has had before you. It is up to you how you take on this monumental task.

Sincerely,
Sean
Boston Latin School
Boston, MA

Empathy

Dear Sean,

Empathy is one Golden Rule I find myself appreciating more and more as I get older. It is the heart of my moral code, and it is how I understand the Golden Rule, not simply as a call of sympathy of charity, but as something more demanding, a call to stand in somebody else's shoes and see through their eyes.

Like most of my values, I learned about empathy from my mother. She disdained any cruelty, thoughtlessness, or abuse of power, whether it expressed itself in the form of racial prejudice, or bullying in the school-yard, or workers being under paid. Whenever she saw a hint of such behavior in me, she would look me square in the eyes and ask, "How do you think that would make you feel?" I find myself returning again and again to my mother's simple principle—"How would that make you feel," as a guidepost for my politics.

As a country, we seem to be suffering from an empathy deficit. I believe a stronger sense of empathy would tilt the balance of our current politics in favor of those who are struggling, the powerless, the oppressed. Talk is cheap, like any value empathy must be acted upon.

Barack Obama

Gratitude

Dear President Obama:

I am writing this letter to you to first of all commend you on your election as President of the United States of America. As a person of mixed heritage, I was extremely proud to see a man of color be elected to the highest office in our country. I cannot tell you how proud I was to go to the voting booth with my six-year-old brother and my mom to be a witness to this historic event. As a result of this, I feel a personal responsibility to continue to make my ten year old voice heard. I feel that the most important issue at this time facing my community is in the area of race relations and education.

As a fifth grader, I attend Open Magnet Charter School in the Los Angeles Unified School District in California. I am surrounded daily by children of all ethnicities. We are learning to be a "community of learners" who are secure, independent, and responsible citizens. I cannot tell you how excited I am to go to school everyday. It is truly an adventure to attend a school where you are learning math, literature, science, art and music. As you know from experience, a quality education is vital to fulfilling your dreams and goals. How can a person attend a good college without first attending a high school where they can meet the standards to gain admission? My community deserves better, no my country deserves better than this for no child should be forced to ride a school bus for more than an hour and a half just so they can get a quality education.

I am unwilling to give up the idea of a multicultural environment. I want it all. I want to become the type of man who is judged by his qualifications, in other words, education, character, and personality. In general, Mr. President, I want for myself and the children in my community a quality multicultural education where they too someday aspire to be President.

Sincerely yours,
Samuel
Open Magnet Charter
Playa Del Rey, CA

Purpose

Dear Samuel,

I ask you to believe, as it is written in the Declaration of Independence, that all men are created equal in a multicultural environment in America, and that we have unalienable rights, that among these are life and pursuit of happiness. I remember a great lady, Rosa Parks, who believed in the Declaration of Independence. When I sat in a Detroit church, Greater Grace, I was one of the persons eulogizing her spirit. She had decided to exercise the rights afforded to her by the Declaration of Independence when she refused to move from her seat for a white passenger and said no, not because she was tired, but because she was tired of giving in. To say that we are one people is not to suggest that race no longer matters or that the fight for equality has been won. It is to say that there is not a black America and white America and Latino America and Asian America, there is the United States of America. This is the source of our confidence—the knowledge that God calls upon us to shape the individual destiny regardless of race in a multi-cultural setting. God bless us all.

Barack Obama

Human Rights

Dear President Barrack Obama,

While the final vote count may lead one to believe that the Declaration's adoption was an easy road all over the world, with respect to the United States, it was not. In order to gain the nation's approval, Eleanor Roosevelt, a member of the Commission on Human Rights, had to deliver a speech, convincing the U.S. government that the Declaration was not a treaty or a form of international law. It simply was an international expression of the rights of all human beings and there would be no legal obligations to follow it. The reason that this had to be clarified is that at the time, the United States was not following many of the articles within the Declaration. Until 1965, "Jim Crow Laws" promoting institutional inequality among races existed in the country.

However, it has been 60 years, and based on your election, President Obama, it is apparent that the "Jim Crow Laws" no longer plague this nation. As your inauguration took place 41 days after the Declaration's anniversary, I believe that, as president your primary concern should be to the freedoms outlined in the Declaration. In the past 60 years, I fear, that rather than correcting our defiance of the document, we have simply been changing the way we go about resisting these rights. It is time for the United States of America, which has for so long been a symbol to the world of liberty, hope and morality, to act as if the Universal Declaration of Human Rights were law and to not only guarantee these rights to our citizens, but to spread them around the world in a way that does not take more away than it gives.

In the world today some of the most atrocious and obvious human rights abuses from the U.S. relate to our War on Terror. While this is most certainly an important issue that must be addressed, as a nation, we cannot let international human rights be defied by our actions.

One of the greatest concerns I have about our human rights violations is the existence of Guantanamo Bay. The U.S. government is currently detaining suspects here without following U.S. or international law. Many of the detainees were arrested without being charged for a specific crime, even though, according to article 9 of the Declaration: "No one shall be subjected to arbitrary arrest, detention or exile." In the six years since Guantanamo has held detainees, only two cases have been adjudicated and less than 25 others have been officially charged. Article 10 of the Declaration states: "*Everyone is entitled in full to a fair public hearing by an independent and impartial tribunal, in the determination of his rights and obligations of any criminal charges against him,*" yet people are being held at Guantanamo Bay without even the hope of a trial. The U.S. government has assumed these people are guilty when "*everyone charged with a penal offence has the right to be resumed innocent until proved guilty according to law in a public trial at which has had all the guarantees necessary for his defense*" is not only guaranteed by the Declaration, but also has been established by the United States Supreme Court. Therefore, as one of your actions as President, I sincerely hope that you will close Guantanamo Bay, and find more humane and legal method of charging suspects.

Sincerely,
Emily
Boston Latin School
Boston, MA

Dignity

Dear Emily,

The United States was founded on the idea that all people are endowed with inalienable rights and that all people are created equal. And that principle has allowed us to work to perfect our union at home while standing as a beacon of hope to the world. Today, that principle is embodied in agreements Americans helped forge—the Universal Declaration of Human Rights, the Geneva Conventions, and treaties against torture and genocide—and it unites us with people from every country and culture.

When the United States stands up for human rights, by example at home and by effort abroad, we align ourselves with men and women around the world who struggle for the right to speak their minds, to choose their leaders, and to be treated with dignity and respect. We also strengthen our security and well being, because the abuse of human rights can feed many of the global dangers that we confront—from armed conflict and humanitarian crises, to corruption and the spread of ideologies that promote hatred and violence.

I believed in these words four years ago, I believe in them today, and I believe we have made real progress in upholding our commitment to human rights not only with our words, but with our actions.

On January 22 of 2009, on my second day in office, I issued an Executive Order that put an end to the inhumane interrogation techniques that were being used at Guantanamo Bay. Now, some Americans may not support this. Some Americans believe these inhumane methods, such as water boarding were effective. But to them I say this: Water boarding is inhumane, and it is torture. It's contrary to America's traditions. It's contrary to our ideals. That's not who we are. That's not how we operate. We don't need it in order to prosecute the War on Terrorism. And, we did the right thing by ending that practice.

If we want to lead around the world, part of our leadership is setting a good example. America's moral example must always shine for all who yearn for freedom and justice and dignity.

Barack Obama

III.

Environment

"I believe in evolution, scientific inquiry, and global warming. Maybe there are a couple of holdouts in the Washington White House that don't believe in climate change. But there are 10,000 scientists who believe that maybe we should do something about it."
—Barack Obama

Cooperation

Dear President Obama,

Did you know that not everybody is fortunate enough to have clean water whenever they need it? Today, we as youth tend to take everything for granted, so that really makes us careless with our resources. Another thing is, because we have all these benefits, we don't really think much about other people's opinions and needs. Also, instead of spending all our time as TV or video game addicts, we could gather a bunch of friends and organize a fundraiser to raise money for those who are less fortunate. However, I think the global/environmental problem needs to be dealt with.

Trees around the world are disappearing, despite our efforts to protect them. Our use of paper is quite extravagant. I've noticed that when taking notes, my fellow classmates write a couple of lines, but the next day, a new sheet would be used. That use of paper is extremely wasteful, as if you only write half a page of notes per day and use a new sheet everyday, over a four day period that is four pieces of paper gone. You can manage to fit four days of notes on one piece of paper. You can recycle them, and that's one thing that can really help.

Another thing to think about is the idea of using electricity. Have you ever left home, and realized after a while that you forgot to turn off your lights? Well, that really wastes electricity. Also, have you ever noticed how some of the streetlights (like along the highway) are still on sometimes even when the sun is out and shining? Like the lights-on-at-home-but-no-people-at-home issue, this problem is also really wasteful. If everybody paid closer attention to the usage of electricity, you could save a lot energy. Water is the same thing. Saving water and electricity is good for you!

The first step in the process is to actually realize that we need to improve our ways of life. The key point in doing these is so that our life, as well as the lives around us, will all be improved. After all, making other people happy makes ourselves feel happy!

Sincerely,
Evan
Boston Latin School
Boston, MA

Leadership

Dear Evan,

    Yes, I am aware we all need to improve our life and use resources wisely. I recall a lady, Rosa Parks, who set an example for us all. There is a lesson in her example— a lesson for as adults and parents must demonstrate a positive, leadership example for young people to follow. If we are going to request our young generation to preserve, conserve, protect and be fiduciary of our resources, then we adults must set an example as teachers, parents, and individuals in addressing our resources or energy needs.

    We can't continue to settle for piecemeal or bite-sized solutions to our energy crisis. We need a national and global commitment. We must choose to change. Just imagine what we can do together. We can choose to rise together, working smarter, and thinking anew. We can do that. This is America—a country defined by the principles of the Declaration of Independence and the determination to believe in and work for things unseen.

Barack Obama

Prioritize

Dear Mr. President,

    I hope you will read this letter with interest. I just want to share what I have to say. I think your #1 priority should be solving the problem of pollution. As I speak, pollution is damaging many things and hurting the environment. We should continue in our marvelous way of creating hybrids but I think first, you should reason with the source. I think that you should come together with all the business owners whose factories are contributing to the mess that is continuing to unravel at our feet. Reason with all these people, and come to an agreement that will satisfy them and the country. Urge them to see what is happening, show examples of what they can make and what will happen if they start over and rethink. After you have done this, go and see how far they have come and help them make success. When you have finished this, move on to solve other problems in the economy and other things that are threatening the U.S.A. I hope you will take a little bit of time to read this letter and consider what I'm saying. Thank you for your time.

Sincerely,
William
Hill Campus of Arts and Science
Denver, CO

Harmony

Dear William,

Your letter has inspired me to respond. Pollution and the economy go hand in hand. As we solve the economy's issues, we are at the same time investing in clean energy enterprises that will employ thousands of Americans and preserve our earth. The economy is a one of my highest priorities but improving our economic situation goes right along with reducing our harmful effects on the environment. We cannot continue to allow high levels of pollution to damage the planet that we will leave behind for future generations. I have faith we will get it right this time for us all.

Barack Obama

Plan

Dear President Obama,

Some changes in America that I would like to see would be gun violence, gangs, and Global Warming. One of the first changes in America that I would like to see is eliminating gun violence because many people die in the U.S. everyday from guns.

Secondly, global warming is affecting our climate, which brings the topic of pollution. Big companies dump waste into our lakes, which is our drinking water source for the city. Biohazards are affecting both humans and aquatic animals in the lakes. And I don't want to get sick or worse die. To make this world a better place you should start new programs, which include a law that requires the use of a battery-backup car, hydrogen based cars, or filtered exhaust cars. This will both reduce the gasoline we use for our car and will reduce greenhouse gases produced by cars. I want my future to be happy and I don't want to have colder winters and hotter summers every year.

I want you to think these ideas over, and I know that they are best for us the children. Gangs and guns hurt people like me, and pollution will kill us all in the end if it isn't slowed down. I will try to help my future all I can, and I hope you do all you can to save the earth.

Sincerely,
David
Swift School
Chicago, IL

Peace

Dear David,

Your letter raises two separate concerns: violence in our nation and our environmental problems, but both are connected to one subject, and that is the economy. Yes, we need more cops on the streets. Yes, we need fewer guns in the hands of people who shouldn't have them. Yes, we need more outstanding teachers in the classroom. Yes, we need more opportunities to reduce crime so that many of our young people will not resort to crime and violence. Those opportunities come from a stabilized economy. This new economy must consider the new possibilities of a greener economy that reduces our pollution levels.

We can't simply turn to the strategies of the past.

We are living through an age of fundamental economic transformation. We may not find a cure-all plan, but yes we can, and yes we will address the gun violence and threat of global warming.

Barack Obama

Global Warming

Dear President Obama,

I believe that in our world today we need to teach everyone about recycling, including garbage, and about ways to help our economy and our environment. Our amounts of pollution that we release into the air every year is causing Global Warming. We need to teach younger and older children about even the smallest of ways that they could harm our earth and try to teach and enrich them with ways to help reduce the damage. We need to talk to them about saving water, using alternative fuels, energy saving light bulbs, planting trees, driving Hybrid cars and much more. The more we damage our surroundings the harder our solutions can get. People like teachers could start asking kids about what they think some solutions could be. They can lead us to newer technologies if they were ever asked what they think by somebody who cares. Talking about new laws to help protect those certain harmful things and work on enforcing the ones already made even more. If we want to last hundreds of decades, more we will need to drastically change our living environment or the ways that we survive. The world is in need of help and its future can be the children who are being educated in this time.

All people have amazing ideas, but we need to stop for a second and ask all the kids in the world what they think and then if one has a great idea, then we can enforce it. I think in your first year or first 100 days to start off your presidency, you need to listen to what us kids have to say and make us feel like we belong and that someone who cares is listening and can give us all hope. You can be a good president by solving problems and making fair judgments, but you are only great when you listen to those who trust you and do something about it. The United States needs a leader to believe in and we chose you to carve the path of our future. The U.S. is ready for change; all you need to do is inform us.

Sincerely,
Katherine
Hill Campus of Arts and Science
Denver, CO

Preservation

Dear Katherine,

I am inspired to listen and respond to your letter. To make this planet better, we must make America better. To make America better, we must make ourselves better. I alone cannot do this. If we work together than we can make a change. The time to act is now. There is no better time. We cannot afford to wait for change. We must be about change. We must change the ways that we confronted this issue in the past in order to minimize pollution to our communities, rivers, lakes, and our worldly environment.

To do so, we can begin with energy. We have fallen behind. We must make this economy energy efficient. By starting there, we will reduce pollution and conserve our resources. Individually, we can all do something to protect our environment, but collectively we can make bigger changes like preserving our drinking water, reducing pollution, and conserving the earth's resources. We know the country that harnesses the power of clean, renewable energy will lead the 21st century. And yet it is China that launched the largest effort in history to make their economy energy efficient. We invented solar technology, but we've fallen behind countries like Germany and Japan in producing it. New hybrids roll off our assembly lines, but they will run on batteries made in South Korea.

I do not accept a future where the jobs and industries of tomorrow take root beyond our borders, and I know you don't either. It is time for America to lead again and be one of the global leaders in the 21st Century.

Barack Obama

Cooperation

Dear President Obama,

I am a ten-year old boy from Des Moines, Iowa. My dream for the whole world is to have clean and healthy oceans and rivers so that all the people on the planet can enjoy them. Sadly, just ONE percent of the ocean is protected, which is ineffectual in the conservation of our water! Ecosystems we don't even know about are at risk of disappearing. In the last twenty years, we have done more damage to our planet than ever before. If we don't stop, our oceans will be uninhabitable to all those beautiful and amazing creatures!

I think the solution to the problem is simple. We need to increase the size and numbers of our protected breeding grounds so that the fish could reproduce. If we build up the supply, there would be more fish. This would help the economy. When the fish are migrating, the fisherman could catch them. We could feed more people for a cheaper price. We could also encourage fishermen to start using different nets with bigger net holes. This would prevent catching juveniles before they had mated.

My second idea is to plant trees. Trees help the ecosystems in a variety of ways. One of these ways is by preventing erosion. Planting trees along rivers would help farmers keep their soil and in turn keep our rivers clean. If we have dirty rivers, then all of the pollutants flow directly into the ocean.

My final suggestion I have is to focus on coral reef conservation. Coral reefs are important to our earth. One advantage of coral reefs is that they will provide important ecotourism thus helping economies flourish. Scientists say Coral may provide life saving medical drugs for cancer and reduce global warming. Furthermore, coral reefs provide a makeshift barricade from hurricanes and typhoons.

The advantages of saving our rivers and oceans are limitless. In the next decade, we will see that water conservation is not only vital for our environment's survival but ours as well.

Sincerely,
Luke
Downtown School
Des Moines, Iowa

Building

Dear Luke,

Your concern and the concern of so many other Americans is recognition that the threat from climate change is serious. Rising sea levels threaten every coastline. More powerful storms and floods threaten every continent. More frequent drought and crop failures breed hunger and conflict in places where hunger and conflict already thrive. On shrinking islands, families are already being forced to flee their homes as climate refugees. The threat to our environment is urgent, and it is growing.

It is true that for many years, mankind has been slow to respond to or even recognize the magnitude of the climate threat. It is true of our own country as well. We recognize that. But Luke, this is a new day. It is a new era. And there is much that can be done to reduce our negative impact on the environment.

I'm talking about the energy and climate bill that the United States House of Representatives passed in June of 2009, and the national policies that have gone into effect over the past four years to increase fuel economy and reduce green house gas pollution. I'm talking about giving businesses incentives to update their buildings to waste less energy. Folks in Pennsylvania have done this. They're designing building that save more energy with energy efficient lighting and windows to heating and cooling. This won't just cut down on energy pollution to our air, rivers, and oceans; it can save us billions of dollars on our energy bills.

We have to build on these accomplishments, because there is nothing to be gained from celebrating our progress, when there is so much progress yet to be made.

We need an all-of-the-above strategy that relies less on foreign oil and more on American-made energy: solar, wind, natural gas, biofuels, and more. That's the strategy we're pursuing. It's why I went to a plant in North Carolina earlier in March of this year, 2012, where they're making trucks that run on natural gas and hybrid trucks that go further on a single tank. We need to extend the tax credits for clean energy companies like the plant in North Carolina and others like TPI in Newton, Iowa. TPI is building wind turbines that are part of powering 10 million

49

American homes by wind alone. These industries are on the rise. These are the clean energy industries of America's future.

So, Luke, we know what needs to be done. We know that our planet's future depends on a global commitment to permanently reduce greenhouse gas pollution. We know that if we put the right rules and incentives in place, we will unleash the creative power of our best scientists, engineers, and entrepreneurs to build a better world for you to grow up in and a better world for future generations as well.

Barack Obama

Recycling

Dear President Barack Obama,

To make the world a better place, the global lesson that I would teach is a lesson about recycling. Why do we recycle? We recycle because we want to prevent global warming as much as possible. Although putting a piece of unwanted paper or a can of any sort in a recycling bin seems like it cannot help a global crisis, it actually can. It builds up to stop global warming from getting worse. A small movement could actually become something extraordinary. How does recycling actually help global warming? Recycling helps global warming because it allows the factories to make less products out of plastic and other materials, which results in reduced amount of greenhouse gases released into the air by the factories. Greenhouse gases are bad for our environment because they increase the temperature of our Earth.

Recycling helps global warming also because it reduces landfills in number and size. A landfill is known as a dump. A landfill is filled with disposal waste. Landfills are bad for our environment because there are some materials that take a long time to decompose. For example, plastic takes a long time to break down. It is estimated that some plastic takes about 250 years to break down. The more plastic we put into landfills, the more landfills we will need. Animals will be affected by landfills because all the landfills are taking up their homes.

Also, the more we recycle, the fewer trees we will need to cut down. Trees can help to reduce global warming greatly because they consume carbon dioxide in the air and produce oxygen. Less carbon dioxide in the air can help cool off our earth more effectively, thus help reduce global warming. Did you know that by recycling a ton of paper, you are actually saving 17 trees, 380 gallons of oil, 3 cubic yards of landfill space, 4000 kilowatts, and 7000 gallons of water? From these numbers Mr. President, you can see the power of recycling. Recycling by everybody is a good way to start preventing global warming. It is your responsibility to take part in helping the earth, your one and only beloved home. Mr. President, before you throw away something, we need to think twice to see if we could recycle it. If we all work together, we will make a great difference in saving our home, the earth.

Sincerely,
Sophia
Boston Latin School
Boston, MA

Participation

Dear Sophia,

You are absolutely right that each and every person doing their part can make a difference in our fight against global climate change. While we need dramatic actions by governments and nations all over the world to reduce greenhouse gas pollution, energy waste, and carbon emissions, we also need the participation of every American to do the same.

It is true that for too many years, mankind has been slow to respond to or even recognize the magnitude of the climate threat. It is true of our own country as well. We recognize that. But, this is a new day. It is a new era. And, I am proud to say that the United States has done more to promote clean energy and reduce carbon pollution in the last eight months than at any other time in our history.

Yes, climate change may be the greatest challenge facing not only the United States of America, but also facing every citizen of every nation and every living thing on this Earth. This journey is long. The journey is hard. And, we do not have much time left to make it. It is a journey that will require each of us to persevere through setbacks, and fight for every inch of progress, even when it comes in fits and starts. So let us begin. For if we are flexible and pragmatic; if we can resolve to work tirelessly in common effort, then we will achieve our common purpose: a world that is safer, cleaner, and healthier than the one we found; and a future that is worthy of our children.

Difficulty is no excuse for complacency. Unease is no excuse for inaction. And, we must not allow the strive for perfection to become the enemy of progress. Each of us must do what we can when we can to grow our economies without endangering our planet—and we must all do it together.

Barack Obama

Conservation

Dear President Obama,

The world is in trouble and the kids in my generation and those that follow will bear the health, economic and environmental consequences. The most important thing we can do to change America is to reduce our dependence on petroleum products and to restrict the damaging practices that are ruining our air, our water, our Earth and our long-term prospects for survival.

Congress needs to pass laws to prohibit drilling in the Alaskan wilderness and offshore. We need laws to force factories to run cleaner and car companies should be prevented from making cars that get poor gas mileage. Plastics containing harmful chemicals are everywhere and should be banned. Company executives that allow their companies to pollute the air or water or our bodies should be fined or sent to jail. They need to know they can't get away with it.

We also need to conserve energy and we need to focus on alternatives to oil such as wind farms, solar fields and sun towers. We need to change how we think about our own energy use and vote for politicians that support responsible energy laws.

Our overdependence on oil for heat, light, transportation and cheap plastic is to blame for global warming, loss of animal habitats, higher cancer rates, wars and famine and will eventually lead to our own extinction. We're running out of time. We're counting on you President Obama to help us change the world.

With Best Wishes for the Future,
William
Boston Latin School
Boston, MA

Lessons

Dear William,

Your letter brings to mind the devastating BP oil spill in 2010 that threatened and continues to threaten the environmental vitality and sustainability of the Gulf of Mexico. As we responded to the oil spill, we moved quickly on steps to ensure that such a catastrophe never happened again. I've said before that producing oil here in America is an essential part of our overall energy strategy. But all drilling, including drilling for natural gas must be safe.

We have a supply of natural gas that can last America for 100 years or more until we find alternative energy sources. My administration will take every possible action to safely develop this energy even further. Experts believe this will support more than 600,000 jobs by the end of the decade. I'm requiring all companies that drill for gas on public lands to disclose the chemicals they use. Because America will develop this resource without putting the health and safety of our citizens at risk. The development of natural gas will create jobs and power trucks and factories that are cleaner and cheaper, proving that we don't have to choose between our environment and our economy.

We also need to reform our government's relationship with oil and gas industries. For years, there has been a scandalously close relationship between oil companies and the agency that regulates them. That is why we decided to separate the people who permit the drilling from those who regulate and ensure the safety of the drilling. We also decided that it's time to stop subsidizing an industry that clearly doesn't need it. We've subsidized oil companies for a century. That's long enough. Its time to end the taxpayer giveaways to an industry that rarely has been more profitable and double down on a clean energy industry that never has been more promising.

Since I became President, America has nearly doubled our uses of renewable energy, like solar power and wind power. So this country's on the path to more energy independence, and that's good for everybody. Our progress does not stop here though. There is more to be done, and we are determined to act. Together, we will meet our responsibility to future generations.

Barack Obama

Resourcefulness

Dear President Obama,

I understand what you are saying, that the world that we are living in today is not all that great. I know you are saying that if we work together than we can make a change. You are right; there is time for change, if we want our planet to last—for instance, garbage. People that litter are the ones destroying this world. They do not know that all garbage that is thrown in the streets is being thrown in the lakes, rivers, ponds and oceans. This contaminates a citizen's water just by throwing trash in the streets where it travels through the sewer systems into main waterways and back to individual homes.

Pollution is the introduction of contaminants into the environment that cause harm or discomfort to humans or other living organisms, or that damage the environment. This pollution can be in the form of chemical substances, or energy such as noise, heat or light. When this world contains pollution, our world is dying, our world will not survive if this is still processing. Hopefully, we can make a change by not being filthy litterers.

Civilization as we know it is coming to an end soon. Oil is also one of the problems. Oil is increasingly plentiful, increasingly scarce and expensive. I feel that there definitely needs to be a BIG change in this world, everything is going wrong. Except, bless those who are trying, who save energy and clean up for this planet. Over the past quarter century, we have come to realize that there is more to life than material goods and services, that "some of the best things in life are free." The pleasure we derive from breathing fresh air, drinking pure water, and enjoying the beauty that nature has provided is priceless and must not be sacrificed. We have come to appreciate the importance of our environment. I will help make this change, by any way as possible. As well as I already do, I do not litter, and I pickup any trash that I see on the ground. I do not want our world to die. You are the most wonderful thing that happened to this world, President Barack Obama.

Sincerely,
Dianna
Breithaupt Career & Technical Center
Detroit, MI

Innovation

Dear Dianna,

Your concern is a recognition that the threat from climate change is real, and I'm glad you agree that America is ready for a BIG change, especially when it comes to our current sources of energy.

It is true that for too many years, mankind has been slow to respond to or even recognize the magnitude of the climate threat. It is true of our own country as well. We recognize that. But this is a new day. It is a new era. And I am proud to say that the United States has done more to promote clean energy and reduce carbon pollution in the last eight months than at any other time in our history.

We've proposed the very first national policy aimed at both increasing fuel economy and reducing greenhouse gas pollution for all new cars and trucks. We're moving forward with our nation's first offshore wind energy projects. We're investing billions to capture carbon pollution so that we can clean up our coal plants.

We used to have just a few dozen manufacturing facilities attached to the wind industry. Today, we have nearly 500 facilities in 43 states employing tens of thousands of American workers.

It's advancements like these that will take America into a clean and sustainable future. And through advancements and investments in clean energy technologies like solar and wind power, bio-fuels and fuel-efficient cars, our dependence on foreign oil has gone down every single year I've been in office. Every single year. America is now producing more domestic oil than any time in the last eight years, but we're also producing more natural gas. We're producing more bio-fuels than anytime in our history. We're laying the foundation for some of our nation's first offshore wind farms. Since I became President, America has nearly doubled our uses of renewable energy, like solar power and wind power.

So this country's on the path to more energy independence, and that's good for Americans today, and for Americans tomorrow.

Barack Obama

IV.

Social Concern

Activism / Family / Parenting

*"We also must remember that there is nothing wrong with young people.
We must show them the way."*
—Rosa Parks

Courage

Dear President Barack Obama,

If I was President Barack Obama there would be a lot of global lessons I would teach. One thing I would tell the youth is to always stay positive. When you stay positive you never get down when you mess up. I would also tell them to never say I can't. When you say I can't, you stop trying. Those are some of the things I would teach the youth.

Sincerely,
LaDamien
Belle Chasse Academy
Belle Chasse, Louisiana

Ability

Dear LaDamien,

We, the people of America, have the right to pursue our happiness. This idea was framed in the Declaration of Independence. Our individual rights are endowed by our Creator. The essential idea of the Declaration of Independence is that we are born free with certain unalienable rights. Each of us has the power of thought that gives us the ability to change our nation and our world for the better. We can be free thinkers. We can be positive thinkers. Yes we can. This idea has been taken for granted among our schools, individuals and families. We can rise together. If we choose to change, just imagine what we can do when we exercise the power of positive thought. We can do that, because this is America. Because the Declaration of Independence and the Bill of Rights say we can. Yes, we can choose.

Barack Obama

Power of Thought

Dear President Obama,

If I was President Barack Obama, one global lesson I would teach today's youth is the power of thought. To think before you act, think about the outcome of any situation, and most of all think about is it worth losing everything or will those actions help you become successful.

As President Barack Obama, I will use examples of people's lives to describe events that could have turned out badly if people didn't use the power of thought. For example, robbers end up in jail because they don't use the power of thought before stealing or harming others.

In conclusion, today's youth should understand and remember if you make mistakes, as we all do, you can use the power of thought to solve the situation.

Sincerely,
Chaz
Ingham Academy
Lansing, MI

Perseverance

Dear Chaz,

Many Americans have taken what this country offers for granted. We have resisted change. If we choose the power of thought to think positively, just imagine what we could accomplish. We must eliminate the cynical thinking that we cannot, and replace it with the mantra, "Yes we can." Each one of us will have to work at it by studying harder, working smarter, and thinking anew. We'll have to slough off bad habits and reform our schools to be open to more critical thinking instead of memorization. The power of thought can get us there. We must revamp and reform our education system so our young people will understand the basic values of self-determination, power of choice, self-restraint, perseverance, power of one, responsibility, to be global lessons as older generations have understood them in the past.

Barack Obama

Parenting

Dear President Obama,

The change I would like to see in my family is respect. My mother is a single parent and life is really heavy on her. She tries to get my father to pay child support after he's been in and out of jail. Now that he's out, he does nothing and he doesn't even give money when we need it. My mother always needed help with my little brother and me, but now life has got harder. I hate to see my mother cry, but I see her crying all the time. She cries in the car, at work and at home. Different things that we used to have we don't have any more like a lot of food, cable, and my mother even had to turn her cell phone off because her boss cut her hours. My mother goes through a lot everyday for me, my little brother, sister and my sick grandmother.

I feel my little brother goes to the best school in Washington, D.C. Arch Bishop Carroll High School—with a scholarship, everything paid for except uniforms and transportation, but he doesn't want it. This is his first year at the school. He gets in trouble everyday, fighting with the teachers and talking really disrespectful. My little brother is out of control; he doesn't listen to anyone at all.

President Obama, I know there is nothing that you can really do, but these are just some changes within my family that I want to happen. I really love my family, but sometimes it's hard to sit in my house or even be around my little brother because he is so disrespectful. I try to tell him that drugs and alcohol are not the way to go. Thank you for letting me share, for listening to me, and for reading the changes that I want to happen in my family.

Sincerely,
Renice
Ballou S.T.A.Y. HS
Washington, D.C.

Support

Dear Renice,

Being a single parent is a huge challenge for many Americans. Children that have two parents to raise them, and contribute to their lives are blessed. Like many men today, I grew up without a father in the house. My mother and father divorced when I was two years old. It was women, then, who provided the balance in my life that kept my family afloat. We know the statistics say that children who grow up without a father are nine times more likely to commit crimes and drop out of school. They are likely to have behavioral problems. The foundation of our community is weaker because of these statistics. We need families to raise our children. We need fathers to realize that responsibility does not end at conception.

As a community, we need to help all mothers, such as yours Renice, who are raising children by themselves. The mothers who drop their kids off at school, go to work, take care of the home, cook dinner, help kids with homework, and do all the other jobs that come with being a parent, are doing the work of two parents. . I know the toll that being a single parent took on my parent. Yes, your brother needs attention. Whatever, help can be provided at home is the first step. I trust he will realize that he needs to take advantage of his education at Arch Bishop Carroll High School. He will have to listen to those around him who want the best for him, like your mother and his teachers in school. A lot of kids don't have these same chances today. There is no margin of error in most young people's lives.

We must set examples of excellence for our children. If we want to set high expectations for them, we have to set high expectations for ourselves. That's how we build and rebuild that foundation.

Barack Obama

Self-Reliance

Dear Mr. President,

Who would've thought that the United States of America would have its first black president? I wouldn't have thought that any African/American would have the courage and the strength to do what you did. Through all of your speeches you were able to convince the United States of America that you are the right person to send into the White House next. Through your speeches you made some very remarkable quotes. One of them is, "*Today we begin in earnest the work of making sure that the world we leave for the children is just a little bit better than the one we inhabit today.*" Through this I think you were telling us that we the children are the future. What we do today will have a big impact on what the future holds for us. To me this quote means that what the people of today leave for us is what we use to make the world a better place for the future.

My parents have always told me that everything they do right now is for us. Everything they sacrifice is for us. When they keep telling me that I begin to understand more about why I have a big impact on what is to come. I begin to understand how important we are to the world. Through them telling me this I understand the importance of education. I understand it is important for me to try to achieve my goals. I know that if I work hard every day to achieve my goals not only my parents will be proud of me, but I will be proud of me too. What we do today is to help the future generations. If we succeed today then that will help the future generation also succeed. It will help them come up with new ideas to help the world become better and better. Also, that my parents just want to make sure that before they leave the world, it is just a little bit better than the way it is right now. That is what you said means to me.

One thing I will commit to doing better for the future generations is make sure that I succeed in what I do and try to help other succeed as well. I would try to do something that would not only help myself but also help others as well. I know that if I do that, I would be keeping my commitment.

Jeneba

Confidence

Dear Jeneba,

Our Nation has been profoundly shaped by ordinary Americans who have volunteered their time and energy to overcome extraordinary challenges. From the American Revolution and the Seneca Falls Convention to the everyday acts of compassion and purpose that move millions to make change in their communities, our Nation has always been at its best when individuals have come together to realize a common vision. As we continue to pursue progress, service and social innovation will play an essential role in achieving our highest ambitions—from a world-class education for every child to an economy built to last.

Now I know that Americans are going through some hard times. Many folks have lost their jobs, and are struggling to make ends meet. At times like these, we look to the example of past generations before us—our grandparents, our great-grandparents. They knew that the next generation's success would only be possible if they felt a responsibility to each other and to the future of their country, and they knew our way of life would only endure if we felt that same sense of shared responsibility. That's how we'll reduce our deficit. That's an America built to last.

We can do this. I know we can, because we've done it before. At the end of World War II, when another generation of heroes returned home from combat, they built the strongest economy and middle-class the world has ever known. They shared the optimism of a nation that had triumphed over a depression and fascism. They understood they were part of something larger, that they were contributing to a story of success that every American had a chance to share, the basic American promise that if you worked hard, you could do well enough to raise a family, own a home, send your kids to college, and put a little away for the future.

Sustaining the American Dream has never been about standing pat. It has required each generation to sacrifice, and struggle, and meet the demands of a new age. And now, it's our turn. We know what it takes to compete for the jobs and industries of our time. We need to out-innovate, out-educate, and out-build the rest of the world. We have to make America the best place on Earth to do business. We need to take responsibility for our deficit and reform our government.

Some people say that Americans have lost their sense of traditions and values, but to them, I say, look at what Americans are doing everyday. Hard work—that's a value. Looking out for one another—that's a value. The idea that we're all in it together—that I am my brother's keeper; I am my sister's keeper—that is a value. That's how our people will prosper.

Barack Obama

Equality

Dear Mr. President,

Congratulations on your victory to become not only the president, but the first African American president of our country. There are a lot of things that I think you should change now that you are president and here is the most important one.

My family is different from most of the families in my school because instead of having a mom and dad, I have two moms instead. I think my family is just as good and loving as anyone's and my moms raised my little brother and me to be good kids. We do our homework and we get good grades and we are nice to everyone. My moms have good jobs and they love us both a lot. So Mr. President I don't think its fair that my parents can't be married like other kids parents just because they are gay. It makes me feel left out and sad for my moms that our family isn't allowed to do the same things as other families.

My mom says that it doesn't matter if she and mommy can get married or not because we are still a family but I think our country would be better if no one was left out. We learned about Martin Luther King Jr. and how he said that all American should be treated the same. I know he was talking about African Americans back then but I think he would mean everyone today. I think that everyone should be able to get married to whoever they want even if they are gay or not. Then my moms would be allowed to get married like everyone else. President Obama I think the most important thing for you to do is to make it legal for all gay people to get married because family is the most important thing.

Sincerely,
Audrey
Northeast Academy Charter School
Denver, CO

The Golden Rule

Dear Audrey,

You are right that there is nothing more important than family—nothing more important to each of us individually, and nothing more important to us as a nation. As a nation, we're founded on the belief that all of us are equal and each of us deserves the freedom to pursue our own version of happiness, to make the most of our talents, to speak our minds, to not fit in. Most of all, to be true to ourselves. That's the freedom that enriches us all. That's what America's all about.

And that's why as your president, I've always been adamant that gay and lesbian Americans should be treated fairly and equally, and I've always stood on the side of broader equality for the LGBT community. And now, over the course of my own evolution on this issue, I think it's important for to affirm that I think same-sex couples should be able to get married. But, my own personal affirmation is not enough. More remains to be done to ensure every single American is treated equally, regardless of sexual orientation or gender identity. Moving forward, my Administration will continue its work to advance the rights of LGBT Americans. As we reflect on how far we have come and how far we have yet to go, let us recall that the progress we have made is built on the words and deeds of ordinary Americans.

From generation to generation, ordinary Americans have led a proud and inexorable march toward freedom, fairness, and full equality under the law—not just for some, but for all. Ours is a heritage of citizens who fought to build for themselves and their families a Nation where no one is a second-class citizen, no one is denied basic rights, and all of us are free to live and love as we see fit.

To take on this issue, I think the best thing that we can do, Audrey, is to go back to the Golden Rule: we must treat others the way we would like to be treated. As long as we live by that rule, America will always be a nation of freedom for all.

Barack Obama

Determination

Dear President Obama,

Indubitably the world in which we live is riddled with flaws and is far from the golden utopia in fairy tales. There are elements beyond our control, such as those of nature. We can build dams or create sturdier buildings, but ultimately we are at the mercy of nature's desire.

However, we are not entirely helpless against the plagues threatening our world. Global Warming, poverty, hatred and lack of education. These are all demons jeopardizing the harmony and vitality of the world. Perhaps these are too formidable for us to eliminate, but that is not an excuse to not try. Just as we do not know the full extent of nature's power, we have yet to see the full extent of human power against the aforementioned global issues. It is imperative that we, as a nation, make a commitment to minimize our delirious effect on the environment. The operative word is "we." In order to maximize the results and create as healthy an environment for our posterity as possible, each person must be willing to make sacrifices and adjustments in his or her life.

Fortunately, poverty is not as imminent for America as it is for other nations, but with the current economic state, everyone is suffering. People must shed their selfish skin and assume one of altruism. We must learn to support each other. Donations to charities and shelters must be increased.

Possibly even more damaging than poverty is the evil of hatred. Far too often over the course of history has hatred prevailed and caused irreparable harm. Within our own nation and globally, hatred has been allowed to fester and metastasize like a disease. It must stop now. The beauty of this world is that it consists of an elected group of people. However, this diversity in culture or thought often is the cause of conflicts. People fear the unknown. We must take strides in order to elevate the level of tolerance. We must smother it before it is allowed to grow, which means focusing our attention on the children. They must be taught history from both sides so that they receive the full picture and are not manipulated into believing one side. Greg Mortenson dedicated his life to building schools in the Middle East for kids who otherwise would never receive an education. His goal is to fight terror with books. His philosophy is brilliant. We must build bridges between nations and learn to understand and respect the differences.

In addition to educating about cultures, there must be an increase of academic teaching. As a nation we need to put more emphasis on the young. We need to instill motivation to learn and pursue higher education. Not only that, but we need more Greg Mortensons who will devote their time and effort to helping those obtain an education, who otherwise would not be able to do so.

After participating in the W.E.B. Dubois Society, which essentially examines race relations and the achievement gap, I came to the realization that if any change is going to be made, it is going to depend on the youth. Therefore, I will commit to continue tutoring children younger than myself, with the hope that the individual will benefit and in turn give back to the community in some way. Not only will I help them academically, but to the best of my ability, I will convey to them the importance of respecting and tolerating others so that perhaps some of the hate invading our world will be eliminated.

Sincerely,
Michelle
Boston Latin School
Boston, MA

Education

Dear Michelle,

Difficulty is no excuse for complacency. Unease is no excuse for inaction. And we must not allow perfection to become the enemy of progress. Yes, the issues that you have outlined in your letter-poverty, global climate change, prejudice, education are enormous challenges, but we are determined to act. And we will meet our responsibility to future generations.

One of our highest priorities is to provide our nation's children with an education that they can use, and of which we can be proud. As a nation, we have an obligation to make sure that all children have the resources they need to learn: quality schools, good teachers, the latest textbooks, and the right technology. That's why instead of just pouring money into a system that's not working, we repealed the No Child Left Behind Act and replaced it with the most meaningful reform our public schools have seen in a generation.

We need our education system to equip our children to become the engineers, scientists, and innovators that this country, and this planet needs to tackle the most daunting challenge of our time: climate change. We need the next generation of students to further the developments of clean, alternative energies and green technologies that will lead us into a sustainable future where we don't have to sacrifice the environment for our economy.

Above all, we need to keep in mind that we as Americans are in this together, and when we act together, there is nothing the United States of America cannot achieve. That's why my administration has proclaimed days like Education and Sharing Day, National Volunteer Week, and signed the Serve America Act. In all of these efforts, we are reminded how volunteer work can expand opportunity not only for those in need, but also for those who give. Service can teach valuable skills that pave the way to long-term employment and stay with volunteers throughout their careers and lives.

These acts embody the idea that time and again, during moments of trial, Americans have demonstrated a fundamental commitment to compassion, cooperation, and goodwill toward others—doing not what is easy, but what is right.

These qualities have come to define us, and as we prepare today's students to become tomorrow's leaders, let us foster values that have sustained our country for generations.

Barack Obama

Role Model

Dear President Obama,

First, I would like to congratulate you on your presidential win and say that I am pleased to call you my president. I want to state a problem to you that I think needs to change in America sometime in your term, and that is Abortion. This issue has been a problem since Roe v. Wade and has been since then, it never fade away unless we think of doing what is right and that is to ban abortion. You said that Change will happen, and I think that first we need to change the minds of women of aborting their unborn.

I understand that not all women think like me but if they are educated with the process of abortion that they will understand the harm that it does to the infant. I see my community filled with pregnant teenage girls from ages 14-18, they all have kept their babies or have put them up for adoption, and I believe they are role models for other women or teens that have a planned or unplanned baby. My mother got pregnant at the age of fifteen, and I am thankful that she decided to raise me and not abort the life process. Many women or teens would have these procedures done to get rid of their problems, but they do not know they create more problems.

President Obama, I think that you should look at the point of view of the infant that is living in the bodies of these women and think if they will ever see the light of day. My mother made the right choice of taking responsibility of her actions. I was not planned, but she understood that it was not my fault I came into this world neither are the other infants. Those infants deserve life and have those rights according to the 9th amendment. Please take the time to think about those who are waiting to be here. Thank you for your time President Obama.

Sincerely,
Cindy
Gertz-Ressler HS
Los Angeles, CA

Trust

Dear Cindy,

Thank you for your letter and congratulations. I understand that the topic of abortion and a woman's right to choose raises a lot of emotions and opinions from many Americans, and each of us has a right to those opinions and beliefs.

In recent months, I have heard people speaking about too much government regulation and involvement in people's lives. In this instance, as a president that is sworn to uphold the law, I have to say that no government should be able to make laws over a woman's body. Every woman should be in control of the decisions that affect her health.

I know this may bring about heated arguments between some Democrats and Republicans, or some liberals and conservatives. But, we don't need another political fight about ending a woman's right to choose, or getting rid of Planned Parenthood, or taking away access to affordable birth control. Every woman should have the right to control their own health choices, just as men do.

The duty of the government is to protect and uphold the rights and integrity of every citizen-no matter their, race, religion, or sex. The United States as a nation is better off when women are treated fairly and equally in every respect, whether it is the salary you earn or the health decisions you make.

Barack Obama

Family

Dear President Obama,

I grew up with not just one mother, but with two. When my mom was pregnant with my brother, she worked in a hospital. While she worked there, she met this incredible African American woman Emma Goodwin. Emma became Ommy to us. My mother and Ommy connected and got to know one another. Soon, my brother was born and my mom needed someone to help with my brother. She needed someone good to take care of my older brother, which made her think of Ommy. Two years later, I was born and Ommy became my second mother. Ommy still watched us while my mom worked. my mom got a big promotion that brought us to Charlotte, North Carolina. This was very sad. Our move made us leave our very close loved friend, Ommy, who had become a family member. Each year for New Years, Ommy would catch the bus and come visit. I grew up with an incredible woman in my life. If I could love her so much, it taught me it doesn't matter about your skin color. It matters about the person.

Ommy grew up around the 1920's in Lamar, South Carolina. This was a time when African Americans didn't have the same rights as white women, men and children have today. Ommy had to go into the back of the store just for a bottle of Nehi, instead of a Coca Cola. Ommy told us that African Americans weren't permitted to drink Coca Cola in Lamar, South Carolina.

I got to visit Ommy during Thanksgiving and was inspired by her hope for the future. As a white American that is loved by an African woman, I am looking to you to lead everyone—to see as I see—with NO color. I'll always love Ommy. She'll fill a large part of my hart forever and she will always be my Ommy.

Sincerely,
Spencer
Carmel Middle School
Charlotte, NC

Example

Dear Spencer,

Thank you for your letter and your and your family's story. Unfortunately, Ommy grew up in and experienced a darker time in our country's history where not all Americans were treated equally and were considered second-class citizens because of their skin color.

When future generations hear these stories of pain and progress and struggle and sacrifice, I hope they will not think of them as somehow separate from the larger American story. I want them to see it as central— an important part of our shared story— as a call to see ourselves in one another. A call to realize that a nation does not mean a collection of people that come from the exact same race, religion, culture, class, or sexual orientation. Neither does a family. A family does not have to meet a standard of one culture or one race, or one mother and one father. A family is about the lives and the love that you share together.

I'm sure Ommy will tell you, with time, you're going to see that our differences are a source of pride, and a source of strength. You'll look back on the struggles you faced, as I'm sure Ommy does now, with compassion and wisdom. And that's not just going to serve you, but it will help you get involved to make this country a better place. It'll mean that you'll be more likely to help fight discrimination, not just against people of different races, but discrimination in all forms.

As a nation, we're founded on the belief that all of us are equal and each of us deserves the freedom to pursue our own version of happiness, to make the most of our talents, to speak our minds, to not fit in. Most of all, to be true to ourselves. That's the freedom that enriches us all. That's what America's all about.

I'm glad we have stories of families like yours. May we remember these stories, and may we live up to their examples.

Barack Obama

V.

Power of Change

"You must be the change you wish to be in the world."
—Gandhi

"I had asked others to make a change, but an opportunity was given to me. I knew someone had to take the first step.
—Rosa Parks

"Change will not come if we wait for some other person or some other time. We are the ones we've been waiting for."
—Barack Obama

Teaching

Dear President Barack Obama,

I'm concerned about students not getting a good education. We need better and safer school environments. Some students are not getting a good education.

Sincerely,
Aryies
Loving Elementary
Detroit, MI

Decisions

Dear Aryies,

We know that education is everything to our children's future. We know that they will no longer just compete for good jobs with children only from Michigan, but with children from India and China and all over the world. We know the work and the studying and the level of education requires a global outlook.

It's up to us parents to instill this ethic of excellence in our children to create a a environment of responsibility. It's up to us to say to our daughters, don't ever let images on TV tell you what you are worth, because I expect you to dream without limit and reach for those goals. It's up to us to tell our sons, those songs on the radio may glorify violence, but in my house we give glory to achievement, self-respect, and hard work. It's up to us to set these high expectations. And that means meeting those expectations ourselves. That means setting examples of excellence in our own lives.

Barack Obama

Service

Dear President Barack Obama,

First, I would like to see a decrease in pollution. We should have more cars that run on electricity or natural gas on the streets. We should have cleaner water and better ways to reduce litter. We need more programs that help clean up and rebuild cities and towns. I would love to see more energy efficiency in homes, schools, cities and towns. The earth is becoming more and more polluted. Sooner or later we may be wearing gas masks on our streets. We need to act fast and smart.

Second, I want to see all educational needs met. We need better, cleaner and safer schools. Schools should have freshly prepared, highly nutritious lunches. Teachers should receive better incomes. There should be more programs for students and parents. We must help our youth now or they will fail.

President Obama, this is what needs to happen. You as well as I know that we need things to change for the better. I hope you will consider these changes when you step into office.

Yours truly,
Jahari
M. V. Leckie Elementary
Washington, D.C.

Growth

Dear Jahari,

Thank you for your letter and your concern. I want you to know that it is one of my goals as president to finally free America from the tyranny of oil. Our nation will harness homegrown, alternative fuels like ethanol and spur the production of more fuel-efficient cars. We will set up a system for capping greenhouse gases. We will turn this crisis of global warming into a moment of opportunity for innovation, and job creation, and an incentive for business that will serve as a model for the world. We will be the generation that makes future generations proud of what we did here.

We will be the next generation that reforms and improves our education system. We will reshape our economy to compete in the digital age. We will set high standards for our children's schools and give them the resources they need to succeed. We will recruit a new army of teachers and give them better pay and more support in exchange for more accountability. We will make college more affordable, we will invest in scientific research, and we will lay down broadband lines through the heart of inner cities and rural towns all across America.

Barack Obama

Hard Work

Dear President Obama,

Congratulations on your hard-won victory. The voters have expressed confidence in your leadership and now you face an array of unprecedented challenges. With the election behind us, it is time for all Americans to put aside their differences and work together. *As George Washington, Abraham Lincoln, and John F. Kennedy promised independence, change, and freedom, you, as well, are next in line of presidency to continue what these great people have left behind.* America has suffered a deadly scar of hatred, violence, depression, and death. Therefore, "She" decided to put you in the presidency office to bring what you promise, "change." One of the changes I am concerned about is taxes.

Sincerely,
José
Gertz-Ressler H.S.
Los Angeles, CA

Conviction

Dear José,

I'd like to recall the life of a tall, gangly, self-made Springfield lawyer, Abraham Lincoln, who tells us that a different future is possible. He tells us that there is power in words. He tells us that there is power in conviction—That beneath all the differences of race and religion, faith, we are one people. He tells us that there is power in hope.

That's why I'm committed to serve America. Not just to hold an office, but to gather with you to transform a nation. I see a future of endless possibility stretching before us. I can see that you sense, as I do, that the time is now to shake off our slumber, and slough off our fear, and make good on the debt we owe past and future generations. I'm ready to take up the cause, and march with you, and work with you. Together, starting today, let us finish the work that needs to be done, and usher in a new birth of freedom on this Earth.

And part of keeping my promise to change will mean keeping my promises to the American people. As I promised before, the middle class and our low-income individuals will not bear a tax—that is my goal and that is my aim. And yes we can make this happen because we are choosing hope over fear. We're choosing unity over division and sending a powerful message that change is here in America.

Barack Obama

Excel

Dear President Barack Obama,

Thank you for your courage and perseverance throughout your life. Your achievement of becoming the first African American President has proven to me that when my mom or dad tells me that I can do anything it is true. It is the greatest feeling in the world to know that success is truly possible in any area I choose.

To make a better tomorrow for my generation we new must begin by making today better. As not only a minority group, but as for our nation and world as one, we have excelled in unmatchable measures, but we can still be better and it is vital that we continue to grow.

That quote of yours means that in the present world citizens must inaugurate the action of improvement in our world. Your target audience may have been those in adulthood but we as children and adolescents have a great impact on our future as well. In our world now, you will find gang members and mafia members walking down most streets, sitting in offices, fighting in courtrooms as lawyers, and ruling as judges. We need a change.

I can honestly commit to being better and to making a difference. I will attend school each day possible solely looking to receive my education with a spirit of joy. I make the commitment to help someone daily.

I will encourage others all that I can, including myself, to courageously soar toward their aspirations.

I am unequivocally appreciative of you sharing your motivational words of wisdom. In reading them a word loudly rang from each corner of my head, that word was try. They enlightened me and refreshed my view on many things.

Sincerely,

Drew

Northeast Academy Charter

Denver, CO

Solidarity

Dear Drew,

In moving America forward, the best agenda starts with education. Whether you're conservative or liberal, Republican or Democrat, practically every economist agrees that in this digital age, a highly educated and skilled workforce will be the key not only to individual opportunity, but to overall success of our economy as well. We cannot be satisfied until every child in America—and I mean every child—has the same chances for good education that we want for our own children. When we start improving education, we start addressing the root causes of some of our nation's problems—drugs, violence, and crime.

How many times in the last year has an inner city child been lost at the hands of another child? How many times have our hearts stopped in the middle of the night with the sound of a gunshot or a siren? How many teenagers have we seen hanging around on street corners when they should be sitting in a classroom? How many are sitting in prison when they should be working, or as least looking for a job? How many in this generation are we willing to lose to poverty, violence, or addiction? How many?

We should take every step necessary to build a strong foundation for our children. But we should also know that even if we do; even if we meet our obligations as fathers and parents; even if Washington does its part, too, we will still face difficult challenges in our lives. There will be days of struggle and heartache. The rains will still come and the winds will still blow. And that is why Jose, the final lesson we must learn, the greatest gift we can pass on to our children, is the gift of a good education that teaches our students to excel beyond good because they can be the best.

Barack Obama

Commitment

Dear President Barack Obama,

There are many changes that need to be made in this country. Now it is your duty as the new president of the United States to make these changes happen. As youth today in America, we have seen what happens when the importance of the individual person is forgotten. We are growing up in a society where science and technology are vital not only in war and medical fields but also in environmental and economic endeavors. In order for America to be competitive with other countries of wealth and great intelligence, changes must be made to educational systems from early childhood up to college level academics.

I do not know a great deal about politics or foreign relations. I feel that it is ironic that Americans spend such a large sum of money donating to charities to further the education of children in other countries, when improvements are needed for schools in America. High school graduation rates have been declining significantly and as a result the success of our country will decline. This has to be fixed.

For elementary and high school grade levels a common curriculum making classes, such as English, Math, Science, Foreign Language, Culture, Economics, and Government, mandatory world only help to improve American society. In order for these changes to be made, decisions about education need to be instituted throughout America, and they need to be instituted quickly. America must not fall behind, especially in an age where a new development can either benefit the well-being of all people or destroy many lives.

What I ask of you, Mr. President, is that once you come into office, that you be a president for the people. If America is ever going to be this great land of opportunity, our children must be given access to all the tools they need to fulfill the goals set for them. With a more educated people, America will be a stronger country. I want to live in a country where the people are actively working to improve their lives and the lives of others, not constantly fighting against restraints such as money or poor education. For our nation to succeed and for the dreams of many American children to be within their reach, this education system needs to change. Mr. President, you can make this possible.

Sincerely,
Deirdre

Improvement

Dear Deirdre,

Thank you for your compassionate letter and concern. As we move forward as one nation and one family, there are significant changes America must make: EDUCATION, SCIENCE, TECHNOLOGY, and ENERGY. Investments in these four key areas would go a long way in making America more competitive. Of course, none of these investments will yield results overnight. All will be subject to controversy. Investment in research, development and education will cost money at a time when our federal budget is already stretched. Increasing the fuel efficiency of American cars or instituting performance pay for public-school teachers will involve overcoming the suspicions of workers who already feel embattled. Arguments over the wisdom of school vouchers or the viability of hydrogen fuel cells won't go away anytime soon.

It's also time to redesign our schools, not just for the sake of working parents, but also to help prepare our children for a more competitive world. Countless studies confirm the educational benefits of strong pre-school programs, which is why even families who have a stay-at-home parent often seek them out. The same goes for longer school days, summer school and after school programs. We shall consider all of these as we move forward in the 21ˢᵗ Century, because in order to build a strong foundation for ourselves and our children, we take every consideration and every step that improves our great nation.

Barack Obama

Vision

Dear Mr. President,

For as long as I can remember, Americans have been starved; they are emaciated and ravenous not because of food shortages or droughts but because of our infatuation with the pursuit of happiness. We want to be happy; we strive for it, we saturate our lives with the longing and reaching for that unattainable end. And that pursuit of happiness is the root of all our troubles, from the economic crisis to the obesity epidemic to the yawning gap between the lower and higher classes. While the idea of every American having the "unalienable right" to "the pursuit of happiness" is a sound and just one, the methods by which Americans seek this happiness are founded in the treacherous illusions our society thrusts upon us from birth on. There illusions tell us that happiness is founded in wealth, beauty and a carefree life. We believe wealth is the key to happiness, so mammoth American companies value money over people; a greedy mentality that recently drove our affluent economy into the ground. Teenagers, despairing over the waiflike models in the pages of glossy magazines, either starve themselves to ghosts or eat their insecurities away. And the rich, afraid of the truth of the world will stain their "perfect" lives, look the other way when a homeless man humbly asks for change.

And so we starve. The rich businessman, having thought of only money his whole life, hungers for meaning to fill his empty mansions. The anorexic woman, never thin enough, yearns for someone to take her hand and tell her that she's beautiful the way she is; and the homeless man craves for simply a kind look, a helping hand, and acknowledgment of his humanity.

I want this to change. I want America to become the place it was always meant to be—a place where the pursuit of happiness does not breed greed, ignorance and resentment but generosity, understanding and love. I want my children and grandchildren to grow up in a world where happiness is most often found in love and caring for others, rather than one where the words "ignorance is bliss" are treated as a common lifestyle.

You have provided hope to millions of Americans; hope that after years of despair, we can yet again rebuild our country. Hope that our children can have a shot at a good education; that our tired troops can come home from war; that we can push back the tide of indifference to heal our broken environment. And you have provided hope to me that America no longer need be a world undone, that we won't have to starve anymore. That is the change I want to see you make in the home I was born and raised in. I understand that you're not Superman, or, for that matter, God, and that you can't make everything right. But I'm asking you to try.

Sincerely,
Elizabeth
Boston Latin School
Boston, MA

Virtue

Dear Elizabeth,

You have made a very poignant observation concerning the greed that has so recently done so much damage to the lives of so many Americans. The greed on Wall Street and the unacceptable practices by financial institutions cannot be tolerated by my administration or by Americans in the 21ˢᵗ Century. That's not the America I see or want for ourselves or our children. We need to rebuild our economy on a sound footing of responsibility and accountability.

I'm confident that we have the talent and the resources to create a better future, a future in which the economy grows and prosperity is shared. What's preventing us from shaping that future isn't the absence of good ideas—it's the absence of a national commitment to take the tough steps necessary to make America more competitive—and the absence of a new consensus around the appropriate role of government in the marketplace.

We have an obligation and a responsibility to be investing in our students and our schools. We must make sure that people who have the grades, the desire and the will, but not the money, can still get the best education possible. We need to internalize this idea of excellence in all of our affairs and what we do. Not many folks spend a lot of time trying to be excellent. We have started to slough off the old practices and begin anew, but we have a long road ahead of us filled with trials and changes. Together, we will meet the challenges we face, and together we will overcome them.

Barack Obama

Forgiveness

Dear President Obama,

As a child, I was very fortunate. I started school when I was three, and I was exposed to make the right decisions from the start. *I never had to worry, because my family cared about me.* However, **a _lot_** of other people in the world do not have this privilege of someone caring for him or her. If we, as one of the most developed nations in the world, continue to let this happen, the world will be left worse than it is today. As America, we have to work together to make each childhood one to remember and learn from. We can achieve this by opening up homes and designating committed volunteers so that every child will have a place to live and a caring "parent." We can start with our own country, and slowly expand to other nations. I personally can't bear to see those millions of children who endure life without homes and families. It's not fair that KIDS suffer like this. *I will, as an adult, dedicate my life to helping the underprivileged. I think that every child, no matter the age, race, wealth, or gender, should be able to enjoy their childhood and learn to be the best person possible.* I hope I have been able to clarify what I think is the first step towards making today's world better for tomorrow's future. President Obama, I feel that you are the unsurpassed man for making this happen, and I am ready for change!

Sincerely,
Pooja,
Hill Campus of Arts & Science
Denver, CO

Selflessness

Dear Pooja,

It is good to hear from a young man who is selflessly committed to a cause greater than himself.

Our Nation has been profoundly shaped by Americans, like you, who have volunteered their time and energy to overcome extraordinary challenges. From the American Revolution and the Seneca Falls Convention to the everyday acts of compassion and purpose that move millions to make change in their communities, our Nation has always been at its best when individuals have come together to realize a common vision. As we continue to pursue progress, service and social innovation will play an essential role in achieving our highest ambitions—from an economy built to last to a world-class education for every child.

The responsibility of providing every child with a quality education falls on the shoulders of all of us. Government leaders, citizens, parents and students must be willing to do what's necessary to give every child a chance to succeed. That responsibility begins not in our classrooms, but in our homes and communities. It's family that first instills the love of learning in a child. Only parents can make sure the TV is turned off and homework gets done. Our schools share this responsibility. When a student walks into the classroom, it should be a place of high expectations and high performance for all children.

The responsibility for bettering America falls on each of us. Time and again, during moments of trial, Americans have demonstrated a fundamental commitment to compassion, cooperation, and goodwill toward others—doing not what is easy, but what is right. These qualities have come to define us, and as we prepare today's students to become tomorrow's leaders, let us nourish the qualities and virtues that have sustained our country for generations.

Barack Obama

Hope

Dear President Obama,

You made the statement, "Today we begin in earnest the work of making sure that the world we leave our children is just a little bit better than the one we inhabit today." This statement is important to me because it gives me hope that I will see change in the world we live in. I hope to see more tolerance of each other. I hope to see myself growing in a United States that will truly be united. This country is made up of so many different cultures and races, and I hope to see us unite as one. The one thing I will commit to do to leave the world better for future generations is to always be fair and to treat my fellow man like I want to be treated. President Obama, you have made history by being the first African American president and I am proud to be of the age to understand the significance of this event. I feel hope that I will become an adult in a world that has no boundaries because of my color, my language, or my culture. I feel hope.

Sincerely,
Kelsey
Western Branch Middle School
Chesapeake, VA

Cooperation

Dear Kelsey,

America is built upon differences—different races and cultures, different religions and political parties. These differences should not divide us; they should strengthen us. And our government leaders in both parties should be the first ones to lead by that example. We may have differences in policy, but we all believe in the rights enshrined in our Constitution. We may have different opinions, but we believe in the same promise that says this is a place where you can make it if you try. We may have different backgrounds, but we believe in the same dream that says this is a country where anything is possible. No matter who you are. No matter where you come from.

We need to end the notion that two parties must be locked in a perpetual campaign of mutual destruction, that politics is about clinging to rigid ideologies instead of building consensus around commonsense ideas. New laws will only pass with support from Democrats and Republicans. We will move forward together, or not at all—for the challenges we face are bigger than party, and bigger than politics.

Kelsey, your letter brings to mind one of my proudest possessions: the flag that the SEAL team took with them on their mission to get bin Laden. On it are each of their names. Some may be Democrats, some may be Republicans, some may be independents, but that doesn't matter. All that mattered that day was the mission. No one thought about politics. No one thought about themselves. More than that, the mission only succeeded because every member of that unit trusted each other, because you can't charge up those stairs into darkness and danger unless you know there's somebody behind you, watching your back. So it is with America.

Each time I look at that flag, I'm reminded that our destiny is stitched together like those 50 stars and 13 stripes. No one built this country on their own. This Nation is great because we built it together. This Nation is great because we worked as a team. This Nation is great because we got each other's backs. And if we hold fast to that truth, in this moment of trial, there is no challenge too great, no mission too hard. As long as we are joined in common purpose, as long as we maintain our common resolve, our journey moves forward, and our future is hopeful, and the state of our Union will always be strong, Kelsey.

Barack Obama

Unity

Dear President Obama,

I would like to see if you can also restore our position as global leader in the world. Your election success opened a giant door of opportunity for all of us of the non-white race. I have been planning to become President of the United States since I was a small child, and thanks to you, this is possible.

The policies of President Bush have both, put us in an economic downturn, and a worldview as a rogue nation. The war in Iraq has divided this nation's peoples as children of both pro-war and antiwar gets shipped off to fight a war that is over, put us in a huge economic burden, and open for attack. As you mentioned, we need to cooperate with Russia, not fight her and her people. The cold war is over and I feel al if we still haven't moved on.

It pains my father each time there is a new report about soldiers dying in Iraq. Children in his view could contribute so much more. As I mentioned earlier, the war in Iraq divided this nation's peoples much like it did during the Vietnam War…" *A house divided cannot stand by itself,"* in respect of Abraham Lincoln. I hope to see that you reunite the people of America so that we can reunite with the rest of the world. We all need to work together like you said in order to make the world a better place to live for future generations.

Sincerely,
Jose
Roosevelt, H.S.
Washington, DC

Victory

Dear Jose,

Seven and a half years ago, when you were still a young man in elementary school making plans to be president, President Bush announced the beginning of a military operation in Iraq. Much has changed since that night. A war to disarm a state become a fight against an insurgency. Terrorism and sectarian warfare threatened to tear Iraq apart. Thousands of Americans gave their lives. Tens of thousands have been wounded. Our relations abroad were strained. Our unity at home was tested. These, Jose, are the rough waters we encountered during one of America's longest wars.

It's harder to end a war than begin one. Indeed, everything that American troops have done in Iraq—all the fighting, and all the dying, the bleeding and the building, and the training and the partnering—all of it led us to a great moment in our nation's history. The moment when I, as your President and the Commander and Chief of our brave troops, could announce that our mission in Iraq is over. I can tell you I have few prouder moments as president than when I stood in front of hundreds of service men and women, our beloved brothers and sisters at Fort Bragg on December 21, 2011 and was able to say, "Welcome home."

Now, Iraq's not a perfect place. It has many challenges ahead. Be we're leaving behind a sovereign, stable, and self-reliant Iraq with a representative government, that was elected by its people. We're building a new partnership between our nations. We're ending a war, not with a final battle, but with a final march toward home. This is an extraordinary achievement nearly nine years in the making.

Our achievement in Iraq did not come without hard work and sacrifice. Those words only begin to describe the costs of this war, and the courage of the men and women who fought it. We know too well the heavy costs of this war. More than 1.5 million Americans have served in Iraq. Over 30,000 Americans have been wounded, and those are only the wounds that show. Nearly 4,500 Americans have made the ultimate sacrifice. And, like your father, I feel the pain of these costs. A pain I'm reminded every time I sign a condolence letter or meet a family member whose life has been turned upside down.

Even as we honor those who made the ultimate sacrifice, we reaffirm our commitment to care for those who served alongside them, the veterans who came home. This includes our newest generation of veterans, from Iraq and Afghanistan. Part of ending a war responsibly is standing by those who fought it. We have to serve them and their families as well as they have served us. We have a responsibility to learn from their service and commit to the hard work and make the sacrifices needed to lead America in this young century as a beacon of strength, peace, and long lasting prosperity.

Barack Obama

United

Dear President Barack Obama,

During the entire election process, I heard you say change and how things are going to be different. Well I can't wait to see it. I'm a senior in high school and all I hear is that the economy is going down, prices are going up and getting money for college is going to be harder than ever.

America, in a way, is in a worse position than my community. Innocent people are dying and people all around the world are losing their loved ones. Then, you turn around and you have people sitting on the ground, cold and begging. I'm not going to sit here and say that this is all Bush's fault. You can't put the blame on one person. We all need to come together and work this problem out.

I would like to see more jobs in the community. Unemployment is at an all time high right now. I would also like to see a cleaner world. The world could be so much fresher and beautiful if we took better care of it. Basically, I want everything you talked about.

I'm ready to see the new and improved America. From now on, only positive things are going to be said about America from now on. I'm just happy that America chose you to lead us to a new beginning. I just wished that I was old enough to have voted.

Sincerely yours,
Angel
John J. Pershing High
Detroit, MI

Diligence

Dear Angel,

Thank you for you letter. I share your both your concerns and your enthusiasm to see change in America. So many of the problems America is facing today are rooted in an economy that has faltered and failed us. And now, we are left trying to find a way to build an economy built to last. Fortunately, we know how to build that economy and it starts with tax reform, spending, job creation, and innovation. So let's get to work.

First, Government has to start living within its means, just like families do. We have to cut the spending we can't afford so we can put the economy on a sounder footing and give our businesses the confidence they need to grow and create jobs. Also, we need Congress to stop giving tax breaks to companies that ship jobs overseas and use that money to cover moving expenses for companies that bring jobs back to America.

Second, Congress should help the millions of Americans who have worked hard and made their mortgage payments on time refinance their mortgages at lower rates and save at least $3,000 a year.

Third, Congress should help small-business owners by giving them a tax break for hiring more workers and paying them higher wages. Small businesses are the engine of economic growth in this country. We shouldn't be holding them back; we should be making it easier for them to succeed.

Fourth, if Congress fails to act soon, clean energy companies will see their taxes go up and could be forced to lay off employees. These companies are putting Americans to work. We used to have just a few dozen manufacturing facilities attached to the wind industry. Today, we have nearly 500 facilities in 43 states employing tens of thousands of American workers. Not only are these companies creating jobs, they're helping to break our dependence on foreign oil. Congress should extend these tax credits.

And finally, Congress should help our veterans returning from Iraq and Afghanistan by creating a veterans' job corps. Our men and women in uniform have served this country with honor. Now it's our turn to serve them.

I ran for President because I believed in an America where ordinary folks could get ahead, where if you worked hard, you could have a better life. That's been my focus since I came into office, and that has to be our focus now.

Barack Obama

Can

Dear President Obama,

As the President of the United States, I would like for you to build fewer jails and more schools. More schools will prevent people from saying they can't do this or can't do that. I also think that you should extend the school day because it will give students more time to learn. I would also like to see more police during weekday mornings because sometimes it is not safe to go to school. I would also like to see more neighborhood patrollers to protect the children around my community.

Last, but not least, I would like to see teachers put forth more of an effort in helping students that don't want to learn.

Sincerely,
Angela
John J. Pershing H.S.
Detroit, MI

Challenge

Dear Angela,

The need for greater capacity in our correctional facilities is evidence of the fact that we are not adequately addressing the root causes of crime in our country. As a nation, we have an obligation to make sure our children have the resources they need to learn in an environment with: quality schools, good teachers, the latest textbooks, and the right technology. As your President, I have worked tirelessly and will continue to work tirelessly to make sure that every child—children in inner cities, children in rural areas, children in suburbs—every child—is not left behind and is not only receiving a quality education, but can feel safe going to school.

I know the city of Detroit has been through struggle and is facing a lot of challenges, Angela, but there are stories of Americans facing adversity and difficulty and overcoming it all over the nation that we can look to for inspiration.

Take for instance, the story of Booker T. Washington High School in Memphis, Tennessee. This is a school in the middle of a tough neighborhood in south Memphis. There's a lot of crime; there's a lot of poverty. And just a few years ago, only about half of the students at the school graduated. Just a handful went off to college each year. But folks came together to change all that.

Under the leadership of a dynamic principal and devoted teachers, they started special academies for ninth graders, because they found that that's when a lot of kids were lost. They made it possible for students to take AP classes or vocational courses. Most importantly, they didn't just change the curriculum; they created a culture that prizes hard work and discipline and that shows every student that they matter. Today, four out of five students at the school earn a diploma. Seventy percent continue their education, many the first in their families to go to college.

So Booker T. Washington High School is no longer a story about what's gone wrong in education. It's a story about how we can set it right when we come together as a community, as a people with a common purpose and common goal. Together, we can make the changes we want to see.

Barack Obama

VI.

Economy

"We must adapt to changing times and still hold to unchanging principles."
—Jimmy Carter

"The one unchangeable certainty is that nothing is certain or unchangeable."
—John Kennedy

Participation

Dear President Obama,

President Barack Obama's line, "Today, we begin in earnest the work of making sure that the world we leave our children is just a little bit better than the one we inhabit today." means that adults need to take steps to help the environment and not make it any worse than it is today. Adults should not waste electricity or fuel, and they should recycle everything they can. Helping the environment today will only make things better for future generations.

Electricity is wasted in every household and probably in every workplace on a daily basis. People should turn off lights during the daytime and use the natural daylight that comes into their houses and offices. If curtains were pulled open and lights were turned off everyone would still be able to do their everyday activities. Using lights when the natural daylight is available is a waste of electricity and money.

My parents always talk about how they walked everywhere as kids, but today they drive everywhere. Adults could save on fuel and create less pollution if they took fewer trips in their cars and actually walked places.

One thing I will commit to do to leave the world better for the future is clean up litter. If I see litter on the ground, I will pick it up and put it in the trash. I know that picking up trash may be a small thing, but it will help the environment because trash won't get blown into other areas like oceans and harm the animals and fish that live there. If everyone picked up trash, it would make our world a cleaner place to live in.

President Obama, there are a lot of things people can do to help make the world a better place. Adults of today can do their part by teaching their children about conserving electricity and fuel, and recycling everything they can. Everyone can do something to help our environment whether it's picking up trash or turning off a light. By taking care of our planet now, this will leave it a better place for future generations.

Sincerely,
Ryan
Boston Latin School
Boston, MA

Teach

Dear Ryan,

Yes, we as adults or parents must teach young people like you and future generations to come. The first is setting an example of excellence for our children—because if we want to set high expectations for them, we've got to set high expectations for ourselves. It's great if you have a job; it's even better if you have a college degree. It's a wonderful thing if you are married and living in a home with your children, but don't just sit in the house and watch Sports Center all weekend long. That's why so many children are growing up in front of the television. As parents, we've got to spend more time with our children, and help them with their homework, and replace the video game or the remote control with a book once in a while. That's how we build that foundation.

If parents are taking their responsibilities seriously to be there for their children, Ryan, and set high expectations for them, and instill in them a sense of excellence and empathy, then our government should meet them half way and move along with them in a support role all along the way.

Barack Obama

Self-Determination

Dear President Barack Obama,

Thank you. Really, I thank you for what you have done and will do for our nation. I am only 12 years old but I if I were 18 or older I would have voted for you on Election Day, hands down. I have heard some of your speeches and, not surprisingly, your greatly influencing words have persuaded other people to do just what you are asking them. I realize we must all help our education, racial relations, communities, families, and most importantly, each other. Working together will make the world a better place for us, and hopefully our future generations.

Right now America is going through an economic crisis. These problems have been caused by many factors including high oil prices, higher food prices, and increased unemployment. Some of these major problems were caused by other minor ones, or the other way around. Let's review the causes and effects of these impacting difficulties...

Since 1999, the price of oil has always been rising in a considerably large amount.

Because of the quickly rising oil prices, the cost of food has increased too. The main causes of this, other than the rising gas prices, are the world population growth and the many idled farmlands.

It has been predicted that at least 20 million jobs will be lost by the end of 2009 due to this crisis—mostly in "construction, real estate, financial services, and the auto sector."

Another source for this national depression, I think, is the war in Iraq. About six hundred billion dollars of taxpayer's funds have been spent just for the Iraqi War. This year's monthly spending in Iraq is approximately twelve billion dollars and the cost of deploying one man into the war costs three hundred and ninety thousand dollars. Also, 20% of these men fighting for our country have already been injured.

President Barack Obama, I do understand it may be hard to find the perfect place to begin, but why don't you just start right here. Start at places where you know people need help. I know as well that getting our men out of Iraq will not be as easy as it seems. We cannot just say "We're leaving," and walk out on an unstable country that is now unpredictable because of us, your very own U.S. of A. We all need your help, somewhere in the world and we will understand if we are the last on your list. Please just work your disciplinary well-educated thing of intelligence to get us out of trouble and into a satisfactory relief. I wish you every bit of luck to help facilitate our country once again.

Thank you, for now and forever,
Sophia
Boston Latin School
Boston, MA

New World

Dear Sophia,

One of my promises was to make arrangements to start withdrawing our troops from Iraq, to bring our brave service men and women home and to end the waste of America's resources. This war has contributed to the economic strain put on so many Americans, and now is the time to start making the changes to relieve this burden.

Yes, we need to provide immediate help to families who are struggling in places like Michigan, Ohio, Massachusetts, but we also need a serious plan to create new jobs and industry. We can't simply return to the strategies of the past. For we are living through an age of fundamental economic transformation. Technology has changed the way we live and the way the world does business.

The collapse of the Soviet Union and the advance of capitalism have vanquished old challenges to America's global leadership, but new challenges have emerged, from China and India, eastern Europe and Brazil. Jobs and industries can move to any country with an Internet connection and willing workers. Michigan's children will grow up facing competition not just from California or South Carolina, but also from Beijing and Bangalore.

A few days ago, I saw a picture of this new reality during a visit to Google's headquarters in California. Toward the end of my tour, I was brought into a room where a three-dimensional image of the earth rotated on a large flat-panel monitor. Across this image, there were countless lights in different colors. A young engineer explained that the lights represented all of the Internet searches taking place across the world, and each color represented a different language. The image was mesmerizing—a picture of a world where old boundaries are disappearing; a world where communication, connection, and competition can come from anywhere. We can change, we must change for America, and yes we will prepare ourselves to change now.

Barack Obama

Gratitude

Dear Mr. President,

I am a sixth grader here at Carmel Middle School in Charlotte, NC. First of all, let me start off by saying I am very happy that you are our next president. November 4, 2008, had to be the greatest day in history. To me it was like the world stopped for a minute, and everybody pulled together and went out to vote.

Mr. Obama, I can sit here and tell you all the things that are going wrong in the world, but I won't. Mr. Obama, I may be only a child, but I read the paper and watch the news just like everybody else. I am concerned about this economy.

My mom and dad both got laid off their jobs, and so did a lot of my friends' parents. This made Christmas hard this year (2008), but I think I got lucky. My mom was able to get me something for Christmas, and something is always better than nothing. I kind of feel sad for the kids who might not have Christmas this year. My mom always taught me to be happy for the small things I get. To be honest with you Mr. Obama, all I wanted for Christmas was for my mom to have a job where she won't be laid off. That way it can be Christmas everyday, meaning that my mom and other parents can have money to pay bills and take care of the kids. So, President Obama, I hope and I pray that you have a very good plan for the economy. Merry Christmas and Happy New Year to you and your family. See you in 2009.

Thank you,
Y-vonne
Carmel Middle School
Charlotte, NC

Faith

Dear Y-vonne,

I am glad to know you had a good Christmas and the support of your parents. Rather than fear the future, we must embrace it. I have no doubt that America can compete—and succeed—in the twenty-first century. And I know that, more than anything else, success will depend not on our government, but on the dynamism, determination, and innovation of the American people. In your home town of Charlotte, it was the educational and private sector that helped turn lumber into the wagons that sent this country west; that built the tanks that faced down Fascism; and that turned out the automobiles that were the cornerstone of America's manufacturing boom. Let us reach for what we know is possible. A nation healed a world repaired, an America that believes again.

Barack Obama

Responsibility

Dear President Obama,

The USA Today reports in an article entitled, "U.S. Manufacturing Jobs Fading Away Fast" that manufacturing job loss accelerated since the year 2000. The Center for America Progress also says, "In January 2001, manufacturing jobs lost another 11,000 in its 42nd monthly decline in a row. There is no excuse for ignoring manufacturing. During the last few years, our family bought items such as cameras, microwave ovens, televisions and toasters. They were all made in China or Mexico. My parents told me that they used to be manufactured in the U.S.A. This means Americans have lost millions of manufacturing jobs.

As the president, you can change this trend. In order to create new manufacturing jobs, you may need to form a commission of experts and representatives of corporations to brainstorm. The experts can advise how to do it and the corporations can help build new factories here in the United States of America.

In addition to building new factories and creating new jobs, *you may need to change the education system so that Americans can be educated and trained well enough to fit the new jobs.*

Several previous presidents have ignored these issues. However, if you are able to pull off this new "New Deal" and make America even greater in the world, I believe you will be remembered as one of the greatest U.S. presidents in history.

Sincerely,

Diana

Anthony Hyde Elementary

Washington, D.C.

Modernization

Dear Diana,

As your president for the past four years, I have made changing this trend of sending jobs overseas one of my highest priorities.

As you've seen Diana, the last few decades haven't been easy for manufacturing in this country. New technology has made businesses more efficient and productive—and that's good—but it's also made a lot of jobs obsolete. The result has been painful for a lot of families and a lot of communities. Factories where people thought they'd retire have left town. Jobs that provided a decent living have been shipped overseas. And the hard truth is that a lot of those jobs aren't coming back. But that doesn't mean we have to settle for a lesser future. I don't accept that idea. In America, there's always something we can do to create new jobs and new manufacturing and new security for the middle class.

Now, Congress and my administration have been working hard to get the things done that will bring jobs back to the United States, and we've also been working to get rid of the policies that have allowed jobs to be lost. We're holding meetings with business leaders on how we can help them bring jobs back to America. We're passing laws that stopped a tax hike on hard working Americans like your parents. We're helping small business owners hire more workers by giving them tax breaks. We're investing in clean energy companies that are paving the way into a future industry that will provide millions of jobs.

Not only are we helping the companies that are providing the jobs, we're helping by educating the people who are going to fill these jobs. To compete in a global economy, we must advance and educate our workforce. We have an obligation and a responsibility to invest in our students and schools. With the changing economy, opportunities are rising for employment. This is the moment when we must build on the wealth that open markets have created and share its benefits more equitably. My administration has already lined up companies that want to help by forming partnerships with community colleges. Together, they are becoming community career centers, places that teach people skills that businesses are looking for.

These reforms will help people get jobs that are open today. You're right when you said Diana, that to prepare for the jobs of tomorrow, our commitment to skills and education has to start now. It's a challenge we have to face head on and one we must not be discouraged by. Because in America, we don't give up, we get up.

Barack Obama

Resiliency

Dear President Obama,

I think of America much differently than I did about 6 years ago. Six years ago, I thought America was a place where a person could just walk in and start a great life with lots of jobs and homes available. Pretty much I thought that America was a great place to come in and start a new life. Now when I think of America I think of a country that is at war, and spending billions of dollars a year on that war and digging itself deeper into debt. I think of a country that has a struggling economy, and is clearly in a recession, but the government won't admit it. With the struggling economy, comes unemployment at its highest rate in years. I see lots of people struggling to pay off their credit card debts, and finding themselves deeper in debt. I see people having trouble paying their mortgages, and even struggling to pay for everyday things like gas and groceries. Instead of coming to this country for a new life, I see more people having banks being forced to foreclose on their homes that they can't afford. President Obama, I am tried of the last 8 years of Washington, the war and the struggles at home. My family and I were very proud to vote for on Election Day, and being a black family it was great to see you be the first African American president elected in the history of the country. President Obama, my family and I are counting on you to turn this country around, by ending the war and help stabilize the economy. I think you can handle it, and obviously, the majority of the country thinks you can do it as well.

Sincerely,
Sebastian
Boston Latin School
Boston, MA

Sustainability

Dear Sebastian,

I share your feelings and your concern. I ran for president because I believed in the idea of "Yes, we can." I ran for President because I believed in an America where ordinary folks could get ahead, where if you worked hard, you could have a better life. That's been my focus since I came into office, and that has to be our country's focus now.

It's one of the reasons why we're working to reduce our Nation's debt. Government has to start living within its means, just like families do. We have to cut the spending we can't afford so we can put the economy on a sounder footing and give our businesses the confidence they need to grow and create jobs.

It's one of the reasons that we finally ended the war in Iraq after nine long years of fighting a war that has cost Americans so dearly. For nine years we fought an insurgency that cost us nearly one trillion dollars and 4,500 American lives. These costs have immeasurably strained our economy and weigh heavy on our hearts. I made America and you a promise in my campaign to get our troops out of Iraq, and at Fort Bragg, California on December 21, 2011, we welcomed our returning troops home.

My belief is the reason Congress and I are working hard to bring jobs back to the United States by giving tax breaks to small businesses so they can hire more workers, especially our veterans returning from war. It's the reason we're investing in clean energy companies that are the future for a clean energy economy that will provide millions of jobs.

It's the reason I prevented a tax increase for millions of middle class Americans. We shouldn't put the burden of an entire country's debts on the backs of folks who've already borne the brunt of the recession. It's not reasonable, it's not right, and it's not respectable.

Together, we are making the changes that will not take us back to an economy weakened by job outsourcing, bad debt, phony financial profits, and a draining war overseas. Together, we are moving forward and have laid out a blueprint for an economy that's built to last, an economy built on American manufacturing, American energy, skills for American workers, and a renewal of the American values of fair play and shared responsibility.

As long as we continue to move forward, I promise you Sebastian, you will once again see America as a place where people can work hard and have a great life just as you envisioned.

Barack Obama

Balance

Dear President Barack Obama,

When you said, "Today we begin in earnest the work of making sure that the world we leave our children is just a little bit better than the one we inhabit today." that meant so much to me that honestly worlds cannot express the way that I felt. The reason I said it means so much to me is because today in the society that we live in is hard on everyone who lives in the United States especially for those who live in the state of Michigan. My reason for saying that is because it seems as if all the jobs in Michigan are being taken away and shipped over seas. In my eyes the future looks dim because jobs are being taken away, the tuition for college is rising higher and higher each and every year.

Now-a-days it is much harder for the youth and future generations to get a job or even pursue their dreams of going to college and become successful in the near future due to money problems whether it be because they don't have a job or their parents don't have one either to pay for or help pay for college tuition. The way I look at life now and how I look at how the future for me, my peers, and future generations to come may be totally different from how other youths may look at it. I look at life as being as easy as you want it to be whether you want to look at it in that way or not. Being totally honest I feel that there are ways to get around all the problems that the world is in and that the world will go through only if everyone in the United States can find a way to come together and work together as one.

One thing that I will do to leave the world better for future generations is to help the youth to further their educations. I will start up on my own business to help my youth and further generations to come with education whether it's to do tutorial programs, scholarship programs, financial aid programs for those who can't afford to pay for college or if they don't have the right things in order for them to get loans. I will try my best to help those in need of being helped because if I ever need help I want someone to reach out their hand and tell me it's going to be ok because they will help me just as I helped people.

Sincerely,
Tammy
Northwestern H.S.
Detroit, MI

Necessity

Dear Tammy,

I see it as my greatest responsibility and highest priority to ensure that you and every child in America can look towards to a future that is bright and full of promise instead missed opportunities and misguided politics.

I understand the problems you're facing. I've met so many Americans who are out there pounding the pavement looking for work only to discover that they need new skills. And I've met a lot of employers who are looking for workers, but can't find ones with the skills they're looking for.

So, we should be doing everything we can to put higher education within reach for every American, because at a time when the unemployment rate for Americans with at least a college degree is about half the national average, it's never been more important. Republicans, democrats, and economists alike agree that in this digital age, a highly educated workforce is the key to a successful economy.

But here's the thing: college has also never been more expensive. Students who take out loans to pay for college graduate owing an average of $25,000. For the first time, Americans owe more debt on their student loans than they do on their credit cards. For many working families, the idea of owing that much money means that higher education is simply out of reach for their children.

In the face of this challenge, there are things that Congress and my administration can do: we can stop the interest on student loans from going up, we can extend tax credits for students, and we can put universities and colleges on notice that if they keep raising tuition, their funding from taxpayers will go down.

A college education is an economic imperative that every family in America should be able to afford. Higher education should not and cannot be a luxury-not in America.

Barack Obama

VII.

War/Crime/Non-Violence & Justice

"Mankind must put an end to war or war will put an end to mankind."
—John F. Kennedy, Jr.

"I object to violence because it appears to do good, the good is only temporary, the evil it does is permanent."
—Gandhi

"There is nothing good in war except its ending."
—Unknown

"It is better to win the peace and to lose the war."
—Bob Marley

Honor

Dear President Obama,

It is an honor for me to be able to write a letter to you. What I would like to write to you about is how you can make the world a better place. First, you should end the war with Iraq by giving each country land, an equal share, of what they want.

Sincerely,
Olivia
John J. Pershing Elementary
Dallas, TX

Integrity

Dear Olivia,

Thank you for you letter. I have a plan that will bring our combat troops home. Letting the Iraqis know that we will not be there forever is our last, best hope to pressure the Sunni and Shia to come to the table and find peace.

Also, there is one other thing that is not too late to get right about this war, and that is the homecoming of the men and women—our veterans—who have sacrificed the most. Let us honor their valor by providing the care they need and rebuilding the military they love. Let us be the generation that begins this work.

I promised you and the American people that I will be a President who ends this war in Iraq and finally brings our troops home and who restores our moral standing. I'll be the president who understands that 9/11 is not a way to scare up votes, but a challenge that should unite America and the world against the common threats of the twenty-first century— common threats of terrorism and nuclear weapons, climate change and poverty, genocide and disease. I made promises to this nation, and as your president, I will uphold them.

Barack Obama

Global Lessons / Non-Violence

Dear President Obama,

My concern about the world is gang violence around communities. Why? Because there are many teenagers involved in gangs. These young people do not focus on their futures. This problem impacts our society and people in communities that do not know how to protect themselves from gangs. How does this impact our communities? It impacts our community because it gives it a bad image, mostly for the families. It affects families because if they have a family member joining a gang, then later on they might die. It also costs the city or community money to repair, fix and repaint the areas where gangs have caused trouble. The trouble that gangs start makes others hate them more, which they do to get attention. That also makes them stronger and powerful.

Another impact would be the control they have of guns and weapons, which is a fear that people have. Most gangs have access to weapons, which makes them more violent, so the safety for others drops. Protection provided by the city does not always work because of highly increased violence that exists out there. More innocent deaths have occurred because of gang violence. That is why we need to create and/or give inspiration to young teenagers about global lessons.

We have to teach young teenagers lessons that would inspire them to become successful and to convince them to stay out of gangs. The first lessons I would teach teenagers would be to always stay in school up to high school graduation. Why? Because this way they could have a decent job that requires a high school diploma. It may not pay that much, but a least they won't become bums or criminals.

Another great lesson would be to be a good role model to others, even to strangers. If this happens there would be less violence and more good citizens. One last lesson would be to respect others as you would like to be respected. It would help people to understand to respect each other and to judge people correctly. These would be my lessons to teach them, and I hope they would follow them. My lessons could change the minds of those that are in gangs or others that want to join them. Not only do I want these lessons to help those in gangs, but also people that want to become someone in life. Learning from these lessons, I hope the world could become a better place.

Sincerely,
Rufino
Central City Value H.S.
Los Angeles, CA

Unity

Dear Rufino,

E pluribus Unum—"out of many, we are one. These are the words inscribed on the Great Seal of the United States. We must apply these words to live by with fundamental changes in government to restore the faith of the American people in our system. We can do better, but government can't solve all our problems.

Better education policies and the application of them can improve our schools. Parents must provide the guidance our children need by being involved with their children, their schools and communities along with the government to make changes to help address the violence we face. The violence may be in our families, our home, streets or the community. The problems you cite—gangs, guns, drugs, abuse— are resolvable. There are changes to be made, and we must make this change happen.

In these times and times before, the American people are not the problem; they are the answer. The values that we as a nation hold dear such as, faith and family, service and citizenship, community and country, responsibility and respect, are what make America strong and give meaning to our lives. This leads us to believe change is possible and always will be when we apply those values and have faith in the process. Yes we can, yes we have, and yes we will. Change shall be for the good of us all. Our leaders along with our young people must stand tall with every American to bring about these global lessons. Remember Rufino, out of many, we are one.

Barack Obama

Care

Dear President Barack Obama,

My name is Chris Walters. I am 11 years old. I live in New Orleans, Louisiana. I want people to do better things for themselves. Do people have to shoot and kill all the time for no reason? See, with people killing all the time, other people will have more difficulty in life. So I just want people to stop the violence in this world. I hope it stops because then people will have less violence and students will have more time in life to do work at school. Then they can go to college. And I want to thank you President Obama.

Sincerely,
Chris
New Orleans College Prep.
New Orleans, LA

Community

Dear Chris,

I understand the pain you feel, and I am happy to know you care about the welfare of others. I started my career as a community organizer on the south side of Chicago and witnessed first hand the destructive nature of youth violence and gang activity on our children and entire communities. We, as one people, must end the dangerous cycles of youth violence. As president, I support the innovative, public health-based local programs in Chicago that have proven effective in breaking the cycle of youth violence. Programs like this can make a difference all across the country. When we get involved in our communities and neighborhoods, we are taking steps to insure that our youth are safe and have meaningful opportunities to keep them in school and out of trouble.

I am committed to you. Our youth and families can take back our neighborhoods from drugs, end dangerous cycles of youth violence and keep drugs off America's streets. I ask you and all who you know to be committed with me and our government. Together we can break the cycle of violence and transform our community to perfecting our country and our union as one.

Barack Obama

Respect

Dear President Obama,

To start, I wish you great prosperity in your upcoming term as president of our great nation. It is a privilege to live in a country where we have countless freedoms, rights, and opportunities. Although the United States of America is one of the greatest nations in the world, there are still many improvements that can be made. I know I am only a kid in some people's eyes, but I have the same mature views on our nation's biggest issues as any adult. With many concerns such as the war in Iraq, it is obvious that even a nation as great as ours leaves much to be desired.

Although the war in Iraq is a tough issue to decide on, it still needs to be ended so it will not effect the present and future generations of American adults. There are many devastating effects from this battle that alter the lives of every American citizen. The death total of over four thousand has devastated several military families, some of them right in our own backyards. There has also been an increase in the taxes we as citizens have to pay, which definitely takes a toll on everyday life. The rising gas prices that occurred as a result of those higher prices, Americans stopped putting their money into local, national, and international businesses, which caused an obvious drop in those companies' profits. This drop, in turn, caused a weakness in our nation's economy, complicating the lives of every person in this country.

I hope the White House will take these issues to thought and put an end to the economic and war issues that face our country today. I hope for a successful and productive presidency for the years to come.

Sincerely,
Leah
Western Branch Middle School
Washington, D.C.

Empathy

Dear Leah,

Thank you for your well wishes and words of concern. Each one of us can make a change. Even though you are a kid, this should never stop you from helping when you know how to make a difference. I learned this from my mother. She would ask me, "How would you feel if something that was not right was done to you?" This question alone caused me to think. I learned the rule of empathy, and I used it today in my politics and my relationships.

This war in Iraq must end, and as the Commander in Chief, I have vowed to responsibly end this war and bring our brave troops home. I empathize with our soldiers and their families, American citizens, and the people of Iraq. We must let Iraq govern itself. I have committed to the year 2010 to withdraw all troops from Iraq, leaving Iraq as a sovereign nation and an ally of our country. This war has taken a toll on our economy and lives, as you have said, for too long. Now is the time for action.

Barack Obama

Peace

Dear President Obama,

There are many changes I would like to see now that you are the president. I would like to see peace in America. There were two wars and George Bush led both. One war with Iraq and the other with Afghanistan. With Barack Obama as the president I want to see no war.

Those are many changes I would like to see, now that you are the president.

Sincerely,

Naeez

Determination

Dear Naeez,

When I ran for President of the United States, I made a promise to the American people. I swore that I would end the war in Iraq. So, on my first day in office, I directed my national security team to undertake a comprehensive review of our strategy in Iraq to determine the best way to strengthen that foundation, while strengthening America's national security. I made a commitment to America that as the Commander in Chief of the U.S. military I would end our combat mission and make a transition that would give the Iraqis full responsibility and control over their country. On December 21, 2011, I made good on those commitments.

As we approach our 10th year of combat in Afghanistan, there are those who are understandably asking tough questions about our mission there. But, we must never lose sight of what's at stake. As we speak, al Qaida continues to plot against us, and its leadership remains anchored in the border regions of Afghanistan and Pakistan. We will disrupt, dismantle, and defeat al Qaida, while preventing Afghanistan from again serving as a base for terrorists.

Since we ended the war in Iraq, we are now able to apply the resources necessary to go on the offense. In fact, over the last 3 and half years, nearly a dozen al Qaida leaders and hundreds of al Qaida's extremist allies have been either killed or captured around the world. Within Afghanistan, I've ordered the deployment of additional troops. They are fighting to break the Taliban's momentum. As with the surge in Iraq, these forces will be in place for a limited time to proved the space for the Afghans to build their capacity and secure their own future. As was the case with Iraq, we cannot do for Afghans what they must do for themselves.

The tide of war is receding Naeez, and now comes the time for America to use all elements of our power including our diplomacy, our economic strength, and the power of America's example.

Barack Obama

Justice

Dear President Barack Obama,

My name is Rachel. I am in the 7th grade at New Orleans College Prep. I am very concerned with my country. I want to stop all of the violence that is happening in the United States. I care about the U.S.A.

I want to see less violence in the world today, because hundreds of people are going to jail and hundreds of people are getting killed. You don't want to see your family and friends going to jail and getting killed. That is very heartbreaking. There will be more people being nice to each other and the world will be a better place.

I also want drugs to leave this country because that is the main thing that is going wrong. People just think that it's okay to take drugs. That's just not how it works. We can start a club and think of some ideas to make the world a better place, and try to help people with their problems.

I want to thank you President Obama for listening to what I had to say because this country needs a lot of help.

Sincerely,
Rachel
New Orleans, LA

Security

Dear Rachel,

Thank you for your letter and for speaking of a problem that has been waiting to be addressed for a long time. Your letter speaks of violence that must be addressed on both a local and national front. Every child, individual, and family deserves to be safe from violence of any kind. I believe that a transformation of conscience and genuine commitment to our every community is needed for all Americans.

When Hurricane Katrina struck New Orleans in 2005, we were glued to our TVs watching not just the devastation of the hurricane itself, but the aftermath that followed. Everybody talked about the loot-ers and the snipers and the endless loops that were played on CNN. But what I mentioned to someone during all of this is that I would love to see somebody take a look at the statistics of homicide rates and violence in the 9th ward of New Orleans before the Hurricane struck. Because violence has always been there, it just wasn't on our television screens.

What's important to understand is that the people of the 9th ward had been abandoned to dilapidated housing, and inadequate schools, and the mayhem, and violence, and drug use that exists in inner cities all across this country. And it's time for us to address these issues head on locally, nationally, and wherever we find disparity and inequality.

What's important is understanding the root causes of these problems. We need to understand that when a gang member shoots indiscriminately into a crowd because he feels someone has disrespected him, we have a problem of morality. Not only do we need to punish this man for his crime, but we need to acknowledge that there is a hole in this person's heart that no government program alone will fill.

The first places to start tackling these problems are in our communities and schools. We need to focus on providing quality education to inner city schools that more often than not lack sufficient supplies, quality teachers, and funding.

We also need to have policies in place that better deal with drug problems among our youth. We need to have an approach that emphasizes prevention, treatment, and is a public health model for reducing drug use in our country. Part of our challenge is getting into schools early and making sure that young people recognize that perils of not only drug use, but also the perils of gang violence.

Solving violence in America will require changes in both government policies and changes in the hearts and minds of our citizens. These issues not only affect the people living in these communities, they affect all Americans. Together, as a country we must work towards reducing drug use and violence in our inner cities.

Barack Obama

VIII.

Spirituality / Religion

"If we suppose to be perfect, we'd all be in trouble, so we rely on God's mercy and grace to get us through."
—Barack Obama

Tolerance

Dear President Obama,

First of all, I would like to congratulate you and your family for winning the 2008 election! With a new president comes hope for a better future and a lot of changes. However, I have found that some things never change.

One thing that I would like to have changed is the racial relations between people of different ethnicities. From times at school when people are made fun of or mocked because they look different to the battlefield where war wins over acceptance. The world would be an overall better place if kids and adults most importantly, could learn to accept different looks, religions, cultures, and pasts and instead of focus on the person now and their positive traits. Not pointing then out or somehow separating the person from society, making them feel like an alien.

Another term might be the word genocide. It has happened a bunch of times, more than it should. The killing of a large group of people belonging to a certain race, ethnic group or a nation is a definition for genocide. Things like this evolve from a small tease of someone's culture.

People can't always accept differences. They are easy to point out differences between things or one another, yet it always seems a little bit harder to find stuff that is the same. Why is this? Is it our lack of acceptance or education? I think it is a mix of both. I think we should teach everyone real history, politics, and different cultures. I think we should set an example by accepting people, and learning from our mistakes.

It might make us think why we go to war with other human beings. They have families too. They have emotions and feelings just like everyone else. They want to fight for their country. And yet, it doesn't help the country. Money is scarce, enemies are found, and innocent people die. I think the best thing to do is to change how people respect each other. From that we can come closer to world peace, long-lasting friendships, and happiness. Opportunities can be given to people of all race, sex and religion. Those people who get paid very little, under the worker's low pay, just because they are from another country will soon be treated just like anyone else. As the saying goes, "Treat others like how you would want to be treated."

In your family, school, community and the world, there should be better racial relationships. I am not saying a place free or anger emotions that is what make us who we are, but more like you tolerate others whether you like them or not. Gangs like in the <u>West Side Story</u> could possibly cease. The United Nations could be more effective in giving aid to places like Darfur or Cambodia. You know what, why go that far across the world, when people here need help? People here in America need help here too. No more racist murders of any murders for that fact.

As you have said that we should make this world a better place, I would also like to say that you can start, not with recycling quite yet, but with racial problems. No more wars and loss of money for weapons and hate, no more people subjected to mockery and hurt feelings. Once you have happy, educated, caring and accepting people, you can do almost anything.

Sincerely,
Michaela
Boston Latin School
Boston, MA

Diversity

Dear Michaela,

I understand the change you seek and the feelings you have as an American wanting one America that is made up of many different types of people. Our nation is not perfect, but it is growing and seeking ways to change for the better. We all have the freedom to make choices. This is the price and promise of citizenship. This is the source of America's confidence—the knowledge that God calls on us to shape an uncertain destiny.

This is the meaning of our liberty and our creed—why men and women and children of every faith and of every race can join in celebration on the day of my inauguration speech. We will mark January 20, 2009, with remembrance of who we are and how far we have traveled. In the year of America's birth in the coldest month, a small band of patriots huddled by dying campfires on the shores and icy rivers. America stood tall during her darkest moment, and she stood tall on the day of accepting me to be her president. I stood before America and told you my story of the brief union between a young man, my father, from Kenya, Africa and a young woman, my mother from Kansas, who weren't well off or well known, but shared a belief in their country and their son, Barack Obama, could achieve whatever they put their mind to. It is that promise that's always set this country apart— that through hard work, each of us can pursue our own individual dreams, but also come together as one nation.

Today, change is happening because American people in the millions voted for change in electing me as their first African-American president. I base my decisions as a citizen and a president on the Declaration of Independence—on the idea that we all created equal, We as a people, have to make our choices to see change upon those ideals of our founding forefathers.

It is that American spirit, the American promise that pushes us forward even when the path is uncertain. It binds us together in spite of our differences and makes us fix our eye not on what is seen, but what is unseen—that better place around the bend. Change is here. We cannot turn back now. As we remember January 20, 2009, people of every creed, color and every walk of life came together. Our destiny is linked together, and together our dreams can be one. We cannot walk alone. Let us keep that promise without wavering. Change is here and is here to stay. I asked that we walk together to continue this change and together we will see it through for my children and your children and children to come. This is hard to do, but we must take one step at a time.

Barack Obama

Optimism

Dear President Obama,

I am from Detroit, Michigan, and I go to school at Beckham Academy. I want to say congrats for you winning the election. How does it feel to win? I'm glad you are the president because you are the first black president. What is it like to be in the White House? I feel that you are a lucky man to win. I am 9 years old. I want to have good luck someday. *I hope that things get better* so my daddy can go to school so he can go to work. I wish he was rich. Good luck as president and help us people.

Your friend,
Jabar
William J. Beckham Academy
Detroit, MI

Hope

Dear Jabar,

Our country's destiny is tied to young people like you and my children and their friends. When it comes to my own daughters, I like them to maintain hope for themselves and for all Americans and never give it up.

Hope is that thing inside us that insists, despite all evidence to the contrary, that something better awaits us if we have the courage to reach for it, and to work for it, and to fight for it.

Hope... hope... is what led me here today—with a father from Kenya; a mother from Kansas; and a story that could only happen in the United States of America. Hope is the bedrock of this nation; the belief that our destiny will not be written for us, but by us; by all those men and women who are not content to settle for the world as it is, who have the courage to remake the world as it should be.

Jabar, despite the present conditions, I want you to maintain hope for your daddy and your family. Things will be better for the family. I will do what I can to help families in America to move forward. Keep hope alive.

Barack Obama

Serenity—Cooperation

Dear President Obama,

Since you have been elected president of the United States, you must find ways to run the country, but must also help citizens make the world a better place. There is a lot of conflict with religion in the world today. These religious wars have been going on throughout history and never seem to really end. Ever since the terrorist attacks, the Taliban, and the Al Qaeda, the country has had a different outlook on Islamic people. There is still anti-Semitism going on in the world in many places around the world, especially the middle-east. If I were you, Mr. President, I would make it clear that religion isn't something that one can judge another on.

Ever since the war in Iraq and Afghanistan started, many citizens of the United States changed their opinion of Muslims. Suddenly, people who followed Islam found themselves in danger all because of a terrorist group. Because of the attack on the World Trade Center Muslims were considered terrorists and people who are not to be trusted. This is still going on today, and I am not saying that this is an unnecessary fear. After all, it was a group of Islamic terrorists that were (and still are) causing significant confusion and terror in the world. The war in Iraq is a great example. But I would try to teach the world that religion is not what should be looked at. the terrorists are using Muslim people who are convinced under indoctrination that what they are doing is the right thing to do. Really the terrorists are those who were brainwashed to do "the right thing." But terrorists and Muslims cannot be put together necessarily. Islam is just a religion, and most of the Muslim population is against what is going on. But they are still suffering because of what is going on, so I would change that if I were you, Mr. President. I would embrace the Muslim population and convince the world that religion is just a belief. It is not something you can use for hatred.

Along with the hate of Islam by many, anti-Semitism is still very active in the U.S., as well as the world. Another example of religious lessons that I would have to teach to the world is that there is no reason why innocent people should be hated for no apparent reason except their beliefs. Anti-Semitism was always a big thing in the world and it is still going on today. There are neo-Nazis who respect Hitler and what he did. In the Middle East, persecution of Jews is ongoing. People in the United States were not directly involved with World War II, so they didn't know what it was like for the Jewish families in the concentration camps during the Holocaust. All we have ever heard are stories, and people have not been convinced. Arabs think that Israel should be destroyed, whether or not for religious reasons. There are constant Jewish stereotypes in the United States, and I speak for myself. It is time for religion to be put away in politics and society. As President Barack Obama, I would make it clear that religious persecution is something that is breaking our society apart, and I would teach that it is time to dismiss religious views and look at who is actually responsible to what is happening in the world.

Sincerely,
Mick
Boston Latin School
Boston, MA

Righteousness

Dear Mick,

Thank you for your letter and your message of tolerance and understanding. One of the most important things to remember about the tragic events of September 11, 2001 is that it was not a religion that attacked us that September day. It was al-Qaeda led by Osama bin Laden.

And seeking justice against bin Laden and al-Qaeda must remain a focus of the United States. Ending the Iraq War allowed us to strike decisive blows against our enemies. From Pakistan to Yemen, the Al Qaeda operatives who remain are scrambling, knowing they can't escape the reach of the United States of America. From this position of strength, we've begun to wind down the war in Afghanistan. Ten thousand of our troops have come home. Twenty-three thousand more will leave by the end of the summer. The tide of war is receding and peace is on the horizon.

As the tide of war recedes, a wave of change has washed across the Middle East and North Africa, from Tunis to Cairo, from Sana's to Tripoli. A year ago, Gadhafi was one of the world's longest serving dictators, a murderer with American blood on his hands. Today, he is gone. And in Syria, I have no doubt that the Asad regime will soon discover that the forces of change cannot be reversed and that human dignity cannot be denied.

While it's ultimately up to the people of the region to decide their fate, we will advocate for the values that have served our own country so well. We will stand up against violence and intimidation. We will stand up for and protect the rights and dignity of all human beings: men, women, and children, Christians, Muslims, and Jews.

As extremists try to inspire acts of violence within our borders, we are responding with the strength of our communities, with the courage of our nation, with respect for the rule of law, and with the conviction that American Muslims are a part of our American family. No matter what occurs Americans will not sacrifice the liberties we cherish or hunker down behind walls of suspicion, mistrust, and fear.

Barack Obama

Change

Dear President Barack Obama,

On November 4, 2008, a great thing happened: you were elected the President of the Unites States of America. First, I would like to say congratulations! Now it's time for you to accomplish the great things that you have promised to our nation so that we can live in a better society. Further, fulfilling your promise will help or youth want to do something with their lives such as obtaining an education so that they can better themselves as well as their future.

However, there is an economic crisis that is rising. There are many jobs that are being moved out of our community and our state. We can start by budgeting our money in a correct manner that way we can have more jobs in the U.S.

President, you will give us a brighter future because anything is possible at this moment. I want to be able to go to school with the supplies that I need, books so that I can learn, and teachers who will be there to teach me because that's what they love doing not just for the money. I want to be something in life.

In addition, you said that you will lower taxes for the middle class and the poor and then tax the rich. As good as this sounds this kind of goes against capitalism, the very kind of market our country has thrived on since the beginning. I firmly believe that the rich deserve their money.

However, this may have a good affect on the future of our country. I certainly hope so. You stand today at the head of a movement that believes deeply in the change you have claimed as the mantle of your campaign. In order to change, you then have to deliver the change you have promised. It's your time and chance to listen to the voice of the people and decide.

Sincerely,
Shiloh
John J. Pershing H.S.
Detroit, MI

Perseverance

Dear Shiloh,

I want to thank you for your letter and congratulations. Four years ago, I came into the presidential office in the worst recession our nation has seen in over 50 years. The mortgage industry had collapsed, the auto industry was on the verge of collapse, and millions of Americans had lost their jobs and their houses.

Over the past few years, we have made strides to overcome this recession, and today I am proud to say that we have created 3 million American jobs and have cut the national deficit by two trillion dollars. But I want to talk to you about Shiloh, is not only what we have done, but we will continue to do to improve the American economy and the American way of life.

First of all, we need to return to the American values of fair play, self-determination, and shared responsibility. It is not right to raise the taxes for millions of Americans, and then turn around and give a tax break to the wealthiest 1 percent of Americans. We shouldn't put the burden of deficit reduction on the backs of folks who've already borne the brunt of the recession. It's not reasonable, and it's not right. If we're going to ask seniors or students or middle class Americans to sacrifice, then we have to ask corporations and the wealthiest Americans to share in that sacrifice.

For years, the Government has spent more money than it takes in. The result is that we have overdrawn and overextended our Nation's credit card. We've created debt that, unless we act, will weaken our economy, cause higher interest rates for families, and force us to scale back things like education and Medicare. That's why we need a managed and balanced approach to cutting the deficit. We need a committed approach that goes after waste in the budget and gets rid of pet projects that cost billions of dollars, and we need an approach that asks everybody to do their part.

Every American must do their part to lead this nation into a future that is not defined by making a quick buck at the expense of millions of Americans, but a future that is sustained by self-responsibility and long-term prosperity.

Barack Obama

IX.

Community

"I think about America and those who built it... Like Lincoln and King, who laid down their lives in the service of perfecting an imperfect union."
—Barack Obama

"The vision of a world community is based on justice."
—Henry Kissinger

Community

Dear President Obama,

I am one of the many citizens of the United States.

As a young teen living in an urban neighborhood, I think that there should be a change within my community. This change should be getting our youth off the streets and for them to keep their selves occupied with after school activities. Nowadays, the youth is just in too much trouble.

This argument has gone on for years. It is not time to stop discussing the matter and take action. I've seen it all. Kids joining gangs and getting forced to steal and fight because it's the only choice they have in making friends. Everyday when I come home, I see young kids on the corner of my block trying to wait to do something wrong. This is why America should always have options open for our youth. I know that you are too busy trying to make the world a better place but the youth is America's "voice to be." Everyday when I turn on the news I see communities gathering up for a vigil because their child has died for being at the wrong place at the wrong time.

My opinion is that you should give a fair amount of money to each state (including Alaska and Hawaii). Each state should use this money to open new after school, community centers, and libraries around the neighborhood. I thank you in advance because I know that you have a lot of things and people to take care of. As Publilius Syrus once said, "Never promise more than you can perform." This quote tells me that if you know you can't finish something then don't make a promise and start it.

Sincerely,
Temi
Boston Latin School
Boston, MA

Participation

Dear Temi,

It is important that we all, and parents, get involved with our children's education early and often. Whenever we do, we will create a proactive community and a healthy community. We help our children and our neighbors by ensuring that our youth are doing productive activities after school is out.

We must protect the future by being involved with our youth. Change is always possible if you're willing to work for it, and fight for it, and above all, believe in it. Remember out of many, there's one—one community, one America, one world.

Barack Obama

Responsibility

Dear President Obama,

As a member of the Detroit community, I have seen many horrible things that I believe you, as the new president, should be able to change. The first issue that I would like to discuss is the number of people receiving a stable high school and college education. This percentage is not very high. America is a country that gives people opportunities that the members of my community are not taking as an advantage. The second issue that I would like to address is the number of blacks, compared to other races, receiving an education. This percentage is also very low. I believe that this percentage should increase by the end of your term as president. These two very important issues need to be addressed as soon as possible.

The amount of education offered in our community taken advantage of by teens is not very high. There are too many high school and college dropouts that are not doing very well. Unfortunately, a lot of those people, join gangs, take drugs, or do many things that are against the law. A lot of those people end up in jail or getting killed. Because of what these dropouts do puts our community in a state of chagrin. The amount of people not receiving an education is unbelievable. I believe that any person should take advantage of every educational opportunity that he/she receives.

The number of blacks in our community, compared to other races that are not receiving an education, is very low. As a member of the African American community, this exasperates me. Most of the African American people in the world are of the hoi polloi. I believe that if more blacks received an education, a lot more of the members of the African American community would be affluent. As president, I believe that you should be able to increase the percentage of blacks receiving an education.

I hope that you are able to address the issues related to general education.

Sincerely,
Vera
Bates Academy
Detroit, MI

Quality

Dear Vera,

Your letter raised several points. To change and better our community, we must have an educated community. I believe it is time to lead a new era of mutual responsibility in education—one where we all come together for the sake of all of our children's success.

The typical school day is a throwback to the curriculums of the 20th Century and is not on par with other developed countries around the world. Our young Americans will have to spend more learning time to make up what they are lacking, especially the struggling students. It is important to gain knowledge and skills for the 21st Century. Longer school days or longer schools years can help provide additional learning time for students to close the achievement gap. But our youth must also get involved themselves to improve their futures. As our young people make the decision to take the responsibility for their futures, my administration will meet them half way. With one step toward each other, positive results are not difficult to achieve.

When we as a society pretend that poor children will fulfill their potential in dilapidated, unsafe schools with outdated equipment and teachers who aren't trained in the subjects they teach, we are perpetrating a lie on these children and on ourselves. We need both cultural transformation and government action—a change in values and a change in policy—to promote the kind of society we want.

Barack Obama

Change

Dear Mr. President,

I would like to first congratulate you on your groundbreaking victory. You have inspired me to reach all of my goals, and essentially assume your role by opening new doors for the next generations. Thank you once again. Some changes I would like to see in America are as follow: affordable healthcare, better homes in better communities, more shelters in the Washington D.C. area, and better education in the inner cities.

Affordable healthcare plays an important role, especially in African American communities. We can barely afford it, and at the same time, we have foreigners coming over and buying the best healthcare. Now, I have nothing against foreigners, but I do have a problem with them coming over and living better then the hard working Americans. I will admit that some Americans are not as hard working as others are, but the majority of us are and deserve the same opportunities.

Another change I would like to see is more quality homes in better communities. There are too many good families out here working a hard 9 to 5 job that deserve better homes, and can only afford a two-bedroom apartment in the inner city. There are too many African Americans dying in their communities plagued with violence. The stagnant wages and lack of affordable housing in better communities lead to Washington, D.C. residents living below the poverty line.

Thirdly, I would like to see a change in poverty and homelessness in the Washington, D.C. area. Nearly 1 out of 5 DC residents live below the poverty line (*U.S. Census Bureau, 2005 American Community Service*) There are hundreds of homeless people in the Washington D.C. area.

Because there are, only a few shelters in Washington D.C. not all of the homeless people can be accommodated. YOU DO THE MATH!

Lastly, I would like to see a change in the educational system. We as inner city children are not receiving the same quality as neighboring counties. Washington D.C. ranks below average compared to all the school systems in the United States. In conclusion, by changing affordable healthcare, better homes in better communities, more shelters in the Washington D.C. area, and better education in the inner cities. I believe that we can have a better America.

Sincerely,
Vincent
Roosevelt S.H.S.
Washington, D.C.

Goals

Dear Vincent,

Thank you for your letter and your concern for this nation. During my time as your president, I, along with Congress and the American people, have sought to address the issues you have described.

For years, America's healthcare system has been in dire need of reform, and as president, I have stood up to that challenge. The health insurance law I signed into law last year in 2011, will address the rising costs that are affecting millions of people, which is part of the reason that nonpartisan economists have said that repealing the health care law would add a quarter of a quarter of a trillion dollars to our deficit.

The healthcare reform law that we passed last year and was recently upheld by the Supreme Court of the United States, requires all insurance plans to cover preventative care at no cost. That means free check-ups and basic services that are imperative for preventing illness. My administration and members of Congress fought for this because it saves lives, and its saves money for families, for business, for government, for everybody. By upholding this law, we are making prescription drugs cheaper for seniors and giving uninsured students a chance to stay on their parents' coverage.

To address the rest of your letter, the government and the rest of the United States cannot abandon its own people in inner cities and low-income areas any longer. We cannot ignore the violence, and poverty, and chaos that exist in our own communities. And part of addressing that problem comes in the reform of our education system. For less than 1 percent of what our Nation spends on education each year, we've convinced nearly every State in the country to raise their standards for teaching and learning, the first time that's happened in a generation. As a nation, we have an obligation to make sure that all children have the resources they need to learn: quality schools, good teachers, the latest textbooks, and the right technology.

Our country still has a long journey ahead that will be difficult and require work from every American. But if you are willing to continue to work with me, we can achieve our goals for this great country.

Barack Obama

Hope

Dear President Obama,

I would like to start out by congratulating you on winning the election! This has been the most historical and exciting election most Americans have probably experienced, and I'm sure that many of us, including me, will remember this for the rest of our lives. We didn't elect you simply because of your optimistic attitude and easy-going smile; we elected you because you give us hope. With that hope, comes the readiness for change, "change we can believe in."

America has always been the home of the rich, the poor and people of different religion and race. However, for many people who are struggling with every day, it may not seem that way for them. There are more poor people in this country than there are millionaires, or people with any significant amount of money for that matter. While the rich have an easy time, buying the latest technology or just hanging out and having a relaxing day, the poor, especially the homeless, try to scrape up enough money to survive. for those who have lost their jobs and simply cannot find work, finding the money is extremely hard to them.

This isn't America; I know this isn't what our country is. We don't just allow people who are less fortunate than others to fend for themselves. We help them, and make it so that they don't have to struggle each and every day. You were elected with the hope that this change could be brought along for the lower class, to make their life better and easier. Another change that I would like to see happen in America is health care. I would like to grow up to become a doctor someday, and I find it awful that many Americans are living with healthcare issues. Of course health care isn't exactly affordable these days, but if that is the case, then that means that the many of Americans who are living close to poverty each day don't have one. Healthcare should be for everyone, no matter how much money you have or don't have.

When you were running for president, you used three words, which many Americans will probably never forget. These small, three words were able to give us hope. They were: "Yes We Can." Change does not come easy, I am aware of that. But I am also aware of the fact that you will try your best to create changes that will help many Americans. The changes you have talked about aren't the only ones that we believe in. You, President Obama, are a change in America. "Change we can believe in" was you motto, and true to that, we believe in you, and what you can do to make America a better place.

Sincerely,
Beverly
Boston Latin School
Boston, MA

Responsibility

Dear Beverly,

I agree with you when you say that America is not the country that stands idly by and allows people less fortunate than others to fend for themselves. That's not who we are. We've had to make hard choices as a nation. I had to make the difficult decision to bail out the banking and auto industries. Too much was at stake to let them fail.

We have a choice to make as a nation. We can either settle for a country where a shrinking number of people do really well while a growing number of Americans barely get by, or we can restore an economy where everyone gets a fair shot, everyone does their fair share, and everyone plays by the same set of rules. What's at stake aren't upper-class values or middle-class values, but American values. And we have to reclaim them.

For years, America's healthcare system has been in dire need of reform, and as president, I have kept my promise to address this issue. For too long, families have suffered because a family member got sick, and the healthcare costs were too much of a financial burden. American's livelihoods should never be threatened because of an illness. The health insurance law I signed into law last year in 2011, will slow the rising costs that are affecting millions of people, which is part of the reason that nonpartisan economists have said that repealing the health care law would add a quarter of a quarter of a trillion dollars to our deficit.

The healthcare reform law that we passed last year, requires all insurance plans to cover preventative care at no cost. That means free check-ups, free mammograms, immunizations, and other basic services. We fought for this because it is the American way. This program saves lives, and its saves money for families, for business, for government, for everybody, because it's a lot cheaper to prevent an illness than to treat one. As we speak, this law is making prescription drugs cheaper for seniors and giving uninsured students a chance to stay on their parents' coverage.

We know that change does not come easy, Beverly. But we also know that when Americans stand together to make their country a better place, there is nothing we cannot achieve.

Barack Obama

Fulfillment

Dear Mr. President,

I'm very glad that you won the election to be the President of the United States of America. When you said, "Today we begin in earnest the work of making sure that world we leave our children is just a little bit better than the one we inhabit today," it made me think of a lot of ways that we can make our country better. I'm glad that you're now the president because now you can accomplish the things you promised and make the world a better place for my generation and others.

When you were running for president you promised to make changes to the health care system. I hope you do because my sister is diabetic and my parents have to pay a lot of money for her doctors' visits and insurance. It uses up a lot of my parents money that they could use for other bills and to save for me and my sister to go to college, which is also very expensive. I think one of the first things you should do as president is to create a better health care system that will help people pay for their medical bills. Not only will that help families like mine, but it will also be good for the economy because people will have more money to buy things.

I hope you will commit to your promises and make these changes. I'm sure you will be a great president.

Yours Truly,
Avery
Western Branch Middle School
Chesapeake, VA

Commitment

Dear Avery,

Over the past four years, my Administration and Congress have worked to make sure that the promises I made to you and the American people during my campaign did not go unfulfilled. Four years ago, our country was facing rising costs in health care that were straining people's wallets, and insurance companies were refusing to cover people with pre-existing conditions. It wasn't right, and we had to something about it. And, so we did.

In 2011 we passed the Affordable Health Care Act. As part of the healthcare reform law that I signed last year, all insurance plans are required to cover preventative care at no cost. That means free check-ups, free mammograms, immunizations, and other basic services. We fought for this because it saves lives, and its saves money for families, for business, for government, for everybody. That's because it's a lot cheaper to prevent an illness than to treat one.

As we speak, the Healthcare Law is making prescription drugs cheaper for seniors and giving uninsured students a chance to stay on their parents' coverage. This is a law that I fought for and will protect because it's good for the American people's finances and it's good for the American people's health.

I will not go back to the days when health insurance companies had unchecked power to cancel your policy, deny your coverage, or raise your rates without notice. I made that promise to the American people, and I will keep that promise.

Barack Obama

X.

Unity / New World Order

*"There is not a liberal America and a conservative America—
there is the United States of America. There is not a black America
and a white America and Latino America and Asian America—
there's the United States of America."*

*"The walls between languages, races and tribes, Christian and Muslim
and Jew cannot stand. There are the walls we must tear down..."*

"People of the world—this is our moment. This is our time."
—Barack Obama

Help

Dear President Obama,

Will you change the way the economy is running because we need changes in our community. It is depressing to see so many abandoned homes in our neighborhoods. Neighborhoods are going down everyday because people are being evicted from their homes because they are losing their jobs everyday. I hope you can help out.

Sincerely,
Antrice
William J. Beckham Academy
Detroit, MI

Egalitarianism

Dear Antrice,

Our public education system is the key to opportunity for millions of children like you and their families to build a prosperous and sustainable economy. It needs to be the best in the world. Paving the way to this economy starts with building an education system that is effective for all students. One of my particular concerns is the growing achievement gap between middle and low-income students, which has continued to expand despite some overall national achievement gains.

We have an obligation and responsibility to be investing in every student and every school. We must make sure that people who have the grades, the desire and the will, but not the money can still get the best education. It is our insurance policy for a brighter America. This will change the economy, community and improve our neighborhoods for future generations.

Barack Obama

Listen

Dear President Obama,

In January of 2009, you were inaugurated into office and became America's next leader. With this great power comes great responsibility. The number one responsibility of the new president is to listen to America's people and improve their areas of concern. The major concerns of the people are the country's economic state, education system, and our involvement in the Middle East.

Unfortunately, our county is in a recession. To end this recession, our government should give incentives to underdeveloped businesses so they can grow and employ more people. Then, the minimum wage should be raised by a significant amount so Americans can purchase more items, which will begin to boost our economy. This money can be raised by reducing wasteful government spending, such as no pay raises for senior officials for 5 years. This plan will help resolve our economic state, and lower unemployment rates, something that was promised during the Presidential campaign.

In addition to addressing America's economic state, our country also requires a better education system. America's teachers aren't being compensated enough for the difficult task they perform every day. Teachers' pay should highly increase! This can be achieved by reducing redundant administration. It is just as hard to be a teacher as it is to be a senator.

The New Year can bring the promise of change in America. Hopefully, the ideas presented here will be taken into consideration. These ideas present opportunities for positive change in our economy, education and the military.

Sincerely,
Blake
Western Branch Middle School
Chesapeake, VA

Fair Play

Dear Blake,

Your ideas present opportunities for positive change that will help workers gain higher wages and better benefits. We need once again to level the playing field between organized labor and employers. We have started to address many of your concerns during this economic bailout for banks and other corporations.

We can rise together. If we choose to change, just imagine what we can do. The great auto manufacturers of the twentieth century can turn out cars that run on renewable energy in the twenty-first century. Biotechnology labs can find new cures for diseases. New rail lines and roadways can connect our communities so that goods made in Michigan can be exported around the world. Our children can get a world class education and their dreams of tomorrow can eclipse even our greatest hopes of today. We can choose to rise together. But, it won't be easy. Everyone of us will have to work at it by studying harder, training more rigorously, working smarter, and thinking anew. We'll have to slough off bad habits, reform our institutions, and reengage the world. We can do that, because this is America—a country that has been defined by a determination to believe in, and work for, things unseen.

Barack Obama

Opportunity

Dear President Obama,

As you once said, "Today we begin in earnest the work of making sure that the world we leave our children is just a little better than the one we inhabit today." After hearing this quote, it occurred to me that you were trying to say how it is the responsibility of the people on Earth today to make the place we live better than that of how we found it from our past generations, and to better equip those who will come after we are gone. Also, this quote is referring to how the people of the world today must unite and "fight off" one of the problems of today's society, both in the United States and throughout the world. We have to begin to try to help the world out of as many predicaments as possible to leave our children and our descendants as perfect a world as possible.

In this world we live in, we have many conundrums that we are faced with in day-to-day life. These problems include poverty, war, disagreement, violence, terrorism, corrupt government, and even starvation. I feel that the most important of the issues that are occurring in today's society is poverty. Our time period is considered to be "the modern era" and the "era of technological advancement." If our generations are supposed to match these descriptions, then, poverty must stop. The people in the United States, and all throughout the world, are faced with not having enough money to buy adequate food, resulting in malnutrition, not having proper living quarters, and not having the correct life protection, such as health care, dentistry, and even education. Something I will commit to do to leave the world better for future generations is to volunteer at poverty shelters and raise money for those who have nothing. By volunteering at poverty shelters, this will be my chance to make a difference in helping those in need, through counseling, serving food, and even better equipping them with necessary supplies for day-to-day life. Also, by raising money for those in poverty, it will give them an opportunity to get those things needed for their survival.

President Obama, as you said in your quote, it is our responsibility to better equip the world for those who will come after us, and I intend to do so.

Sincerely,
Mitchell
Carmel Middle School
Charlotte, NC

Progress

Dear Mitchell,

However daunting the challenges we face may seem, I know we can overcome them when we have young people like you who are so willing and eager to make positive changes in our country.

Combating poverty is perhaps one of the most difficult challenges facing our communities, the nation, and the world. I believe the best place to start this battle is in classrooms across the country.

Over the next 10 years, nearly half of all new jobs will require education beyond high school, many requiring proficiency in math and science. And yet today, we've fallen behind in math, and in science, and in graduation rates. As a result, companies like Intel struggle to hire American workers with the skills that fit their needs. If we want to win the global competition for new jobs and industries, we've got to win the global competition to educate our people. We've got to have the best trained, best skilled workforce in the world. That's how we'll ensure that the next Intel, the next Google, the next Apple, or the next Microsoft is created in America and hires American workers.

We must also invest in the building blocks of innovation: education, infrastructure, and research. Technology is advancing everyday, and we need Americans to be in the forefront of that advancement. In a single generation, revolutions in technology have transformed the way we live, work and do business.

That's why I appointed the first ever Chief Technology Office to reduce our digital divide, and why I set a goal of putting a full 3 percent of our Gross Domestic Product, our national income, into research and development. That's the role of government: to provide investment to spur innovation and also to set up common sense ground rules to ensure that there's a level playing field for all comers who seek to contribute their innovations and ideas for a better world.

The ingredients for success and growth are right here in the United States. You and your generation, Mitchell, are testimony to that.

Barack Obama

Diversity

Dear Mr. President,

My name is Kris and I live in Los Angeles, California. I go to school with a lot of different kids. I have friends that are white, black, and Asian. My best friend is Mexican. I think it's a good thing that I my friends are not all the same because it's good to know and be friends with people who aren't exactly like you.

Before you became president you said you were going to bring change to the United States. I think you should start by helping my friend Lorenzo. He has to live with his aunt and uncle because his parents were sent back to Mexico because they were living in the United States illegally. I know people should not break the law, but they are really nice people and they work hard. I feel bad for my friend because he misses his parents a lot, but since he is an American his mom and dad want him to stay here so he can get a better education.

President Obama, I hope there is something you can do to change our laws so people can move to America easier. I hear people saying how they don't like immigrants because they take our jobs, but I think they should remember that we all come from immigrants. I hope that you can change people's minds about this and I promise to help by trying to teach people that it's good to have all different kinds of people in America.

Sincerely,
Kris
Open Magnet Charter
Los Angeles, CA

E Pluribus Unum

Dear Kris,

Your letter brings to mind my visit to Miami Dade Community College to give the commencement address back in March, 2011. The graduates were proud that their class could claim heritage from 181 countries around the world.

Many of the students were immigrants themselves, coming to America with little more than the dream of their parents and the clothes on their back. A handful had discovered only in adolescence or adulthood that they were undocumented. But they worked hard and they gave it their all, and so they earned those diplomas.

At the ceremony, 181 flags—one for every nation that was represented—was marched across the stage. And each one was applauded by the graduates and the relatives with ties to those countries. So when the Haitian flag went by, all the Haitian kids shouted out. And when the Guatemalan flag went by, all the kids of Guatemalan heritage shouted out. But then, the last flag, the American flag, came into view. And everyone in the room erupted in applause.

It was a reminder of a simple idea, as old as America itself: E Pluribus Unum—Out of many, one. We define ourselves as a nation of immigrants—a nation that welcomes those willing to embrace America's ideals and America's precepts.

It's important to recognize that this flow of immigrants has helped make this country stronger and more prosperous. We also recognize that being a nation of laws goes hand in hand with being a nation of immigrants. This, too, is our heritage. This, too, is important and that's why immigration reform has been so important to my Administration.

Barack Obama

Acceptance

Dear President Obama,

When you said, "Today we begin in earnest the work of making sure that the world we leave our children is just a little bit better than the one we inhabit today." you echoed the philosophy that stretches back to the time of Ancient Greece, concerning perfection. Plato, one of those famous Greek philosophers defined perfection as: 1) which is complete—which contains all the requisite parts, 2) which is so good that nothing of the kind could be better, and 3) which has attained its purpose. To the Athenian Greeks, their form of government, democracy seemed to be that perfect government where no man could overthrow the government from the inside.

If we are given the ability to do something in the world for the betterment of mankind, I would attempt to try to stop the paranoia of racism and ethnicity. It seems that people nowadays do not view racism as it originally was, and still call each, "Jews," "Muslims," "blacks," and other terms. Its because of hate and prejudice that seems to be the root of all evil in the world. People are affected by so many stereotypes, putting pressure on them, putting them down, or making them feel alone leading to suicide. If we ended these words of hatred, we may be able to heal the wounded spirit of a nation, of a country, of a people and begin to help others when we have finally helped ourselves. Only then, can the United States return to its ability to help others and make the world a better place. We will not be able to make it perfect despite all our efforts, but if we try it will feel perfect.

Sincerely,
Raymond
Boston Latin School
Boston, MA

Strength

Dear Raymond,

Thank you for your letter and insight into an issue that affects every American. I know there's some people who still think through the prism of race. I'm very familiar with this as I'm sure there are people who think through the prism of race when it comes to evaluating me and my presidency. Sometime they vote for me for that reason, and sometimes they vote against me for that reason. I'm sure that was true during the campaign, and it's true now.

But your words remind us of what Dr. King once said. He said, 'The arc of the moral universe is long but it bends towards justice.' But, it doesn't bend on its own. It bends because each of us, Charles Hamilton Houston, Thurgood Marshall, John Lewis, and then all of you put your hands on the arc and you bend it in the direction of justice. That's our task. *That is what we must do. And I'm confident that that arc will keep on bending in the right direction.*

From the earliest days of our founding fathers, America has been the story of ordinary people who dare to dream. That's how we win the future. That's how Dr. King won the future. He had a dream. He had a vision of America that we have come to realize. There is no Black America, or White America, or Latino America, or Asian America. There is only the United States of America. And, when we act together, there's nothing the United States of America cannot achieve.

Barack Obama

Dedication/Commitment

Dear Barack Obama,

I'm 11 years old, and I'm in 6th grade at Hill Campus of Arts and Sciences in Denver, Colorado. I would like to remind you how the war in Iraq is tearing our world apart. During your presidential term I would love to see a stop to the war in Iraq. I personally don't know anyone serving in the war, but I can't even imagine how I would feel. I would probably feel terribly sad and devastated. It's impossible for me to imagine waking up one day and finding out that a friend or even a family member has died in the war. I hope and pray that I will never have to experience that feeling of loss.

Please consider that one of the first problems you deal with when you're in office is to end the war in Iraq, so it doesn't tear our world apart anymore than it already is. Let's bring our brave soldiers home, where they belong, with their family and friends who love them most. Thank you for your time… it's time for change! Yes We Can!!!

Sincerely,
Emily
Hill Campus of Arts and Sciences
Denver, CO

Duty

Dear Emily,

I made a promise to you, to the American people, and to our service men and women that I would end the war in Iraq. I set out to do this on my first day in office when I had my national security team review our strategy for the war. And, as of December 21, 2011, I made good on that promise.

As President, I have no higher honor than serving as the military's Commander in Chief. But with that honor comes a solemn responsibility, one that gets driven home every time I sign a condolence letter or meet a family member whose life has been turned upside down. No words can ever bring back a loved one who has been lost. No ceremony can do justice to their memory. No honor will ever fill their absence. And so it is my duty, as part of ending the Iraq War responsibly, to stand by those who have returned home from fighting it.

Our freedom endures because of the men and women in uniform who defend it. When they come home, we must serve them as well as they've served us. That includes giving them the care and the benefits they have earned, which is why we've increased annual VA spending every year that I've been President. And it means enlisting our veterans in the work of rebuilding our Nation. With the bipartisan support of this Congress, we're providing new tax credits to companies that hire vets. Michelle and Jill Biden have worked with American businesses to secure a pledge of 135,000 jobs for veterans and their families. I've also proposed a veterans jobs corps that will help our communities hire veterans as cops and firefighters, so that America is as strong as those who defend her.

We know that this generation of heroes has made the United States safer and more respected around the world. For the first time in 9 years, there are no Americans fighting in Iraq. For the first time in two decades, Usama Bin Laden is not a threat to this country. Most of Al Qaida's top lieutenants have been defeated. The Taliban's momentum has been broken, and some troops in Afghanistan have begun to come home. These achievements are a testament to the courage, selflessness, and teamwork of America's Armed Forces and Special Forces like the Navy Seals. At a *time when too many of our institutions have let us down, they exceed all expectations. They're not consumed with personal ambition. They don't obsess over their differences. They focus on the mission at hand. They work together. We have a responsibility to learn from their service. We cannot turn our backs on those who serve this country. We must set the example for future generations that one good deed deserves another.*

Barack Obama

Honor

Dear Mr. President,

I read in your book, *The Audacity of Hope*, how you believe every person should have an opportunity to be all that one can be. You also stated that there is no White America, or Black America, or Latino America, or Asian America. There is only the United States of America. I believe that history and this country should give honor to all those who seek to better this country. It puzzles me that you give credit in your book to a man, a freedom fighter named Malcolm X. You stated that he helped you to understand yourself. I researched who he was and found out that New York Magazine cited him as one of history's most influential men along with Albert Einstein, John F. Kennedy, Moses, and Julius Caesar

This country has not given him a Presidential Medal of Freedom or a Congressional Medal of Honor. I'm not asking for a holiday Mr. President, but this man should be honored. What do you think?

John
Gaston Middle School
Dallas, TX

Reverence

Dear John,

Thank you for your letter and your high regard for our nations history. When I think about our country, I think about America and those who built it, like Abraham Lincoln and Martin Luther King Jr., who laid down their lives in the service of perfecting an imperfect union.

They were great men. Malcolm X is one of those great men. And, it is true that such men should be honored with distinction—distinction such as being honored with a postal stamp commemoration.

Every so often, there are times when America must rise to meet a moment. So it has been for the generations that built the railroad and beat back the depression and battled for civil rights. It is our obligation to learn from their stories, to honor their stories, and most of all, live up to their examples.

Barack Obama

Conscience

Dear President Obama,

You have said many things that inspired people to reevaluate oneself, and will definitely be quoted and remembered from here on out. One quote that has exceptional meaning to me was, "Today we begin in earnest the work of making sure that the world we leave our children is just a little bit better than the one we inhabit today." This one quote brings me back to disturbing images of what our world has come to today, and how our country is buried under many problems we have yet found solutions to. So what problems do the American people face?

We are not the strong country we once were, the country where people from all over the world strive to immigrate to, where they can find a place where there is peace and prosperity. In fact, America is undeniably under stress from crashes in our capitalist economy, and will have to go into a recession. Even though our economic crisis might seem as the big picture, we cannot forget the problems that were already present but is now just merely covered up because people are too used to having them there. Such problems are racism, sexism, violence and discrimination. How many times have we heard in the news that people were killed because of the difference of skin color? How many times have we listened to stories of gangs on streets fighting each other, of discrimination against someone's sexual orientation, race, and etc.? High school students, such as myself, can look into their school and see the subtle and some unsubtle segregation between students. Wherever you are, there is still racism and all these other problems in the world. And yet we can still live in this society without any conscience, and passing on this life to our children? Even though it seems impossible to rid the world of these, the best we can do is try. Just like you have said, President Obama, we have to work in earnest to get things done. All of this starts now. It does not mean it would be easy, but we have to reach for the goal of being peaceful. We cannot lose faith on trying to solve things that some consider inevitable. We cannot settle for the society we are in right now.

Sincerely,
Thu
Boston Latin School
Boston, MA

Unity

Dear Thu,

Thank you for your compassionate and insightful letter. You are right that these problems—racism, sexism, discrimination against sexual orientation and religion—have plagued our nation for centuries. But we must remember that our past does not define us. How we move forward defines us. For nearly four centuries, men and women have immigrated to America's shores in pursuit of religious and personal freedom. Hailing from diverse backgrounds, cultures, and faiths, countless settlers have shared a simple aspiration—to practice their beliefs and ways of life free from prejudice and persecution.

In the United States of America, our freedom and our diversity have been our greatest sources of pride and our greatest strength. Our armed forces, the strongest military force on this earth, is an inspiring example of unity over division when it comes to matters of race, religion, and sexual orientation. Our troops come from every corner of this country—they're black, white, Latino, Asian, Native American. They are Christian and Hindu, Jewish and Muslim. And, yes, we know that some of them are gay. But they take a lesson to heart that keeps them strong and united, and reminds them that they always have each other's backs. And that lesson is: there is no Black America, or White America, of Latino America, or Asian America. There is only the United States of America.

Our nation may have some dark chapters in our history when it comes to the pain and struggles of racism and discrimination that past generations have gone through. When future generations hear these songs of pain and progress and struggle and sacrifice, I hope they will not think of them as somehow separate from the larger American story. I want them to see it as central—an important part of our shared story. A call to see ourselves in one another. A call to remember that each of us is made in God's image and that not one of us is perfect.

That's the history of Americans like Abraham Lincoln, John F. Kennedy, Rosa Parks, and Martin Luther King Jr., and we will preserve that history within the borders of this nation. The history of a people who, in the words of Dr. King, "injected new meaning and dignity into the veins of civilization." May we remember their stories. May we live up to their example.

Barack Obama

President Obama Talks to America's Students

September 8, 2009

The President: Hello everyone—how's everybody doing today? I'm here with students at Wakefield High School in Arlington, Virginia. And we've got students tuning in from all across America, kindergarten through twelfth grade. I'm glad you all could join us today.

I know that for many of you, today is the first day of school. And for those of you in kindergarten, or starting middle or high school, it's your first day in a new school, so it's understandable if you're a little nervous. I imagine there are some seniors out there who are feeling pretty good right now, with just one more year to go. And no matter what grade you're in, some of you are probably wishing it were still summer, and you could've stayed in bed just a little longer this morning.

I know that feeling. When I was young, my family lived in Indonesia for a few years, and my mother didn't have the money to send me where all the American kids went to school. So she decided to teach me extra lessons herself, Monday through Friday—at 4:30 in the morning.

Now I wasn't too happy about getting up that early. A lot of times, I'd fall asleep right there at the kitchen table. But whenever I'd complain, my mother would just give me one of those looks and say, "This is no picnic for me either, buster."

155

So I know some of you are still adjusting to being back at school. But I'm here today because I have something important to discuss with you. I'm here because I want to talk with you about your education and what's expected of all of you in this new school year.

Now I've given a lot of speeches about education. And I've talked a lot about responsibility.

I've talked about your teachers' responsibility for inspiring you, and pushing you to learn.

I've talked about your parents' responsibility for making sure you stay on track, and get your homework done, and don't spend every waking hour in front of the TV or with that Xbox.

I've talked a lot about your government's responsibility for setting high standards, supporting teachers and principals, and turning around schools that aren't working where students aren't getting the opportunities they deserve.

But at the end of the day, we can have the most dedicated teachers, the most supportive parents, and the best schools in the world—and none of it will matter unless all of you fulfill your responsibilities. Unless you show up to those schools; pay attention to those teachers; listen to your parents, grandparents and other adults; and put in the hard work it takes to succeed.

And that's what I want to focus on today: the responsibility each of you has for your education. I want to start with the responsibility you have to yourself.

Every single one of you has something you're good at. Every single one of you has something to offer. And you have a responsibility to yourself to discover what that is. That's the opportunity an education can provide.

Maybe you could be a good writer—maybe even good enough to write a book or articles in a newspaper—but you might not know it until you write a paper for your English class. Maybe you could be an innovator or an inventor—maybe even good enough to come up with the next iPhone or a new medicine or vaccine—but you might not know it until you do a project for your science class. Maybe you could be a mayor or a Senator or a Supreme Court Justice, but you might not know that until you join student government or the debate team.

And no matter what you want to do with your life—I guarantee that you'll need an education to do it. You want to be a doctor, or a teacher, or a police officer? You want to be a nurse or an architect, a lawyer or a member of our military? You're going to need a good education for every single one of those careers. You can't drop out of school and just drop into a good job. You've got to work for it and train for it and learn for it.

And this isn't just important for your own life and your own future. What you make of your education will decide nothing less than the future of this country. What you're learning in school today will determine whether we as a nation can meet our greatest challenges in the future.

You'll need the knowledge and problem-solving skills you learn in science and math to cure diseases like cancer and AIDS, and to develop new energy technologies and protect our environment. You'll need the insights and critical thinking skills you gain in history and social studies to fight poverty and homelessness, crime and discrimination, and make our nation more fair and more free. You'll need the creativity and ingenuity you develop in all your classes to build new companies that will create new jobs and boost our economy.

We need every single one of you to develop your talents, skills and intellect so you can help solve our most difficult problems. If you don't do that—if you quit on school—you're not just quitting on yourself, you're quitting on your country.

Now I know it's not always easy to do well in school. I know a lot of you have challenges in your lives right now that can make it hard to focus on your schoolwork.

I get it. I know what that's like. My father left my family when I was two years old, and I was raised by a single mother who struggled at times to pay the bills and wasn't always able to give us things the other kids had. There were times when I missed having a father in my life. There were times when I was lonely and felt like I didn't fit in.

So I wasn't always as focused as I should have been. I did some things I'm not proud of, and got in more trouble than I should have. And my life could have easily taken a turn for the worse.

But I was fortunate. I got a lot of second chances and had the opportunity to go to college, and law school, and follow my dreams. My wife, our First Lady Michelle Obama, has a similar story. Neither of her parents had gone to college, and they didn't have much. But they worked hard, and she worked hard, so that she could go to the best schools in this country.

Some of you might not have those advantages. Maybe you don't have adults in your life who give you the support that you need. Maybe someone in your family has lost their job, and there's not enough money to go around. Maybe you live in a neighborhood where you don't feel safe, or have friends who are pressuring you to do things you know aren't right.

But at the end of the day, the circumstances of your life—what you look like, where you come from, how much money you have, what you've got going on at home—that's no excuse for neglecting your homework or having a bad attitude. That's no excuse for talking back to your teacher, or cutting class, or dropping out of school. That's no excuse for not trying.

Where you are right now doesn't have to determine where you'll end up. No one's written your destiny for you. Here in America, you write your own destiny. You make your own future.

That's what young people like you are doing every day, all across America.

Young people like Jazmin Perez, from Roma, Texas. Jazmin didn't speak English when she first started school. Hardly anyone in her hometown went to college, and neither of her parents had gone either. But she worked hard, earned good grades, got a scholarship to Brown University, and is now in graduate school, studying public health, on her way to being Dr. Jazmin Perez.

I'm thinking about Andoni Schultz, from Los Altos, California, who's fought brain cancer since he was three. He's endured all sorts of treatments and surgeries, one of which affected his memory, so it took him much longer—hundreds of extra hours—to do his schoolwork. But he never fell behind, and he's headed to college this fall.

And then there's Shantell Steve, from my hometown of Chicago, Illinois. Even when bouncing from foster home to foster home in the toughest neighborhoods, she managed to get a job at a local health center; start a program to keep young people out of gangs; and she's on track to graduate high school with honors and go on to college.

Jazmin, Andoni and Shantell aren't any different from any of you. They faced challenges in their lives just like you do. But they refused to give up. They chose to take responsibility for their education and set goals for themselves. And I expect all of you to do the same.

That's why today, I'm calling on each of you to set your own goals for your education—and to do everything you can to meet them. Your goal can be something as simple as doing all your homework, paying attention in class, or spending time each day reading a book. Maybe you'll decide to get involved in an extracurricular activity, or volunteer in your community. Maybe you'll decide to stand up for kids who are being teased or bullied because of who they are or how they look, because you believe, like I do, that all kids deserve a safe environment to study and learn. Maybe you'll decide to take better care of yourself so you can be more ready to learn. And along those lines, I hope you'll all wash your hands a lot, and stay home from school when you don't feel well, so we can keep people from getting the flu this fall and winter.

Whatever you resolve to do, I want you to commit to it. I want you to really work at it.

I know that sometimes, you get the sense from TV that you can be rich and successful without any hard work—that your ticket to success is through rapping or basketball or being a reality TV star, when chances are, you're not going to be any of those things.

But the truth is, being successful is hard. You won't love every subject you study. You won't click with every teacher. Not every homework assignment will seem completely relevant to your life right this minute. And you won't necessarily succeed at everything the first time you try.

That's OK. Some of the most successful people in the world are the ones who've had the most failures. JK Rowling's first Harry Potter book was rejected twelve times before it was finally published. Michael Jordan was cut from his high school basketball team, and he lost hundreds of games and missed thousands of shots during his career. But he once said, "I have failed over and over and over again in my life. And that is why I succeed."

These people succeeded because they understand that you can't let your failures define you—you have to let them teach you. You have to let them show you what to do differently next time. If you get in trouble, that doesn't mean you're a troublemaker, it means you need to try harder to behave. If you get a bad grade, that doesn't mean you're stupid, it just means you need to spend more time studying.

No one's born being good at things, you become good at things through hard work. You're not a varsity athlete the first time you play a new sport. You don't hit every note the first time you sing a song. You've got to practice. It's the same with your schoolwork. You might have to do a math problem a few times before you get it right, or read something a few times before you understand it, or do a few drafts of a paper before it's good enough to hand in.

Don't be afraid to ask questions. Don't be afraid to ask for help when you need it. I do that every day. Asking for help isn't a sign of weakness, it's a sign of strength. It shows you have the courage to admit when you don't know something, and to learn something new. So find an adult you trust—a parent, grandparent or teacher; a coach or counselor—and ask them to help you stay on track to meet your goals.

And even when you're struggling, even when you're discouraged, and you feel like other people have given up on you—don't ever give up on yourself. Because when you give up on yourself, you give up on your country.

The story of America isn't about people who quit when things got tough. It's about people who kept going, who tried harder, who loved their country too much to do anything less than their best.

It's the story of students who sat where you sit 250 years ago, and went on to wage a revolution and found this nation. Students who sat where you sit 75 years ago who overcame a Depression and won a world war; who fought for civil rights and put a man on the moon. Students who sat where you sit 20 years ago who founded Google, Twitter and Facebook and changed the way we communicate with each other.

So today, I want to ask you, what's your contribution going to be? What problems are you going to solve? What discoveries will you make? What will a president who comes here in twenty or fifty or one hundred years say about what all of you did for this country?

Your families, your teachers, and I are doing everything we can to make sure you have the education you need to answer these questions. I'm working hard to fix up your classrooms and get you the books, equipment and computers you need to learn. But you've got to do your part too. So I expect you to get serious this year. I expect you to put your best effort into everything you do. I expect great things from each of you. So don't let us down—don't let your family or your country or yourself down. Make us all proud. I know you can do it.

Thank you, God bless you, and God bless America.

Epilogue

by
William Alexander Haley
"America's Young Voices"

There is a saying that my father used to have, "Whenever you see a turtle on top of a fence post, you know it had help getting up there." These letters show us that the President of the United States of America had the help and support of the youth to be elected in 2008. Now in 2012, the president needs the help and support of the youth, once again, to stay and follow through for all of us.

I recognize how rare it is to have thousands of young people write the office of the president with a sense of urgency to change America. It is even rarer for the students to write in volumes to an incoming president before he takes office. It is rarest to have access to these young people's letters that are directed to the president of the United States—letters filled with the hope that their country and their president will take notice of their concerns and their desire for change.

Presidential letters are not readily accessible to the public. Therefore, these letters addressed to the president would not ordinarily be known at all due to access restrictions and the obligations of the presidential office. *The Presidential Records and Freedom of Information Acts guarantee public access to recent presidential papers, but only after a suitable period of time has elapsed and a minimum of five years after the administration*

163

has completed its term period and a maximum of twelve years. A president can receive as many as 40,000 – 100,000 letters per week. President Bush received 40,000 plus letters weekly, depending on the crisis or a current event of the nation. *President Obama receives about 65,000 written letters and approximately 100,000 emails every week. Because of this project, the American people now for the first time have a glimpse into the correspondence between a president and his constituents.*

Under the above scenario, our young people's letters, a rare collection accompanied by formulated responses, would not be known of for twenty years (if the president serves an eight-year term). *America cannot effectively or holistically change without the millions of young people's voices being heard or known. This project is a step in honoring the voices of our young future leaders who are preparing to participate in America's voting process.*

This unique volume of letters provides Americans an opportunity to view and understand our young people's outlook and demands on the **economy, religion, education, crime, war, race, violence, justice, environment, and the direction they want to see their country move in.** Their poignant and genuine letters contributed to the "Kids for Obama" social movement that was launched by President Obama during his 2008 campaign in the hope that this nation would take note of their letters and their demands.

President Obama has gotten our young people's attention. The "Kids for Obama" movement and these letters to the president have engineered a path for mankind to prove this country was, and still is committed to *change* and that we should be ready to help our young people and this nation as we continue to move forward. Yes, we can!

William Alexander Haley
CEO, Alex Haley Foundation

Appendix

President Obama's Spiritual Journey to the Whitehouse

Evolution of Thoughts

1859-2008

President Obama's Spiritual Journey
to the Whitehouse

Evolution of Thoughts

1859
Abraham Lincoln –"The best way to destroy an enemy is to make him a friend."

W.E. Dubois—"The hope of civilization lies not in exclusion, but inclusion of all human elements."

2006
Barack Obama—"By ourselves, this change will not happen. Divided we are bound to fail. That beneath all the differences of race and region, faith and station, we are one people."

Barack Obama—"There is not a black America and white America and Latino America and Asian America." "A vision of America finally freed from the past—Jim Crow and slavery, Japanese interment camps… cultural conflict—an America that fulfills Dr. King's promise that be judge not by color of our skin, but by the content of our character."

1863
Frederick Douglas –"If there is no struggle, this is no progress. The struggle may be a moral one, or it may be a physical one but it must be a struggle."

2006
Barack Obama—"We hold these truths to be self-evident... pursuit of happiness. The values of self-reliance and self-improvement and risk taking. The values of drive, discipline, temperance, and hard work. These values are rooted in a basic optimism about life and faith in free will—a confidence that through pluck and sweat, and smarts, each of us can rise above the circumstances of our birth."

1900's
James Weldon Johnson –"My inner life is mine and I shall defend and maintain its integrity..."

2006
Barack Obama—"My mother was the most spiritually awakened person that I've ever known. She instilled in me the values that many learned from Sunday school; honesty, discipline, delayed gratification and hard work.

Booker T. Washington—"More and more we must learn to think not in terms of race or color or language or religion or of political boundaries. There is humanity. That should be considered first; and in proportion as we teach our youths of this county to love all races and all nations, we are rendering the highest service with education can render."

Barack Obama—"We must be careful to keep our eyes on the prize—equal rights for every American. We must continue to expand adoption rights to make them consistent and seamless throughout all 50 states."

1907

Madam C. J. Walker –"I had to make my own living and my own opportunity… Don't sit down and wait for opportunities to come; you have to get up and make them…"

1923

Marcus Garvey –"According to commonest principles of human action, no man will do as much for you as you will do for yourself."

1922

Paul Roberson –"The course of history can be changed but not halted."

1926

Eleanor Roosevelt –"You gain strength, courage and confidence in which you really stop to look fear in the face… you must do the things you think you cannot do."

"No one can make you feel inferior without your consent. You have to accept whatever comes… and that you meet it with courage… with the best you have to give."

October 22, 2006

Barack Obama—"I am not sure anyone is ready to be president before they're president. America is ready to turn the page. America is ready for a new set of challenges. This is our time. A new generation is prepared to lead."

January 8, 2008

Barack Obama—"Change is what America is looking for. Nothing can withstand the power of millions of millions of voices calling for change… You are the changes you have been waiting for."

January 8, 2008

Barack Obama—"There is something happening in America. There is something happening when Americans who are young in age and in spirit—who have never before participated in politics—they know in their hearts that this time must be different."

2006

Barack Obama—"A transformation (race) in attitude has to begin in the home, and in neighborhoods and places in worship, community-based institutions."

"The problem is not that things have gotten better. The problem is that they're not good enough, and we still have a lot of work to do."

1934
Franklin Roosevelt—"The only thing we have to fear is fear itself."

1950's
Ghandi–"You must be the change you wish to see in the world."

Jackie Robinson –"A life is not important except as to the impact it has on other lives."

1955
Martin Luther King Jr.—"The ultimate measure of a person is not where they stand in moments of comfort and convenience, but where they stand at times of challenge and controversy."

2006
Barack Obama—"We must always reserve the right to strike at terrorists wherever they may exist."

February 10, 2007
Barack Obama—"If you join me in this improvable quest, if you feel destiny calling and, as I see, a future of endless possibilities, the time is now to shake off our slumber and slough off our fear. Together let us in a new birth of freedom on this earth."

Barack Obama—"My attitude about the presidency is that you don't want to just be the president. You want to change the country. You want to make a unique contribution. You want to be a great president."

Barack Obama—"There are some who believe we must try to turn back the clock on this new world, that the only chance to maintain our living standards is to build a fortress around America. It is impossible to turn back the tide of globalization… true leadership moved the country forward with confidence and a common purpose… that had the strength to turn moments of adversity into opportunity, the wisdom to see a little further down the road."

Correta Scott King –"There is a spirit and a need and a man at the beginning of every great human advance. Each of these must be right for the particular moment of history, or nothing happens."

Barack Obama –"Change is what's happening in America. We must challenge ourselves to reach for something better, there's no problem we can't solve—no destiny we cannot fulfill… no matter what obstacles stand in our way, nothing can withstand the power of millions of voices calling for a change."

Alex Haley—"When you clench your fist, no one can put anything in your hand, nor can your hand pick anything up."

Barack Obama—"I've always been clear that I'm rooted in the African-American community, but not limited to it."

1960
Malcolm X –"The man who stands for nothing will fall for anything."

Barack Obama—"At some level, your individual salvation depends on collective salvation. It's only when you hitch yourself up to something bigger than yourself that you're going to realize your true potential and the world will benefit from that potential."

John F. Kennedy –"One person can make a difference and every person should try."

Barack Obama—"I can walk into a room of people, whether they're black, white, rural, urban, red state, blue state, and after 30 minutes, engage them in a conversation where they say, 'A lot of what this guy is saying makes sense.'"

1965

Nelson Mandela –"If you talk to a man in a language he understands that goes to his head. If you talk to a man in his language, that goes to his heart."

1968

James Brown –"Say it loud, I'm black and I'm proud."

1990

Minister Louis Farrakhan –"If we can put the names of our faith aside for the moment and look at principles, we will find a common thread running through all the great religious expressions."

2000

Barack Obama—"My mother's simple principle, "How would that make you feel?" as a guide-post for politics. It's not a question we ask ourselves enough, I think; as a country we seem to be suffering form empathy deficit."

November 2, 2006

Barack Obama—"You don't vote for somebody because of what they look like. You vote for what they stand for."

May 31, 2004

Barack Obama—"There are so many different interpretations of Islam as there are so many inter-pretations of Christianity, that to somehow fix or define a religion based on one particular reading of the text is a mistake."

Barack Obama—"It was the struggle of these men and women that had moved me. Rather, it was their determination, self-reliance, a relentless, optimism in the face of hardship. It was that quality, I thought, that joined us as one people. It was that pervasive spirit of hope that tied my own family's story to the larger American story, and my own story to those of the voters I sought to represent."

In Honor of Dr. Otis Stanley

Great Leaders' Steps Toward Change

"Rare do we find men who are willing to engage in hard solid thinking. There is an almost universal quest for every answer and half-baked solutions. Nothing pains someone more than having to think"
—Martin Luther King, Jr.

Great Leaders' Steps Toward Change

"We have a stake in one another …what binds us together is greater than what drives us apart, and … if enough people believe in the truth of that proposition and act on it, then we might not solve every problem, but we can get something meaningful done for the people with whom we share this Earth."

—Barack Obama

The care of human life and happiness, and not their destruction, is the first and only object of good government.
Thomas Jefferson

Any people anywhere, being inclined and having the power, have the right to rise up and shake off the existing government, and form a new one that suits them better. This is a most valuable—a most sacred right—a right, which we hope and believe, is to liberate the world.
Abraham Lincoln

The assertion that "all men are created equal" was of no practical use in effecting our separation from Great Britain and it was placed in the Declaration not for that, but for future use.
Abraham Lincoln

This country, with its institutions, belongs to the people who inhabit it. Whenever they shall grow weary of the existing government, they can exercise their constitutional right of amending it, or exercise their revolutionary right to overthrow it.
Abraham Lincoln

And thus goes segregation, which is the most far-reaching development in the history of the Negro since the enslavement of the race.
Carter G. Woodson

If the human race wishes to have a prolonged and indefinite period of material prosperity, they have only got to behave in a peaceful and helpful way toward one another.
Winston Churchill

I claim that human mind or human society is not divided into watertight compartments called social, political and religious. All act and react upon one another.
Mohandas Gandhi

Our problems are man-made; therefore they may be solved by man. And man can be as big as he wants. No problem of human destiny is beyond human beings.
John F. Kennedy

At the time I was arrested I had no idea it would turn into this. It was just a day like any other day. The only thing that made it significant was that the masses of the people joined in.
Rosa Parks

There are no constraints on the human mind, no walls around the human spirit, and no barriers to our progress except those we ourselves erect.
Ronald Reagan

There is no better than adversity. Every defeat, every heartbreak, every loss, contains its own seed, its own lesson on how to improve your performance the next time.
Malcolm X

The sweltering summer of the Negro's legitimate discontent will not pass until there is an invigorating autumn of freedom and equality.
Martin Luther King, Jr.

Thoughtful Steps Towards…Hope

"Yes, our greatness as a nation has depended on individual initiative, on a belief in the free market. But it has also depended on our sense of mutual regard for each other, of mutual responsibility. The idea that everybody has a stake in the country, that we're all in it together and everybody's got a shot at opportunity. Americans know this. We know that government can't solve all our problems—and we don't want it to. But we also know that there are some things we can't do on our own. We know that there are some things we do better together."

—Barack Obama

America will never be destroyed from the outside. If we falter and lose our freedoms, it will be because we destroyed ourselves.
Abraham Lincoln

The dogmas of the quiet past are inadequate to the stormy present. The occasion is piled high with difficulty, and we must rise with the occasion. As our case is new, so we must think anew and act anew.
Abraham Lincoln

Fourscore and seven years ago our fathers brought forth on this continent, a new nation, conceived in Liberty, and dedicated to the proposition that all men are created equal.
Abraham Lincoln

It is not enough to understand, or to see clearly. The future will be shaped in the arena of human activity, by those willing to commit their minds and their bodies to the task.
Robert Kennedy

One thing is clear to me: We, as human beings, must be willing to accept people who are different from ourselves.
Barbara Jordan

I am trying to show the world that we are all human beings and that color is not important. What is important is the quality of our work.
Alvin Ailey

Racism is still with us. But it is up to us to prepare our children for what they have to meet, and, hopefully, we shall overcome.
Rosa Parks

Education is the passport to the future, for tomorrow belongs to those who prepare for it today.
Malcolm X

The Negro needs the white man to free him from his fears. The white man needs the Negro to free him from his guilt.
Martin Luther King, Jr.

America did not invent human rights. In a very real sense human rights invented America.
Jimmy Carter

Man's greatness consists in his ability to do and the proper application of his powers to things needed to be done.
Frederick Douglass

I am a Republican, a black, dyed in the wool Republican, and I never intend to belong to any other party than the party of freedom and progress.
Frederick Douglass

America, this is our moment. This is our time. Our time to turn the page of the policies of the past.
Barack Obama

We've got a tragic history when it comes to race in this country. We've got a lot of pent-up anger and bitterness and misunderstanding. … This country wants to move beyond these kinds of things.
Barack Obama

Thoughtful Steps Towards...Family

"You know, there's a lot of talk in this country about the federal deficit. But I think we should talk more about our empathy deficit—the ability to put ourselves in someone else's shoes; to see the world through the eyes of those who are different from us—the child who's hungry, the steelworker who's been laid-off, and the family who lost the entire life they built together when the storm came to town. When you think like this—when you choose to broaden your ambit of concern and empathize with the plight of others, whether they are close friends or distant strangers—it becomes harder not to act; harder not to help."

—Barack Obama

All human actions have one or more of these seven causes: chance, nature, compulsions, habit, reason, passion, desire.
Aristotle

One ever feels his twoness-an American, a Negro; two souls, two thoughts, two unreconciled strivings; two warring ideals in one dark body, whose dogged strength alone keeps it from being torn asunder.
W. E. B. Du Bois

The drums of Africa still beat in my heart. They will not let me rest while there is a single Negro boy or girl without a chance to prove his worth.
Mary McLeod Bethune

The steady expansion of welfare programs can be taken as a measure of the steady disintegration of the Negro family structure over the past generation in the United States.
Daniel Patrick Moynihan

Memories of our lives, of our works and our deeds will continue in others.
Rosa Parks

But suppose God is black? What if we go to Heaven and we, all our lives, have treated the Negro as an inferior, and God is there, and we look up and He is not white? What then is our response?
Robert Kennedy

She was the cornerstone of our family and a woman of extraordinary accomplishment, strength and humility. She was the person who encouraged and allowed us to take chances.

In joint statement with his sister, on death of 86-year-old grandmother Madelyn Dunham on eve of US presidential election 2008.
Barack Obama

Change will not come if we wait for some other person or some other time. We are the ones we've been waiting for. We are the change that we seek.
Barack Obama

Americans ... still believe in an America where anything's possible—they just don't think their leaders do.

We live in a culture that discourages empathy. A culture that too often tells us our principle goal in life is to be rich, thin, young, famous, safe, and entertained.

Secularists are wrong when they ask believers to leave their religion at the door before entering into the public square. Frederick Douglas, Abraham Lincoln, Williams Jennings Bryant, Dorothy Day, Martin Luther King—indeed, the majority of great reformers in American history—were not only motivated by faith, but repeatedly used religious language to argue for their cause.

The best judge of whether or not a country is going to develop is how it treats its women. If it's educating its girls, if women have equal rights, that country is going to move forward. But if women are oppressed and abused and illiterate, then they're going to fall behind.

Thoughtful Steps Towards... Young Citizens

"Making your mark on the world is hard. If it were easy, everybody would do it. But it's not. It takes patience, it takes commitment, and it comes with plenty of failure along the way. The real test is not whether you avoid this failure, because you won't.. it's whether you let it harden or shame you into inaction, or whether you learn from it; whether you choose to persevere."
—Barack Obama

It is easier to build strong children than to repair broken men.
Frederick Douglass

An American, a Negro... two souls, two thoughts, two unreconciled strivings; two warring ideals in one dark body, whose dogged strength alone keeps it from being torn asunder.
W. E. B. Du Bois

If you're walking down the right path and you're willing to keep walking, eventually you'll make progress.
Barack Obama

My Alma mater was books, a good library... I could spend the rest of my life reading, just satisfying my curiosity.
Malcolm X

And so, my fellow Americans, ask not what your country can do for you; ask what you can do for your country.
John F. Kennedy

Every human has four endowments—self awareness, conscience, independent will and creative imagination. These give us the ultimate human freedom... The power to choose, to respond, to change.
Stephen Covey

Human progress is neither automatic nor inevitable... Every step toward the goal of justice requires sacrifice, suffering, and struggle; the tireless exertions and passionate concern of dedicated individuals.
Martin Luther King, Jr.

It doesn't do well to open doors for someone who doesn't have the price to get in. If he has the price, he may not need the laws. There is no law saying the Negro has to live in Harlem or Watts.
Ronald Reagan

As human beings, our greatness lays not so much in being able to remake the world—that is the myth of the atomic age—as in being able to remake ourselves.
Mohandas Gandhi

The so-called modern education, with all its defects, however, does others so much more good than it does the Negro, because it has been worked out in conformity to the needs of those who have enslaved and oppressed weaker peoples.
Carter G. Woodson

There is not a liberal America and a conservative America—there is the United States of America. There is not a black America and a white America and Latino America and Asian America—there's the United States of America.
Barack Obama

My job is not to represent Washington to you, but to represent you to Washington.
Barack Obama

Focusing your life solely on making a buck shows a certain poverty of ambition. It asks too little of yourself. Because it's only when you hitch your wagon to something larger than yourself that you realize your true potential.
Barack Obama

We have an obligation and a responsibility to be investing in our students and our schools. We must make sure that people who have the grades, the desire and the will, but not the money, can still get the best education possible.
Barack Obama

Today we are engaged in a deadly global struggle for those who would intimidate, torture, and murder people for exercising the most basic freedoms. If we are to win this struggle and spread those freedoms, we must keep our own moral compass pointed in a true direction.
Barack Obama

Thoughtful Steps Towards... Our Future

"My parents shared not only an improbable love; they shared an abiding faith in the possibilities of this nation. They would give me an African name, Barack, or blessed, believing that in a tolerant America your name is no barrier to success. They imagined me going to the best schools in the land, even though they weren't rich, because in a generous America you don't have to be rich to achieve your potential."

—Barack Obama

It is better to remain silent and be thought a fool than to open one's mouth and remove all doubt.
Abraham Lincoln

The Negro revolution is controlled by foxy white liberals, by the Government itself. But the Black Revolution is controlled only by God.
Malcolm X

You're not supposed to be so blind with patriotism that you can't face reality. Wrong is wrong, no matter who says it.
Malcolm X

Words mean more than what is set down on paper. It takes the human voice to infuse them with deeper meaning.
Maya Angelou

The world is very different now. For man holds in his mortal hands the power to abolish all forms of human poverty, and all forms of human life.
John F. Kennedy

Man must evolve for all human conflict, a method, which rejects revenge, aggression and retaliation. The foundation of such a method is love.
Martin Luther King, Jr.

I believe in human beings, and that all human beings should be respected as such, regardless of their color.
Malcolm X

You don't have to be a man to fight for freedom. All you have to do is to be an intelligent human being.
Malcolm X

Our progress as a nation can be no swifter than our progress in education. The human mind is our fundamental resource.

John F. Kennedy

Where justice is denied, where poverty is enforced; where ignorance prevails; and where any one class is made to feel that society is an organized conspiracy to oppress, rob and degrade them; neither persons nor property will be safe.
Frederick Douglass

A battle lost or won is easily described, understood, and appreciated, but the moral growth of a great nation requires reflection, as well as observation, to appreciate it.
Frederick Douglass

We need to steer clear of this poverty of ambition, where people want to drive fancy cars and wear nice clothes and live in nice apartments but don't want to work hard to accomplish these things. Everyone should try to realize their full potential.
Barack Obama

With the changing economy, no one has lifetime employment. But community colleges provide lifetime employability.
Barack Obama

We need to internalize this idea of excellence. Not many folks spend a lot of time trying to be excellent.
Barack Obama

President Obama's Notable Speeches

2004-2009

Democratic National Convention Speech

Run for the Democratic Nomination Speech

Presidential Nomination Acceptance Speech

Victory Speech

Inauguration Speech

2012 State of the Union Address

Democratic National Convention Keynote Address

July 27, 2004

Thank you so much. Thank you. Thank you. Thank you so much. Thank you so much. Thank you. Thank you. Thank you, Dick Durbin. You make us all proud.

On behalf of the great state of Illinois, crossroads of a nation, Land of Lincoln, let me express my deepest gratitude for the privilege of addressing this convention.

Tonight is a particular honor for me because, let's face it, my presence on this stage is pretty unlikely. My father was a foreign student, born and raised in a small village in Kenya. He grew up herding goats, went to school in a tin-roof shack. His father—my grandfather—was a cook, a domestic servant to the British.

But my grandfather had larger dreams for his son. Through hard work and perseverance my father got a scholarship to study in a magical place, America, that shone as a beacon of freedom and opportunity to so many who had come before.

While studying here, my father met my mother. She was born in a town on the other side of the world, in Kansas. Her father worked on oil rigs and farms through most of the Depression. The day after Pearl Harbor my grandfather signed up for duty; joined Patton's army, marched across Europe. Back home, my grandmother raised a baby and went to work on a bomber assembly line. After the war, they studied on the G.I. Bill, bought a house through F.H.A., and later moved west all the way to Hawaii in search of opportunity.

And they, too, had big dreams for their daughter. A common dream, born of two continents.

My parents shared not only an improbable love, they shared an abiding faith in the possibilities of this nation. They would give me an African name, Barack, or "blessed," believing that in a tolerant America your name is no barrier to success. They imagined—They imagined me going to the best schools in the land, even though they weren't rich, because in a generous America you don't have to be rich to achieve your potential.

They're both passed away now. And yet, I know that on this night they look down on me with great pride.

They stand here—And I stand here today, grateful for the diversity of my heritage, aware that my parents' dreams live on in my two precious daughters. I stand here knowing that my story is part of the larger American story, that I owe a debt to all of those who came before me, and that, in no other country on earth, is my story even possible.

Tonight, we gather to affirm the greatness of our Nation—not because of the height of our skyscrapers, or the power of our military, or the size of our economy. Our pride is based on a very simple premise, summed up in a declaration made over two hundred years ago:

We hold these truths to be self-evident, that all men are created equal, that they are endowed by their Creator with certain inalienable rights, that among these are Life, Liberty and the pursuit of Happiness.

That is the true genius of America, a faith—a faith in simple dreams, an insistence on small miracles; that we can tuck in our children at night and know that they are fed and clothed and safe from harm; that we can say what we think, write what we think, without hearing a sudden knock on the door; that we can have an idea and start our own business without paying a bribe; that we can participate in the political process without fear of retribution, and that our votes will be counted—at least most of the time.

This year, in this election we are called to reaffirm our values and our commitments, to hold them against a hard reality and see how we're measuring up to the legacy of our forbearers and the promise of future generations.

And fellow Americans, Democrats, Republicans, Independents, I say to you tonight: We have more work to do—more work to do for the workers I met in Galesburg, Illinois, who are losing their union jobs at the Maytag plant that's moving to Mexico, and now are having to compete with their own children for jobs that pay seven bucks an hour; more to do for the father that I met who was losing his job and choking back the tears, wondering how he would pay 4500 dollars a month for the drugs his son needs without the health benefits that he counted on; more to do for the young woman in East St. Louis, and thousands more like her, who has the grades, has the drive, has the will, but doesn't have the money to go to college.

Now, don't get me wrong. The people I meet—in small towns and big cities, in diners and office parks—they don't expect government to solve all their problems. They know they have to work hard to get ahead, and they want to. Go into the collar counties around Chicago, and people will tell you they don't want their tax money wasted, by a welfare agency or by the Pentagon. Go in—Go into any inner city neighborhood, and folks will tell you that government alone can't teach our kids to learn; they know that parents have to teach, that children can't achieve unless we raise their expectations and turn off the television sets and eradicate the slander that says a black youth with a book is acting white. They know those things.

People don't expect—People don't expect government to solve all their problems. But they sense, deep in their bones, that with just a slight change in priorities, we can make sure that every child in America has a decent shot at life, and that the doors of opportunity remain open to all.

They know we can do better. And they want that choice.

In this election, we offer that choice. Our Party has chosen a man to lead us who embodies the best this country has to offer. And that man is John Kerry.

John Kerry understands the ideals of community, faith, and service because they've defined his life. From his heroic service to Vietnam, to his years as a prosecutor and lieutenant governor, through two decades in the United States Senate, he's devoted himself to this country. Again and again, we've seen him make tough choices when easier ones were available.

His values and his record affirm what is best in us. John Kerry believes in an America where hard work is rewarded; so instead of offering tax breaks to companies shipping jobs overseas, he offers them to companies creating jobs here at home.

John Kerry believes in an America where all Americans can afford the same health coverage our politicians in Washington have for themselves.

John Kerry believes in energy independence, so we aren't held hostage to the profits of oil companies, or the sabotage of foreign oil fields.

John Kerry believes in the Constitutional freedoms that have made our country the envy of the world, and he will never sacrifice our basic liberties, nor use faith as a wedge to divide us.

And John Kerry believes that in a dangerous world war must be an option sometimes, but it should never be the first option.

You know, a while back—awhile back I met a young man named Shamus in a V.F.W. Hall in East Moline, Illinois. He was a good-looking kid—six two, six three, clear eyed, with an easy smile. He told me he'd joined the Marines and was heading to Iraq the following week. And as I listened to him explain why he'd enlisted, the absolute faith he had in our country and its leaders, his devotion to duty and service, I thought this young man was all that any of us might ever hope for in a child.

But then I asked myself, "Are we serving Shamus as well as he is serving us?"

I thought of the 900 men and women—sons and daughters, husbands and wives, friends and neighbors, who won't be returning to their own hometowns. I thought of the families I've met who were struggling to get by without a loved one's full income, or whose loved ones had returned with a limb missing or nerves shattered, but still lacked long-term health benefits because they were Reservists.

When we send our young men and women into harm's way, we have a solemn obligation not to fudge the numbers or shade the truth about why they're going, to care for their families while they're gone, to tend to the soldiers upon their return, and to never ever go to war without enough troops to win the war, secure the peace, and earn the respect of the world.

Now—Now let me be clear. Let me be clear. We have real enemies in the world. These enemies must be found. They must be pursued. And they must be defeated. John Kerry knows this. And just as Lieutenant Kerry did not hesitate to risk his life to protect the men who served with him in Vietnam, President Kerry will not hesitate one moment to use our military might to keep America safe and secure.

John Kerry believes in America. And he knows that it's not enough for just some of us to prosper—for alongside our famous individualism, there's another ingredient in the American saga, a belief that we're all connected as one people. If there is a child on the south side of Chicago who can't read, that matters to me, even if it's not my child. If there is a senior citizen somewhere who can't pay for their prescription drugs, and having to choose between medicine and the rent, that makes my life poorer, even if it's not my grandparent. If there's an Arab American family being rounded up without benefit of an attorney or due process, that threatens my civil liberties.

It is that fundamental belief—It is that fundamental belief: I am my brother's keeper. I am my sister's keeper that makes this country work. It's what allows us to pursue our individual dreams and yet still come together as one American family.

E pluribus Unum: "Out of many, one."

Now even as we speak, there are those who are preparing to divide us—the spin masters, the negative ad peddlers who embrace the politics of "anything goes." Well, I say to them tonight, there is not a liberal America and a conservative America—there is the United States of America. There is not a Black America and a White America and Latino America and Asian America—there's the United States of America.

The pundits, the pundits like to slice-and-dice our country into Red States and Blue States; Red States for Republicans, Blue States for Democrats. But I've got news for them, too. We worship an "awesome God" in the Blue States, and we don't like federal agents poking around in our libraries in the Red States. We coach Little League in the Blue States and yes, we've got some gay friends in the Red States. There are patriots who opposed the war in Iraq and there are patriots who supported the war in Iraq. We are one people, all of us pledging allegiance to the stars and stripes, all of us defending the United States of America.

In the end—In the end—In the end, that's what this election is about. Do we participate in a politics of cynicism or do we participate in a politics of hope?

John Kerry calls on us to hope. John Edwards calls on us to hope.

I'm not talking about blind optimism here—the almost willful ignorance that thinks unemployment will go away if we just don't think about it, or the health care crisis will solve itself if we just ignore it. That's not what I'm talking about. I'm talking about something more substantial. It's the hope of slaves sitting around a fire singing freedom songs; the hope of immigrants setting out for distant shores; the hope of a young naval lieutenant bravely patrolling the Mekong Delta; the hope of a mill worker's son who dares to defy the odds; the hope of a skinny kid with a funny name who believes that America has a place for him, too.

Hope—Hope in the face of difficulty. Hope in the face of uncertainty. The audacity of hope!

In the end, that is God's greatest gift to us, the bedrock of this nation. A belief in things not seen. A belief that there are better days ahead.

I believe that we can give our middle class relief and provide working families with a road to opportunity.

I believe we can provide jobs to the jobless, homes to the homeless, and reclaim young people in cities across America from violence and despair.

I believe that we have a righteous wind at our backs and that as we stand on the crossroads of history, we can make the right choices, and meet the challenges that face us.

America! Tonight, if you feel the same energy that I do, if you feel the same urgency that I do, if you feel the same passion that I do, if you feel the same hopefulness that I do—if we do what we must do, then I have no doubt that all across the country, from Florida to Oregon, from Washington to Maine, the people will rise up in November, and John Kerry will be sworn in as President, and John Edwards will be sworn in as Vice President, and this country will reclaim its promise, and out of this long political darkness a brighter day will come.

Thank you very much everybody. God bless you. Thank you.

Run for the Democratic Nomination Speech

February 10, 2007

Thank you so much. Praise and honor to God for bringing us together today. Thank you so much. I am so grateful to see all of you.

Let me begin by saying thanks to all of you who've traveled, from far and wide, to brave the cold today.

I'm fired up.

We all made this journey for a reason. It's humbling to see a crowd like this, but in my heart I know you didn't come here just for me. No, you came here because you believe in what this country can be. In the face of war, you believe there can be peace. In the face of despair, you believe there can be hope. In the face of a politics that's shut you out, that's told you to settle, that's divided us for too long, you believe that we can be one people, reaching for what's possible, building that more perfect union.

That's the journey we're on today. But let me tell you how I came to be here. As most of you know, I am not a native of this great state. I moved to Illinois over two decades ago. I was a young man then, just a year out of college; I knew no one in Chicago when I arrived, was without money or family connections. But a group of churches had offered me a job as a community organizer for the grand sum of

$13,000 a year. And I accepted the job, sight unseen, motivated then by a single, simple, powerful idea—that I might play a small part in building a better America.

My work took me to some of Chicago's poorest neighborhoods. I joined with pastors and lay-people to deal with communities that had been ravaged by plant closings. I saw that the problems people faced weren't simply local in nature—that the decision to close a steel mill was made by distant executives; that the lack of textbooks and computers in schools could be traced to the skewed priorities of politicians a thousand miles away; and that when a child turns to violence, I came to realize that there's a hole in that boy's heart no government could ever fill.

It was in these neighborhoods that I received the best education I ever had, and where I learned the meaning of my Christian faith.

After three years of this work, I went to law school, because I wanted to understand how the law should work for those in need. I became a civil rights lawyer, and taught constitutional law, and after a time, I came to understand that our cherished rights of liberty and equality depend on the active participation of an awakened electorate. It was with these ideas in mind that I arrived in this capital city as a state Senator.

It was here, in Springfield, where I saw all that is America converge—farmers and teachers, businessmen and laborers, all of them with a story to tell, all of them seeking a seat at the table, all of them clamoring to be heard. I made lasting friendships here—friends that I see in the audience here today.

It was here we learned to disagree without being disagreeable—that it's possible to compromise so long as you know those principles that can never be compromised; and that so long as we're willing to listen to each other, we can assume the best in people instead of the worst.

It's why we were able to reform a death penalty system that was broken. That's why we were able to give health insurance to children in need. That's why we made the tax system right here in Springfield more fair and just for working families, and that's why we passed ethics reforms that the cynics said could never, ever be passed.

It was here, in Springfield, where North, South, East and West come together that I was reminded of the essential decency of the American people—where I came to believe that through this decency, we can build a more hopeful America.

And that is why, in the shadow of the Old State Capitol, where Lincoln once called on a house divided to stand together, where common hopes and common dreams still live, I stand before you today to announce my candidacy for President of the United States of America.

Now listen, I recognize there is a certain presumptuousness—a certain audacity—to this announcement. I know I haven't spent a lot of time learning the ways of Washington. But I've been there long enough to know that the ways of Washington must change.

The genius of our founders is that they designed a system of government that can be changed. And we should take heart, because we've changed this country before. In the face of tyranny, a band of patriots brought an Empire to its knees. In the face of secession, we unified a nation and set the captives free. In the face of Depression, we put people back to work and lifted millions out of poverty. We welcomed immigrants to our shores, we opened railroads to the west, we landed a man on the moon, and we heard a King's call to let justice roll down like water, and righteousness like a mighty stream.

Each and every time, a new generation has risen up and done what's needed to be done. Today we are called once more—and it is time for our generation to answer that call.

For that is our unyielding faith—that in the face of impossible odds, people who love their country can change it.

That's what Abraham Lincoln understood. He had his doubts. He had his defeats. He had his setbacks. But through his will and his words, he moved a nation and helped free a people. It is because of the millions who rallied to his cause that we are no longer divided, North and South, slave and free. Because men and women of every race, from every walk of life, continued to march for freedom long after Lincoln was laid to rest, that today we have the chance to face the challenges of this millennium together, as one people—as Americans.

All of us know what those challenges are today—a war with no end, a dependence on oil that threatens our future, schools where too many children aren't learning, and families struggling paycheck to paycheck despite working as hard as they can. We know the challenges. We've heard them. We've talked about them for years.

What's stopped us from meeting these challenges is not the absence of sound policies and sensible plans. What's stopped us is the failure of leadership, the smallness of our politics—the ease with which we're distracted by the petty and trivial, our chronic avoidance of tough decisions, our preference for scoring cheap political points instead of rolling up our sleeves and building a working consensus to tackle the big problems of America.

For the last six years we've been told that our mounting debts don't matter, we've been told that the anxiety Americans feel about rising health care costs and stagnant wages are an illusion, we've been told that climate change is a hoax, we've been told that tough talk and an ill-conceived war can replace diplomacy, and strategy, and foresight. And when all else fails, when Katrina happened, or the death toll in Iraq mounts, we've been told that our crises are somebody else's fault. We're distracted from our real failures, and told to blame the other party, or gay people, or immigrants.

And as people have looked away in disillusionment and frustration, we know what's filled the void. The cynics, the lobbyists, the special interests who've turned our government into a game only they can afford to play. They write the checks and you get stuck with the bills, they get the access while you get to write a letter, they think they own this government, but we're here today to take it back. The time for that kind of politics is over. It is through. It's time to turn the page right here and right now.

Now look, we have made some progress already. I was proud to help lead the fight in Congress that led to the most sweeping ethics reform since Watergate.

But Washington has a long way to go. And it won't be easy. That's why we'll have to set priorities. We'll have to make hard choices. And although government will play a crucial role in bringing about the changes that we need, more money and programs alone will not get us to where we need to go. Each of us, in our own lives, will have to accept responsibility—for instilling an ethic of achievement in our children, for adapting to a more competitive economy, for strengthening our communities, and sharing some measure of sacrifice. So let us begin. Let us begin this hard work together. Let us transform this nation.

Let us be the generation that reshapes our economy to compete in the digital age. Let's set high standards for our schools and give them the resources they need to succeed. Let's recruit a new army of teachers, and give them better pay and more support in exchange for more accountability. Let's make college more affordable, and let's invest in scientific research, and let's lay down broadband lines through the heart of inner cities and rural towns all across America. We can do that.

And as our economy changes, let's be the generation that ensures our nation's workers are sharing in our prosperity. Let's protect the hard-earned benefits their companies have promised. Let's make it possible for hardworking Americans to save for retirement. Let's allow our unions and their organizers to lift up this country's middle-class again. We can do that.

Let's be the generation that ends poverty in America. Every single person willing to work should be able to get job training that leads to a job, and earn a living wage that can pay the bills, and afford child care so their kids can have a safe place to go when they work. We can do this.

And let's be the generation that finally tackles our health care crisis. We can control costs by focusing on prevention, by providing better treatment for the chronically ill, and using technology to cut the bureaucracy. Let's be the generation that says right here, right now, we will have universal health care in America by the end of the next president's first term. We can do that.

Let's be the generation that finally frees America from the tyranny of oil. We can harness homegrown, alternative fuels like ethanol and spur the production of more fuel-efficient cars. We can set up a system for capping greenhouse gases. We can turn this crisis of global warming into a moment of opportunity for innovation, and job creation, and an incentive for businesses that will serve as a model for the world. Let's be the generation that makes future generations proud of what we did here.

Most of all, let's be the generation that never forgets what happened on that September day and confront the terrorists with everything we've got. Politics doesn't have to divide us on this anymore—we can work together to keep our country safe. I've worked with Republican

Senator Dick Lugar to pass a law that will secure and destroy some of the world's deadliest weapons. We can work together to track down terrorists with a stronger military, we can tighten the net around their finances, and we can improve our intelligence capabilities and finally get homeland security right. But let us also understand that ultimate victory against our enemies will come only by rebuilding our alliances and exporting those ideals that bring hope and opportunity to millions of people around the globe. We can do those things.

But all of this cannot come to pass until we bring an end to this war in Iraq. Most of you know that I opposed this war from the start. I thought it was a tragic mistake. Today we grieve for the families who have lost loved ones, the hearts that have been broken, and the young lives that could have been. America, it is time to start bringing our troops home. It's time to admit that no amount of American lives can resolve the political disagreement that lies at the heart of someone else's civil war. That's why I have a plan that will bring our combat troops home by March of 2008. Letting the Iraqis know that we will not be there forever is our last, best hope to pressure the Sunni and Shia to come to the table and find peace.

And there is one other thing that is not too late to get right about this war—and that is the homecoming of the men and women—our veterans—who have sacrificed the most. Let us honor their courage by providing the care they need and rebuilding the military they love. Let us be the generation that begins that work.

I know there are those who don't believe we can do all these things. I understand the skepticism. After all, every four years, candidates from both parties make similar promises, and I expect this year will be no different. All of us running for president will travel around the country offering ten-point plans and making grand speeches; all of us will trumpet those qualities we believe make us uniquely qualified to lead the country. But too many times, after the election is over, and the confetti is swept away, all those promises fade from memory, and the lobbyists and the special interests move in, and people turn away, disappointed as before, left to struggle on their own.

That's why this campaign can't only be about me. It must be about us—it must be about what we can do together. This campaign must be the occasion, the vehicle, of your hopes, and your dreams. It will take your time, your energy, and your advice—to push us forward when we're doing right, and to let us know when we're not. This campaign has to be about reclaiming the meaning of citizenship, restoring our sense of common purpose, and realizing that few obstacles can withstand the power of millions of voices calling for change.

By ourselves, this change will not happen. Divided, we are bound to fail.

But the life of a tall, gangly, self-made Springfield lawyer tells us that a different future is possible.

He tells us that there is power in words.

He tells us that there is power in conviction.

That beneath all the differences of race and region, faith and station, we are one people.

He tells us that there is power in hope.

As Lincoln organized the forces arrayed against slavery, he was heard to say this: "Of strange, discordant, and even hostile elements, we gathered from the four winds, and formed and fought to battle through."

That is our purpose here today.

That is why I'm in this race.

Not just to hold an office, but to gather with you to transform a nation.

I want to win that next battle—for justice and opportunity.

I want to win that next battle—for better schools, and better jobs, and better health care for all.

I want us to take up the unfinished business of perfecting our union, and building a better America.

And if you will join with me in this improbable quest, if you feel destiny calling, and see as I see, a future of endless possibility stretching before us; if you sense, as I sense, that the time is now to shake off our slumber, and slough off our fear, and make good on the debt we owe past and future generations, then I am ready to take up the cause, and march with you, and work with you. Today, together, we can finish the work that needs to be done, and usher in a new birth of freedom on this Earth. Thank you very much everybody—let's get to work.

Presidential Nomination Acceptance Speech

August 28, 2008

To Chairman Dean and my great friend Dick Durbin; and to all my fellow citizens of this great nation; With profound gratitude and great humility, I accept your nomination for the presidency of the United States.

Let me express my thanks to the historic slate of candidates who accompanied me on this journey, and especially the one who traveled the farthest—a champion for working Americans and an inspiration to my daughters and to yours—Hillary Rodham Clinton. To President Clinton, who last night made the case for change as only he can make it; to Ted Kennedy, who embodies the spirit of service; and to the next Vice President of the United States, Joe Biden, I thank you. I am grateful to finish this journey with one of the finest statesmen of our time, a man at ease with everyone from world leaders to the conductors on the Amtrak train he still takes home every night.

To the love of my life, our next First Lady, Michelle Obama, and to Sasha and Malia—I love you so much, and I'm so proud of all of you.

Four years ago, I stood before you and told you my story—of the brief union between a young man from Kenya and a young woman from Kansas who weren't well-off or well-known, but shared a belief that in America, their son could achieve whatever he put his mind to.

It is that promise that has always set this country apart—that through hard work and sacrifice, each of us can pursue our individual dreams but still come together as one American family, to ensure that the next generation can pursue their dreams as well.

That's why I stand here tonight. Because for two hundred and thirty two years, at each moment when that promise was in jeopardy, ordinary men and women—students and soldiers, farmers and teachers, nurses and janitors—found the courage to keep it alive.

We meet at one of those defining moments—a moment when our nation is at war, our economy is in turmoil, and the American promise has been threatened once more. Tonight, more Americans are out of work and more are working harder for less. More of you have lost your homes and even more are watching your home values plummet. More of you have cars you can't afford to drive, credit card bills you can't afford to pay, and tuition that's beyond your reach. These challenges are not all of government's making. But the failure to respond is a direct result of a broken politics in Washington and the failed policies of George W. Bush.

America, we are better than these last eight years. We are a better country than this.

This country is more decent than one where a woman in Ohio, on the brink of retirement, finds herself one illness away from disaster after a lifetime of hard work. This country is more generous than one where a man in Indiana has to pack up the equipment he's worked on for twenty years and watch it shipped off to China, and then chokes up as he explains how he felt like a failure when he went home to tell his family the news. We are more compassionate than a government that lets veterans sleep on our streets and families slide into poverty; that sits on its hands while a major American city drowns before our eyes.

Tonight, I say to the American people, to Democrats and Republicans and Independents across this great land—enough! This moment—this election—is our chance to keep, in the 21st century, the American promise alive. Because next week, in Minnesota, the same party that brought you two terms of George Bush and Dick Cheney will ask this country for a third. And we are here because we love this country too much to let the next four years look like the last eight. On November 4th, we must stand up and say: "Eight is enough."

Now let there be no doubt. The Republican nominee, John McCain, has worn the uniform of our country with bravery and distinction, and for that we owe him our gratitude and respect. And next week, we'll also hear about those occasions when he's broken with his party as evidence that he can deliver the change that we need.

But the record's clear: John McCain has voted with George Bush ninety percent of the time. Senator McCain likes to talk about judgment, but really, what does it say about your judgment when you think George Bush has been right more than ninety percent of the time? I don't know about you, but I'm not ready to take a ten percent chance on change.

The truth is, on issue after issue that would make a difference in your lives—on health care and education and the economy—Senator McCain has been anything but independent. He said that our economy has made "great progress" under this President. He said that the fundamentals of the economy are strong. And when one of his chief advisors—the man who wrote his economic plan—was talking about the anxiety Americans are feeling, he said that we were just suffering from a "mental recession," and that we've become, and I quote, "a nation of whiners."

A nation of whiners? Tell that to the proud auto workers at a Michigan plant who, after they found out it was closing, kept showing up every day and working as hard as ever, because they knew there were people who counted on the brakes that they made. Tell that to the military families who shoulder their burdens silently as they watch their loved ones leave for their third or fourth or fifth tour of duty. These are not whiners. They work hard and give back and keep going without complaint. These are the Americans that I know.

Now, I don't believe that Senator McCain doesn't care what's going on in the lives of Americans. I just think he doesn't know. Why else would he define middle-class as someone making under five million dollars a year? How else could he propose hundreds of billions in tax breaks for big corporations and oil companies but not one penny of tax relief to more than one hundred million Americans? How else could he offer a health care plan that would actually tax people's benefits, or an education plan that would do nothing to help families pay for college, or a plan that would privatize Social Security and gamble your retirement?

It's not because John McCain doesn't care. It's because John McCain doesn't get it.

For over two decades, he's subscribed to that old, discredited Republican philosophy—give more and more to those with the most and hope that prosperity trickles down to everyone else. In Washington, they call this the Ownership Society, but what it really means is—you're on your own. Out of work? Tough luck. No health care? The market will fix it. Born into poverty? Pull yourself up by your own bootstraps—even if you don't have boots. You're on your own.

Well it's time for them to own their failure. It's time for us to change America. You see, we Democrats have a very different measure of what constitutes progress in this country. We measure progress by how many people can find a job that pays the mortgage; whether you can put a little extra money away at the end of each month so you can someday watch your child receive her college diploma. We measure progress in the 23 million new jobs that were created when Bill Clinton was President—when the average American family saw its income go up $7,500 instead of down $2,000 like it has under George Bush.

We measure the strength of our economy not by the number of billionaires we have or the profits of the Fortune 500, but by whether someone with a good idea can take a risk and start a new business, or whether the waitress who lives on tips can take a day off to look after a sick kid without losing her job—an economy that honors the dignity of work.

The fundamentals we use to measure economic strength are whether we are living up to that fundamental promise that has made this country great—a promise that is the only reason I am standing here tonight.

Because in the faces of those young veterans who come back from Iraq and Afghanistan, I see my grandfather, who signed up after Pearl Harbor, marched in Patton's Army, and was rewarded by a grateful nation with the chance to go to college on the GI Bill. In the face of that young student who sleeps just three hours before working the night shift, I think about my mom, who raised my sister and me on her own while she worked and earned her degree; who once turned to food stamps but was still able to send us to the best schools in the country with the help of student loans and scholarships.

When I listen to another worker tell me that his factory has shut down, I remember all those men and women on the South Side of Chicago who I stood by and fought for two decades ago after the local steel plant closed. And when I hear a woman talk about the difficulties of starting her own business, I think about my grandmother, who worked her way up from the secretarial pool to middle-management, despite years of being passed over for promotions because she was a woman. She's the one who taught me about hard work. She's the one who put off buying a new car or a new dress for herself so that I could have a better life. She poured everything she had into me. And although she can no longer travel, I know that she's watching tonight, and that tonight is her night as well.

I don't know what kind of lives John McCain thinks that celebrities lead, but this has been mine. These are my heroes. Theirs are the stories that shaped me. And it is on their behalf that I intend to win this election and keep our promise alive as President of the United States. What is that promise?

It's a promise that says each of us has the freedom to make of our own lives what we will, but that we also have the obligation to treat each other with dignity and respect. It's a promise that says the market should reward drive and innovation and generate growth, but that businesses should live up to their responsibilities to create American jobs, look out for American workers, and play by the rules of the road. Ours is a promise that says government cannot solve all our problems, but what it should do is that which we cannot do for ourselves—protect us from harm and provide every child a decent education; keep our water clean and our toys safe; invest in new schools and new roads and new science and technology.

Our government should work for us, not against us. It should help us, not hurt us. It should ensure opportunity not just for those with the most money and influence, but for every American who's willing to work.

That's the promise of America—the idea that we are responsible for ourselves, but that we also rise or fall as one nation; the fundamental belief that I am my brother's keeper; I am my sister's keeper. That's the promise we need to keep. That's the change we need right now. So let me spell out exactly what that change would mean if I am President.

Change means a tax code that doesn't reward the lobbyists who wrote it, but the American workers and small businesses who deserve it. Unlike John McCain, I will stop giving tax breaks to corporations that ship jobs overseas, and I will start giving them to companies that create good jobs right here in America. I will eliminate capital gains taxes for the small businesses and the start-ups that will create the high-wage, high-tech jobs of tomorrow. I will cut taxes—cut taxes—for 95% of all working families. Because in an economy like this, the last thing we should do is raise taxes on the middle-class.

And for the sake of our economy, our security, and the future of our planet, I will set a clear goal as President: in ten years, we will finally end our dependence on oil from the Middle East. Washington's been talking about our oil addiction for the last thirty years, and John McCain has been there for twenty-six of them. In that time, he's said no to higher fuel-efficiency standards for cars, no to investments in renewable energy, no to renewable fuels. And today, we import triple the amount of oil as the day that Senator McCain took office. Now is the time to end this addiction, and to understand that drilling is a stop-gap measure, not a long-term solution. Not even close.

As President, I will tap our natural gas reserves, invest in clean coal technology, and find ways to safely harness nuclear power. I'll help our auto companies re-tool, so that the fuel-efficient cars of the future are built right here in America. I'll make it easier for the American people to afford these new cars. And I'll invest 150 billion dollars over the next decade in affordable, renewable sources of energy—wind power and solar power and the next generation of biofuels; an investment that will lead to new industries and five million new jobs that pay well and can't ever be outsourced. America, now is not the time for small plans.

Now is the time to finally meet our moral obligation to provide every child a world-class education, because it will take nothing less to compete in the global economy. Michelle and I are only here tonight because we were given a chance at an education. And I will not settle for an America where some kids don't have that chance. I'll invest in early childhood education. I'll recruit an army of new teachers, and pay them higher salaries and give them more support. And in exchange, I'll ask for higher standards and more accountability. And we will keep our promise to every young American—if you commit to serving your community or your country, we will make sure you can afford a college education.

Now is the time to finally keep the promise of affordable, accessible health care for every single American. If you have health care, my plan will lower your premiums. If you don't, you'll be able to get the same kind of coverage that members of Congress give themselves. And as someone who watched my mother argue with insurance companies while she lay in bed dying of cancer, I will make certain those companies stop discriminating against those who are sick and need care the most.

Now is the time to help families with paid sick days and better family leave, because nobody in America should have to choose between keeping their jobs and caring for a sick child or ailing parent. Now is the time to change our bankruptcy laws, so that your pensions are protected ahead of CEO bonuses; and the time to protect Social Security for future generations.

And now is the time to keep the promise of equal pay for an equal day's work, because I want my daughters to have exactly the same opportunities as your sons. Now, many of these plans will cost money, which is why I've laid out how I'll pay for every dime—by closing corporate loopholes and tax havens that don't help America grow. But I will also go through the federal budget, line by line, eliminating programs that no longer work and making the ones we do need work better and cost less—because we cannot meet twenty-first century challenges with a twentieth century bureaucracy.

And Democrats, we must also admit that fulfilling America's promise will require more than just money. It will require a renewed sense of responsibility from each of us to recover what John F. Kennedy called our "intellectual and moral strength." Yes, government must lead on energy independence, but each of us must do our part to make our homes and businesses more efficient. Yes, we must provide more ladders to success for young men who fall into lives of crime and despair. But we must also admit that programs alone can't replace parents; that government can't turn off the television and make a child do her homework; that fathers must take more responsibility for providing the love and guidance their children need. Individual responsibility and mutual responsibility—that's the essence of America's promise.

And just as we keep our keep our promise to the next generation here at home, so must we keep America's promise abroad. If John McCain wants to have a debate about who has the temperament, and judgment, to serve as the next Commander-in-Chief, that's a debate I'm ready to have. For while Senator McCain was turning his sights to Iraq just days after 9/11, I stood up and opposed this war, knowing that it would distract us from the real threats we face. When John McCain said we could just "muddle through" in Afghanistan, I argued for more resources and more troops to finish the fight against the terrorists who actually attacked us on 9/11, and made clear that we must take out Osama bin Laden and his lieutenants if we have them in our sights. John McCain likes to say that he'll follow bin Laden to the Gates of Hell—but he won't even go to the cave where he lives.

And today, as my call for a time frame to remove our troops from Iraq has been echoed by the Iraqi government and even the Bush Administration, even after we learned that Iraq has a $79 billion surplus while we're wallowing in deficits, John McCain stands alone in his stubborn refusal to end a misguided war. That's not the judgment we need. That won't keep America safe. We need a President who can face the threats of the future, not keep grasping at the ideas of the past.

You don't defeat a terrorist network that operates in eighty countries by occupying Iraq. You don't protect Israel and deter Iran just by talking tough in Washington. You can't truly stand up for Georgia when you've strained our oldest alliances. If John McCain wants to follow George Bush with more tough talk and bad strategy, that is his choice—but it is not the change we need. We are the party of Roosevelt. We are the party of Kennedy. So don't tell me that Democrats won't defend this country. Don't tell me that Democrats won't keep us safe. The Bush-McCain foreign policy has squandered the legacy that generations of Americans—Democrats and Republicans—have built, and we are here to restore that legacy.

As Commander-in-Chief, I will never hesitate to defend this nation, but I will only send our troops into harm's way with a clear mission and a sacred commitment to give them the equipment they need in battle and the care and benefits they deserve when they come home. I will end this war in Iraq responsibly, and finish the fight against al-Qaeda and the Taliban in Afghanistan. I will rebuild our military to meet future conflicts. But I will also renew the tough, direct diplomacy that can prevent Iran from obtaining nuclear weapons and curb Russian aggression. I will build new partnerships to defeat the threats of the 21st century: terrorism and nuclear proliferation; poverty and genocide; climate change and disease. And I will restore our moral standing, so that America is once again that last, best hope for all who are called to the cause of freedom, who long for lives of peace, and who yearn for a better future.

These are the policies I will pursue. And in the weeks ahead, I look forward to debating them with John McCain. But what I will not do is suggest that the Senator takes his positions for political purposes. Because one of the things that we have to change in our politics is the idea that people cannot disagree without challenging each other's character and patriotism. The times are too serious, the stakes are too high for this same partisan playbook. So let us agree that patriotism has no party. I love this country, and so do you, and so does John McCain. The men and women who serve in our battlefields may be Democrats and Republicans and Independents, but they have fought together and bled together and some died together under the same proud flag. They have not served a Red America or a Blue America—they have served the United States of America.

So I've got news for you, John McCain. We all put our country first. America, our work will not be easy. The challenges we face require tough choices, and Democrats as well as Republicans will need to cast off the worn-out ideas and politics of the past. For part of what has been lost these past eight years can't just be measured by lost wages or bigger trade deficits. What has also been lost is our sense of common purpose—our sense of higher purpose. And that's what we have to restore.

We may not agree on abortion, but surely we can agree on reducing the number of unwanted pregnancies in this country. The reality of gun ownership may be different for hunters in rural Ohio than for those plagued by gang-violence in Cleveland, but don't tell me we can't uphold the Second Amendment while keeping AK-47s out of the hands of criminals. I know there are differences on same-sex marriage, but surely we can agree that our gay and lesbian brothers and sisters deserve to visit the person they love in the hospital and to live lives free of discrimination. Passions fly on immigration, but I don't know anyone who benefits when a mother is separated from her infant child or an employer undercuts American wages by hiring illegal workers. This too is part of America's promise—the promise of a democracy where we can find the strength and grace to bridge divides and unite in common effort.

I know there are those who dismiss such beliefs as happy talk. They claim that our insistence on something larger, something firmer and more honest in our public life is just a Trojan Horse for higher taxes and the abandonment of traditional values. And that's to be expected. Because if you don't have any fresh ideas, then you use stale tactics to scare the voters. If you don't have a record to run on, then you paint your opponent as someone people should run from.

You make a big election about small things.

And you know what—it's worked before. Because it feeds into the cynicism we all have about government. When Washington doesn't work, all its promises seem empty. If your hopes have been dashed again and again, then it's best to stop hoping, and settle for what you already know. I get it. I realize that I am not the likeliest candidate for this office. I don't fit the typical pedigree, and I haven't spent my career in the halls of Washington. But I stand before you tonight because all across America something is stirring. What the nay-sayers don't understand is that this election has never been about me. It's been about you.

For eighteen long months, you have stood up, one by one, and said enough to the politics of the past. You understand that in this election, the greatest risk we can take is to try the same old politics with the same old players and expect a different result. You have shown what history teaches us—that at defining moments like this one, the change we need doesn't come from Washington. Change comes to Washington. Change happens because the American people demand it—because they rise up and insist on new ideas and new leadership, a new politics for a new time.

America, this is one of those moments. I believe that as hard as it will be, the change we need is coming. Because I've seen it. Because I've lived it. I've seen it in Illinois, when we provided health care to more children and moved more families from welfare to work. I've seen it in

Washington, when we worked across party lines to open up government and hold lobbyists more accountable, to give better care for our veterans and keep nuclear weapons out of terrorist hands. And I've seen it in this campaign. In the young people who voted for the first time, and in those who got involved again after a very long time. In the Republicans who never thought they'd pick up a Democratic ballot, but did. I've seen it in the workers who would rather cut their hours back a day than see their friends lose their jobs, in the soldiers who re-enlist after losing a limb, in the good neighbors who take a stranger in when a hurricane strikes and the floodwaters rise.

This country of ours has more wealth than any nation, but that's not what makes us rich. We have the most powerful military on Earth, but that's not what makes us strong. Our universities and our culture are the envy of the world, but that's not what keeps the world coming to our shores. Instead, it is that American spirit—that American promise—that pushes us forward even when the path is uncertain; that binds us together in spite of our differences; that makes us fix our eye not on what is seen, but what is unseen, that better place around the bend.

That promise is our greatest inheritance. It's a promise I make to my daughters when I tuck them in at night, and a promise that you make to yours—a promise that has led immigrants to cross oceans and pioneers to travel west; a promise that led workers to picket lines, and women to reach for the ballot. And it is that promise that forty five years ago today, brought Americans from every corner of this land to stand together on a Mall in Washington, before Lincoln's Memorial, and hear a young preacher from Georgia speak of his dream. The men and women who gathered there could've heard many things. They could've heard words of anger and discord. They could've been told to succumb to the fear and frustration of so many dreams deferred.

But what the people heard instead—people of every creed and color, from every walk of life—is that in America, our destiny is inextricably linked. That together, our dreams can be one. "We cannot walk alone," the preacher cried. "And as we walk, we must make the pledge that we shall always march ahead. We cannot turn back."

America, we cannot turn back. Not with so much work to be done. Not with so many children to educate, and so many veterans to care for. Not with an economy to fix and cities to rebuild and farms to save. Not with so many families to protect and so many lives to mend. America, we cannot turn back. We cannot walk alone. At this moment, in this election, we must pledge once more to march into the future. Let us keep that promise—that American promise—and in the words of Scripture hold firmly, without wavering, to the hope that we confess.

Thank you, God Bless you, and God Bless the United States of America.

Victory Speech

November 5, 2008

If there is anyone out there who still doubts that America is a place where all things are possible; who still wonders if the dream of our founders is alive in our time; who still questions the power of our democracy, tonight is your answer.

It's the answer told by lines that stretched around schools and churches in numbers this nation has never seen; by people who waited three hours and four hours, many for the very first time in their lives, because they believed that this time must be different; that their voice could be that difference.

It's the answer spoken by young and old, rich and poor, Democrat and Republican, black, white, Latino, Asian, Native American, gay, straight, disabled and not disabled—Americans who sent a message to the world that we have never been a collection of red states and blue states; we are, and always will be, the United States of America.

It's the answer that led those who have been told for so long by so many to be cynical, and fearful, and doubtful of what we can achieve to put their hands on the arc of history and bend it once more toward the hope of a better day.

It's been a long time coming, but tonight, because of what we did on this day, in this election, at this defining moment, change has come to America.

I just received a very gracious call from Sen. McCain. He fought long and hard in this campaign, and he's fought even longer and harder for the country he loves. He has endured sacrifices for America that most of us cannot begin to imagine, and we are better off for the service rendered by this brave and selfless leader. I congratulate him and Gov. Palin for all they have achieved, and I look forward to working with them to renew this nation's promise in the months ahead.

I want to thank my partner in this journey, a man who campaigned from his heart and spoke for the men and women he grew up with on the streets of Scranton and rode with on that train home to Delaware, the vice-president-elect of the United States, Joe Biden.

I would not be standing here tonight without the unyielding support of my best friend for the last 16 years, the rock of our family and the love of my life, our nation's next first lady, Michelle Obama. Sasha and Malia, I love you both so much, and you have earned the new puppy that's coming with us to the White House. And while she's no longer with us, I know my grandmother is watching, along with the family that made me who I am. I miss them tonight, and know that my debt to them is beyond measure.

To my campaign manager, David Plouffe; my chief strategist, David Axelrod; and the best campaign team ever assembled in the history of politics—you made this happen, and I am forever grateful for what you've sacrificed to get it done.

But above all, I will never forget who this victory truly belongs to—it belongs to you.

I was never the likeliest candidate for this office. We didn't start with much money or many endorsements. Our campaign was not hatched in the halls of Washington—it began in the backyards of Des Moines and the living rooms of Concord and the front porches of Charleston.

It was built by working men and women who dug into what little savings they had to give $5 and $10 and $20 to this cause. It grew strength from the young people who rejected the myth of their generation's apathy; who left their homes and their families for jobs that offered little pay and less sleep; from the not-so-young people who braved the bitter cold and scorching heat to knock on the doors of perfect strangers; from the millions of Americans who volunteered and organized, and proved that more than two centuries later, a government of the people, by the people and for the people has not perished from this earth. This is your victory.

I know you didn't do this just to win an election, and I know you didn't do it for me. You did it because you understand the enormity of the task that lies ahead. For even as we celebrate tonight, we know the challenges that tomorrow will bring are the greatest of our lifetime—two wars, a planet in peril, the worst financial crisis in a century. Even as we stand here tonight, we know there are brave Americans waking up in the deserts of Iraq and the mountains of Afghanistan to risk their lives for us. There are mothers and fathers who will lie awake after their children fall asleep and wonder how they'll make the mortgage, or pay their doctor's bills, or save enough for college. There is new energy to harness and new jobs to be created; new schools to build and threats to meet and alliances to repair.

The road ahead will be long. Our climb will be steep. We may not get there in one year, or even one term, but America—I have never been more hopeful than I am tonight that we will get there. I promise you: We as a people will get there.

There will be setbacks and false starts. There are many who won't agree with every decision or policy I make as president, and we know that government can't solve every problem. But I will always be honest with you about the challenges we face. I will listen to you, especially when we disagree. And, above all, I will ask you join in the work of remaking this nation the only way it's been done in America for 221 years—block by block, brick by brick, callused hand by callused hand.

What began 21 months ago in the depths of winter must not end on this autumn night. This victory alone is not the change we seek—it is only the chance for us to make that change. And that cannot happen if we go back to the way things were. It cannot happen without you.

So let us summon a new spirit of patriotism; of service and responsibility where each of us resolves to pitch in and work harder and look after not only ourselves, but each other. Let us remember that if this financial crisis taught us anything, it's that we cannot have a thriving Wall Street while Main Street suffers. In this country, we rise or fall as one nation—as one people.

Let us resist the temptation to fall back on the same partisanship and pettiness and immaturity that has poisoned our politics for so long. Let us remember that it was a man from this state who first carried the banner of the Republican Party to the White House—a party founded on the values of self-reliance, individual liberty and national unity. Those are values we all share, and while the Democratic Party has won a great victory tonight, we do so with a measure of humility and determination to heal the divides that have held back our progress.

As Lincoln said to a nation far more divided than ours, "We are not enemies, but friends... Though passion may have strained, it must not break our bonds of affection." And, to those Americans whose support I have yet to earn, I may not have won your vote, but I hear your voices, I need your help, and I will be your president, too.

And to all those watching tonight from beyond our shores, from parliaments and palaces to those who are huddled around radios in the forgotten corners of our world—our stories are singular, but our destiny is shared, and a new dawn of American leadership is at hand. To those who would tear this world down: We will defeat you. To those who seek peace and security: We support you. And to all those who have wondered if America's beacon still burns as bright: Tonight, we proved once more that the true strength of our nation comes not from the might of our arms or the scale of our wealth, but from the enduring power of our ideals: democracy, liberty, opportunity and unyielding hope.

For that is the true genius of America—that America can change. Our union can be perfected. And what we have already achieved gives us hope for what we can and must achieve tomorrow.

This election had many firsts and many stories that will be told for generations. But one that's on my mind tonight is about a woman who cast her ballot in Atlanta. She's a lot like the millions of others who stood in line to make their voice heard in this election, except for one thing: Ann Nixon Cooper is 106 years old.

She was born just a generation past slavery; a time when there were no cars on the road or planes in the sky; when someone like her couldn't vote for two reasons—because she was a woman and because of the color of her skin.

And tonight, I think about all that she's seen throughout her century in America—the heartache and the hope; the struggle and the progress; the times we were told that we can't and the people who pressed on with that American creed: Yes, we can.

At a time when women's voices were silenced and their hopes dismissed, she lived to see them stand up and speak out and reach for the ballot. Yes, we can.

When there was despair in the Dust Bowl and depression across the land, she saw a nation conquer fear itself with a New Deal, new jobs and a new sense of common purpose. Yes, we can.

When the bombs fell on our harbor and tyranny threatened the world, she was there to witness a generation rise to greatness and a democracy was saved. Yes, we can.

She was there for the buses in Montgomery, the hoses in Birmingham, a bridge in Selma and a preacher from Atlanta who told a people that "We Shall Overcome." Yes, we can.

A man touched down on the moon, a wall came down in Berlin, a world was connected by our own science and imagination. And this year, in this election, she touched her finger to a screen and cast her vote, because after 106 years in America, through the best of times and the darkest of hours, she knows how America can change. Yes, we can.

America, we have come so far. We have seen so much. But there is so much more to do. So tonight, let us ask ourselves: If our children should live to see the next century; if my daughters should be so lucky to live as long as Ann Nixon Cooper, what change will they see? What progress will we have made?

This is our chance to answer that call. This is our moment. This is our time—to put our people back to work and open doors of opportunity for our kids; to restore prosperity and promote the cause of peace; to reclaim the American Dream and reaffirm that fundamental truth that out of many, we are one; that while we breathe, we hope, and where we are met with cynicism, and doubt, and those who tell us that we can't, we will respond with that timeless creed that sums up the spirit of a people: Yes, we can.

Thank you, God bless you, and may God bless the United States of America.

Inauguration Speech

January 20, 2009

"My fellow citizens:

I stand here today humbled by the task before us, grateful for the trust you have bestowed, mindful of the sacrifices borne by our ancestors. I thank President Bush for his service to our nation, as well as the generosity and co-operation he has shown throughout this transition.

Forty-four Americans have now taken the presidential oath. The words have been spoken during rising tides of prosperity and the still waters of peace. Yet, every so often the oath is taken amidst gathering clouds and raging storms. At these moments, America has carried on not simply because of the skill or vision of those in high office, but because we, the people, have remained faithful to the ideals of our forbearers, and true to our founding documents.

So it has been. So it must be with this generation of Americans.

'Serious Challenges'

That we are in the midst of crisis is now well understood. Our nation is at war, against a far-reaching network of violence and hatred. Our economy is badly weakened, a consequence of greed and irresponsibility on the part of some, but also our collective failure to make hard choices and prepare the nation for a new age. Homes have been lost; jobs shed; businesses shuttered. Our health care is too costly; our schools fall too many; and each day brings further evidence that the ways we use energy strengthen our adversaries and threaten our planet.

These are the indicators of crisis, subject to data and statistics. Less measurable but no less profound is a sapping of confidence across our land—a nagging fear that America's decline is inevitable, and that the next generation must lower its sights.

Today I say to you that the challenges we face are real. They are serious and they are many. They will not be met easily or in a short span of time. But know this, America—they will be met.

On this day, we gather because we have chosen hope over fear, unity of purpose over conflict and discord.

On this day, we come to proclaim an end to the petty grievances and false promises, the recriminations and worn out dogmas, that for far too long have strangled our politics.

'Nation of 'risk-takers'

We remain a young nation, but in the words of scripture, the time has come to set aside childish things. The time has come to reaffirm our enduring spirit; to choose our better history; to carry forward that precious gift, that noble idea, passed on from generation to generation: the God-given promise that all are equal, all are free, and all deserve a chance to pursue their full measure of happiness.

In reaffirming the greatness of our nation, we understand that greatness is never given. It must be earned. Our journey has never been one of short-cuts or settling for less. It has not been the path for the faint-hearted—for those who prefer leisure over work, or seek only the pleasures of riches and fame. Rather, it has been the risk-takers, the doers, the makers of things—some celebrated but more often men and women obscure in their labor, who have carried us up the long, rugged path towards prosperity and freedom.

For us, they packed up their few worldly possessions and raveled across oceans in search of a new life.

For us, they tolled in sweatshops and settled the West; endured the lash of the whip and ploughed the hard earth.

For us, they fought and died, in places like Concord and Gettysburg; Normandy and KheSahn.

'Remaking America'

Time and again these men and women struggled and sacrificed and worked till their hands were raw so that we might live a better life.

They saw America as bigger than the sum of our individual ambitions; greater than all the differences of birth or wealth or faction.

This is the journey we continue today. We remain the most prosperous, powerful nation on earth. Our workers are no less productive than when this crisis began. Our minds are no less inventive, our goods and services no less needed than they were last week or last month or last year. Our capacity remains undiminished. But our time of standing pat, of protecting narrow interest and putting off unpleasant decisions—that time has surely passed. Starting today, we must pick ourselves up, dust ourselves off, and begin again the work of remaking America.

For everywhere we look, there is work to be done. The state of the economy calls for action, bold and swift, and we will act—not only to create new jobs, but to lay a new foundation for growth. We will build the roads and bridges, the electric grids and digital lines that feed our commerce and bind us together. We will restore science to its rightful place, and wield technology's wonders to raise health care's quality and lower its cost. We will harness the sun and the winds and the soil to fuel our cars and run our factories. And we will transform our schools and colleges and universities to meet the demands of a new age. All this we will do.

'Restoring Trust'

Now, there are some who question the scale of our ambitions—who suggest that our system cannot tolerate too many big plans. Their memories are short. For they have forgotten what this country has already done; what free men and women can achieve when imagination is joined to common purpose, and necessity to courage.

What the cynics fail to understand is that the ground has shifted beneath them—that the stale political arguments that have consumed us for so long no longer apply. The question we ask today is not whether our government is too big or too small, but whether it works—whether it helps families find jobs at a decent wage, care they can afford, a retirement that is dignified. Where the answer is no, programs will end. And those of us who manage the public's dollars will be held to account—to spend wisely, reform bad habits, and do our business in the light of day—because only then can we restore the vital trust between a people and their government.

Nor is the question before us whether the market is a force for good or ill. Its power to generate wealth and expand freedom I unmatched, but the crisis has reminded us that without a watchful eye, the market can spin out of control—that a nation cannot prosper long when it favors only the prosperous. The success of our economy has always depended not just on the size of our gross domestic product, but on the reach of our prosperity; on the ability to extend opportunity to every willing heart—not out of charity, but because it is the surest route to our common good.

'Ready to Lead'

As for our common defense, we reject as false the choice between our safety and our ideas. Our founding fathers, faced with perils we can scarcely imagine, drafted a charter to assure the rule of law and the rights of man, a charter expanded by the blood of generations. Those ideals still light the world, and we will not give them up for expedience's sake. And so to all other peoples and governments who are watching today, from the grandest capitals to the small village where my father was born: know that America is a friend of each nation and every man, woman, and child who seeks a future of peace and dignity, and we are ready to lead once more.

Recall that earlier generations faced down fascism and communism not just with missiles and tanks, but with the sturdy alliances and enduring convictions They understood that our power alone cannot protect us, nor does it entitle us to do as we please. Instead, they knew that our power grows through its prudent use; our security emanates from the justness of our cause, the force of our example, the tempering qualities of humility and restraint.

We are the keepers of this legacy. Guided by these principles once more, we can meet those new threats that demand even greater effort—even greater cooperation and understanding between nations. We will begin to responsibly leave Iraq to its people, and forge a hard earned peace in Afghanistan. With old friends and former foes, we will work tirelessly to lessen the nuclear threat, and roll back the specter of a warming planet. We will not apologize for our way of life, nor will we waver in its defense, and for those who seek to advance their aims by inducing terror and slaughtering innocents, we say to you now that our spirit is stronger and cannot be broken; you cannot outlast us, and we will defeat you.

'Era of Peace'

For we know that our patchwork heritage is a strength, not a weakness. We are a nation of Christians and Muslims, Jews and Hindus—and non-believers. We are shaped by every language and culture, drawn from every end of this earth; and because we have tasted the bitter swill of civil war and segregation, and emerged from the dark chapter stronger and more united, we cannot help but believe that the old hatreds shall someday pass; that the lines of tribe shall soon dissolve; that as the world grows smaller, our common humanity shall reveal itself; and that America must play its role in ushering in a new era of peace.

To the Muslim world, we seek a new way forward, based on mutual interest and mutual respect. To those leaders around the globe who seek to sow conflict, or blame their society's ills on the West—know that your people will judge you on what you can build, not what you destroy. To those who cling to power through corruption and deceit and the silencing of dissent, know that you are on the wrong side of history; but that we will extend a hand if you are willing to unclench your fist.

To the people of poor nations, we pledge to work alongside you to make your farms flourish and let clean waters flow; to nourish starved bodies and feed hungry minds. And to those nations like ours that enjoy relative plenty, we say we can no longer afford indifference to suffering outside our borders; nor can we consume the world's resources without regard to effect. For the world has changed, and we must change with it.

'Duties'

As we consider the road that unfolds before us, we remember with humble gratitude those brave Americans who, at this very hour, patrol far-off deserts and distant mountains. They have something to tell us, just as the fallen heroes who lie in Arlington whisper through the ages. We honor them not only because they are guardians of our liberty, but because they embody the spirit of service; a willingness to find meaning in something greater than themselves. And yet, at this moment—a moment that will define a generation—it is precisely this spirit that must inhabit us all.

For as much as government can do and must do, it is ultimately the faith and determination of American people upon which this nation relies. It is the kindness to take in a stranger when the levees break, the selflessness of workers who would rather cut their hours than see a friend lose their job which sees us through our darkest hours. It is the firefighter's courage to storm a stairway filled with smoke, but also a parent's willingness to nurture a child, that finally decides our fate.

Our challenges may be new. The instruments with which we meet them may be new. But those values upon which our success depends— honesty and hard work, courage and fair play, tolerance and curiosity, loyalty and patriotism—these things are old. These things are true. They have been the quiet force of progress throughout our history. What is demanded then is a return to these truths. What is required of us now is a new era of responsibility—a recognition, on the part of every American, that we have duties to ourselves, our nation, and the world, duties that we do not grudgingly accept but rather seize gladly, firm in the knowledge that there is nothing so satisfying to the spirit, so defining of our character, than giving our all to a difficult task.

'Gift of freedom'

This is the price and the promise of citizenship.

This is the source of our confidence—the knowledge that God calls on us to shape an uncertain destiny.

This is the meaning of our liberty and our creed—why men and women and children of every race and every faith can join in celebration across this magnificent mall, and why a man whose father less than 60 years ago might not have been served at a local restaurant can now stand before you to take a most sacred oath.

So let us mark this day with remembrance, of who we are and how far we have traveled. In the year of America's birth, in the coldest of months, a small band of patriots huddled by dying campfires on the shores of an icy river. The capital was abandoned. The enemy was advancing. The snow was stained with blood. At a moment when the outcome of our revolution was most in doubt, the father of our nation ordered these words be read to the people:

"Let it be told to the future world... that in the depth of winter, when nothing but hope and virtue could survive... that the city and the country, alarmed at one common danger, came forth to meet [it]".

America, in the face of our common dangers, in this winter of our hardship, let us remember these timeless words. With hope and virtue, let us brave once more the icy currents, and endure what storms may come. Let it be said by our children's children that when we were tested we refused to let this journey end, that we did not turn back nor did we falter; and with eyes fixed on the horizon and God's grace upon us, we carried forth that great gift of freedom and delivered it safely to future generations.

Thank you. God bless you. And God bless the United States of America."

State of the Union Address

January 24, 2012

Mr. Speaker, Mr. Vice President, members of Congress, distinguished guests, and fellow Americans:

Last month, I went to Andrews Air Force Base and welcomed home some of our last troops to serve in Iraq. Together, we offered a final, proud salute to the colors under which more than a million of our fellow citizens fought—and several thousand gave their lives.

We gather tonight knowing that this generation of heroes has made the United States safer and more respected around the world. For the first time in nine years, there are no Americans fighting in Iraq. For the first time in two decades, Osama bin Laden is not a threat to this country. Most of al Qaeda's top lieutenants have been defeated. The Taliban's momentum has been broken, and some troops in Afghanistan have begun to come home.

These achievements are a testament to the courage, selflessness and teamwork of America's Armed Forces. At a time when too many of our institutions have let us down, they exceed all expectations. They're not consumed with personal ambition. They don't obsess over their differences. They focus on the mission at hand. They work together.

Imagine what we could accomplish if we followed their example. Think about the America within our reach: A country that leads the world in educating its people. An America that attracts a new generation of high-tech manufacturing and high-paying jobs. A future where we're in control of our own energy, and our security and prosperity aren't so tied to unstable parts of the world. An economy built to last, where hard work pays off, and responsibility is rewarded.

We can do this. I know we can, because we've done it before. At the end of World War II, when another generation of heroes returned home from combat, they built the strongest economy and middle class the world has ever known. My grandfather, a veteran of Patton's Army, got the chance to go to college on the GI Bill. My grandmother, who worked on a bomber assembly line, was part of a workforce that turned out the best products on Earth. The two of them shared the optimism of a nation that had triumphed over a depression and fascism. They understood they were part of something larger; that they were contributing to a story of success that every American had a chance to share—the basic American promise that if you worked hard, you could do well enough to raise a family, own a home, send your kids to college, and put a little away for retirement.

The defining issue of our time is how to keep that promise alive. No challenge is more urgent. No debate is more important. We can either settle for a country where a shrinking number of people do really well while a growing number of Americans barely get by, or we can restore an economy where everyone gets a fair shot, and everyone does their fair share, and everyone plays by the same set of rules. What's at stake aren't Democratic values or Republican values, but American values. And we have to reclaim them.

Let's remember how we got here. Long before the recession, jobs and manufacturing began leaving our shores. Technology made businesses more efficient, but also made some jobs obsolete. Folks at the top saw their incomes rise like never before, but most hardworking Americans struggled with costs that were growing, paychecks that weren't, and personal debt that kept piling up.

In 2008, the house of cards collapsed. We learned that mortgages had been sold to people who couldn't afford or understand them. Banks had made huge bets and bonuses with other people's money. Regulators had looked the other way, or didn't have the authority to stop the bad behavior.

It was wrong. It was irresponsible. And it plunged our economy into a crisis that put millions out of work, saddled us with more debt, and left innocent, hardworking Americans holding the bag. In the six months before I took office, we lost nearly 4 million jobs. And we lost another 4 million before our policies were in full effect.

Those are the facts. But so are these: In the last 22 months, businesses have created more than 3 million jobs.

Last year, they created the most jobs since 2005. American manufacturers are hiring again, creating jobs for the first time since the late 1990s. Together, we've agreed to cut the deficit by more than $2 trillion. And we've put in place new rules to hold Wall Street accountable, so a crisis like this never happens again.

The state of our Union is getting stronger. And we've come too far to turn back now. As long as I'm President, I will work with anyone in this chamber to build on this momentum. But I intend to fight obstruction with action, and I will oppose any effort to return to the very same policies that brought on this economic crisis in the first place.

No, we will not go back to an economy weakened by outsourcing, bad debt, and phony financial profits. Tonight, I want to speak about how we move forward, and lay out a blueprint for an economy that's built to last—an economy built on American manufacturing, American energy, skills for American workers, and a renewal of American values.

Now, this blueprint begins with American manufacturing.

On the day I took office, our auto industry was on the verge of collapse. Some even said we should let it die. With a million jobs at stake, I refused to let that happen. In exchange for help, we demanded responsibility. We got workers and automakers to settle their differences. We got the industry to retool and restructure. Today, General Motors is back on top as the world's number-one automaker. Chrysler has grown faster in the U.S. than any major car company. Ford is investing billions in U.S. plants and factories. And together, the entire industry added nearly 160,000 jobs.

We bet on American workers. We bet on American ingenuity. And tonight, the American auto industry is back.

What's happening in Detroit can happen in other industries. It can happen in Cleveland and Pittsburgh and Raleigh. We can't bring every job back that's left our shore. But right now, it's getting more expensive to do business in places like China. Meanwhile, America is more productive. A few weeks ago, the CEO of Master Lock told me that it now makes business sense for him to bring jobs back home. Today, for the first time in 15 years, Master Lock's unionized plant in Milwaukee is running at full capacity.

So we have a huge opportunity, at this moment, to bring manufacturing back. But we have to seize it. Tonight, my message to business leaders is simple: Ask yourselves what you can do to bring jobs back to your country, and your country will do everything we can to help you succeed.

We should start with our tax code. Right now, companies get tax breaks for moving jobs and profits overseas. Meanwhile, companies that choose to stay in America get hit with one of the highest tax rates in the world. It makes no sense, and everyone knows it. So let's change it.

First, if you're a business that wants to outsource jobs, you shouldn't get a tax deduction for doing it. That money should be used to cover moving expenses for companies like Master Lock that decide to bring jobs home.

Second, no American company should be able to avoid paying its fair share of taxes by moving jobs and profits overseas. From now on, every multinational company should have to pay a basic minimum tax. And every penny should go towards lowering taxes for companies that choose to stay here and hire here in America.

Third, if you're an American manufacturer, you should get a bigger tax cut. If you're a high-tech manufacturer, we should double the tax deduction you get for making your products here. And if you want to relocate in a community that was hit hard when a factory left town, you should get help financing a new plant, equipment, or training for new workers.

So my message is simple. It is time to stop rewarding businesses that ship jobs overseas, and start rewarding companies that create jobs right here in America. Send me these tax reforms, and I will sign them right away.

We're also making it easier for American businesses to sell products all over the world. Two years ago, I set a goal of doubling U.S. exports over five years. With the bipartisan trade agreements we signed into law, we're on track to meet that goal ahead of schedule. And soon, there will be millions of new customers for American goods in Panama, Colombia, and South Korea. Soon, there will be new cars on the streets of Seoul imported from Detroit, and Toledo, and Chicago.

I will go anywhere in the world to open new markets for American products. And I will not stand by when our competitors don't play by the rules. We've brought trade cases against China at nearly twice the rate as the last administration—and it's made a difference. Over a thousand Americans are working today because we stopped a surge in Chinese tires. But we need to do more. It's not right when another country lets our movies, music, and software be pirated. It's not fair when foreign manufacturers have a leg up on ours only because they're heavily subsidized.

Tonight, I'm announcing the creation of a Trade Enforcement Unit that will be charged with investigating unfair trading practices in countries like China. There will be more inspections to prevent counterfeit or unsafe goods from crossing our borders. And this Congress should make sure that no foreign company has an advantage over American manufacturing when it comes to accessing financing or new markets like Russia. Our workers are the most productive on Earth, and if the playing field is level, I promise you–America will always win.

I also hear from many business leaders who want to hire in the United States but can't find workers with the right skills. Growing industries in science and technology have twice as many openings as we have workers who can do the job. Think about that—openings at a time when millions of Americans are looking for work. It's inexcusable. And we know how to fix it.

Jackie Bray is a single mom from North Carolina who was laid off from her job as a mechanic. Then Siemens opened a gas turbine factory in Charlotte, and formed a partnership with Central Piedmont Community College. The company helped the college design courses in laser and robotics training. It paid Jackie's tuition, then hired her to help operate their plant.

I want every American looking for work to have the same opportunity as Jackie did. Join me in a national commitment to train 2 million

Americans with skills that will lead directly to a job. My administration has already lined up more companies that want to help. Model partnerships between businesses like Siemens and community colleges in places like Charlotte, and Orlando, and Louisville are up and running. Now you need to give more community colleges the resources they need to become community career centers—places that teach people skills that businesses are looking for right now, from data management to high-tech manufacturing. And I want to cut through the maze of confusing training programs, so that from now on, people like Jackie have one program, one website, and one place to go for all the information and help that they need. It is time to turn our unemployment system into a reemployment system that puts people to work.

These reforms will help people get jobs that are open today. But to prepare for the jobs of tomorrow, our commitment to skills and education has to start earlier.

For less than 1 percent of what our nation spends on education each year, we've convinced nearly every state in the country to raise their standards for teaching and learning—the first time that's happened in a generation.

But challenges remain. And we know how to solve them.

At a time when other countries are doubling down on education, tight budgets have forced states to lay off thousands of teachers. We know a good teacher can increase the lifetime income of a classroom by over $250,000. A great teacher can offer an escape from poverty to the child who dreams beyond his circumstance. Every person in this chamber can point to a teacher who changed the trajectory of their lives. Most teachers work tirelessly, with modest pay, sometimes digging into their own pocket for school supplies—just to make a difference.

Teachers matter. So instead of bashing them, or defending the status quo, let's offer schools a deal. Give them the resources to keep good teachers on the job, and reward the best ones. And in return, grant schools flexibility: to teach with creativity and passion; to stop teaching to the test; and to replace teachers who just aren't helping kids learn. That's a bargain worth making.

We also know that when students don't walk away from their education, more of them walk the stage to get their diploma. When students are not allowed to drop out, they do better. So tonight, I am proposing that every state–every state–requires that all students stay in high school until they graduate or turn 18.

When kids do graduate, the most daunting challenge can be the cost of college. At a time when Americans owe more in tuition debt than credit card debt, this Congress needs to stop the interest rates on student loans from doubling in July.

Extend the tuition tax credit we started that saves millions of middle-class families thousands of dollars, and give more young people the chance to earn their way through college by doubling the number of work-study jobs in the next five years.

Of course, it's not enough for us to increase student aid. We can't just keep subsidizing skyrocketing tuition; we'll run out of money. States also need to do their part, by making higher education a higher priority in their budgets. And colleges and universities have to do their part by working to keep costs down.

Recently, I spoke with a group of college presidents who've done just that. Some schools redesign courses to help students finish more quickly. Some use better technology. The point is, it's possible. So let me put colleges and universities on notice: If you can't stop tuition from going up, the funding you get from taxpayers will go down. Higher education can't be a luxury—it is an economic imperative that every family in America should be able to afford.

Let's also remember that hundreds of thousands of talented, hard-working students in this country face another challenge: the fact that they aren't yet American citizens. Many were brought here as small children, are American through and through, yet they live every day with the threat of deportation. Others came more recently, to study business and science and engineering, but as soon as they get their degree, we send them home to invent new products and create new jobs somewhere else.

That doesn't make sense.

I believe as strongly as ever that we should take on illegal immigration. That's why my administration has put more boots on the border than ever before. That's why there are fewer illegal crossings than when I took office. The opponents of action are out of excuses. We should be working on comprehensive immigration reform right now.

But if election-year politics keeps Congress from acting on a comprehensive plan, let's at least agree to stop expelling responsible young people who want to staff our labs, start new businesses, defend this country. Send me a law that gives them the chance to earn their citizenship. I will sign it right away.

You see, an economy built to last is one where we encourage the talent and ingenuity of every person in this country. That means women should earn equal pay for equal work. It means we should support everyone who's willing to work, and every risk-taker and entrepreneur who aspires to become the next Steve Jobs.

After all, innovation is what America has always been about. Most new jobs are created in start-ups and small businesses. So let's pass an agenda that helps them succeed. Tear down regulations that prevent aspiring entrepreneurs from getting the financing to grow. Expand tax relief to small businesses that are raising wages and creating good jobs. Both parties agree on these ideas. So put them in a bill, and get it on my desk this year.

Innovation also demands basic research. Today, the discoveries taking place in our federally financed labs and universities could lead to new treatments that kill cancer cells but leave healthy ones untouched. New lightweight vests for cops and soldiers that can stop any bullet. Don't gut these investments in our budget. Don't let other countries win the race for the future. Support the same kind of research and innovation that led to the computer chip and the Internet; to new American jobs and new American industries.

And nowhere is the promise of innovation greater than in American-made energy. Over the last three years, we've opened millions of new acres for oil and gas exploration, and tonight, I'm directing my administration to open more than 75 percent of our potential offshore oil and gas resources. Right now–right now–American oil production is the highest that it's been in eight years. That's right–eight years. Not only that–last year, we relied less on foreign oil than in any of the past 16 years.

But with only 2 percent of the world's oil reserves, oil isn't enough. This country needs an all-out, all-of-the-above strategy that develops every available source of American energy. A strategy that's cleaner, cheaper, and full of new jobs.

We have a supply of natural gas that can last America nearly 100 years. And my administration will take every possible action to safely develop this energy. Experts believe this will support more than 600,000 jobs by the end of the decade. And I'm requiring all companies that drill for gas on public lands to disclose the chemicals they use. Because America will develop this resource without putting the health and safety of our citizens at risk.

The development of natural gas will create jobs and power trucks and factories that are cleaner and cheaper, proving that we don't have to choose between our environment and our economy. And by the way, it was public research dollars, over the course of 30 years, that helped develop the technologies to extract all this natural gas out of shale rock— reminding us that government support is critical in helping businesses get new energy ideas off the ground.

Now, what's true for natural gas is just as true for clean energy. In three years, our partnership with the private sector has already positioned America to be the world's leading manufacturer of high-tech batteries. Because of federal investments, renewable energy use has nearly doubled, and thousands of Americans have jobs because of it.

When Bryan Ritterby was laid off from his job making furniture, he said he worried that at 55, no one would give him a second chance. But he found work at Energetx, a wind turbine manufacturer in Michigan. Before the recession, the factory only made luxury yachts. Today, it's hiring workers like Bryan, who said, "I'm proud to be working in the industry of the future."

Our experience with shale gas, our experience with natural gas, shows us that the payoffs on these public investments don't always come right away. Some technologies don't pan out; some companies fail. But I will not walk away from the promise of clean energy. I will not walk away from workers like Bryan. I will not cede the wind or solar or battery industry to China or Germany because we refuse to make the same commitment here.

We've subsidized oil companies for a century. That's long enough. It's time to end the taxpayer giveaways to an industry that rarely has been more profitable, and double-down on a clean energy industry that never has been more promising. Pass clean energy tax credits. Create these jobs.

We can also spur energy innovation with new incentives. The differences in this chamber may be too deep right now to pass a comprehensive plan to fight climate change. But there's no reason why Congress shouldn't at least set a clean energy standard that creates a market for innovation. So far, you haven't acted. Well, tonight, I will. I'm directing my administration to allow the development of clean energy on enough public land to power 3 million homes. And I'm proud to announce that the Department of Defense, working with us, the world's largest consumer of energy, will make one of the largest commitments to clean energy in history—with the Navy purchasing enough capacity to power a quarter of a million homes a year.

Of course, the easiest way to save money is to waste less energy. So here's a proposal: Help manufacturers eliminate energy waste in their factories and give businesses incentives to upgrade their buildings. Their energy bills will be $100 billion lower over the next decade, and America will have less pollution, more manufacturing, more jobs for construction workers who need them. Send me a bill that creates these jobs.

Building this new energy future should be just one part of a broader agenda to repair America's infrastructure. So much of America needs to be rebuilt. We've got crumbling roads and bridges; a power grid that wastes too much energy; an incomplete high-speed broadband network that prevents a small business owner in rural America from selling her products all over the world.

During the Great Depression, America built the Hoover Dam and the Golden Gate Bridge. After World War II, we connected our states with a system of highways. Democratic and Republican administrations invested in great projects that benefited everybody, from the workers who built them to the businesses that still use them today.

In the next few weeks, I will sign an executive order clearing away the red tape that slows down too many construction projects. But you need to fund these projects. Take the money we're no longer spending at war, use half of it to pay down our debt, and use the rest to do some nation-building right here at home.

There's never been a better time to build, especially since the construction industry was one of the hardest hit when the housing bubble burst. Of course, construction workers weren't the only ones who were hurt. So were millions of innocent Americans who've seen their home values decline. And while government can't fix the problem on its own, responsible homeowners shouldn't have to sit and wait for the housing market to hit bottom to get some relief.

And that's why I'm sending this Congress a plan that gives every responsible homeowner the chance to save about $3,000 a year on their mortgage, by refinancing at historically low rates. No more red tape. No more runaround from the banks. A small fee on the largest financial institutions will ensure that it won't add to the deficit and will give those banks that were rescued by taxpayers a chance to repay a deficit of trust.

Let's never forget: Millions of Americans who work hard and play by the rules every day deserve a government and a financial system that do the same. It's time to apply the same rules from top to bottom. No bailouts, no handouts, and no copouts. An America built to last insists on responsibility from everybody.

We've all paid the price for lenders who sold mortgages to people who couldn't afford them, and buyers who knew they couldn't afford them. That's why we need smart regulations to prevent irresponsible behavior. Rules to prevent financial fraud or toxic dumping or faulty medical devices–these don't destroy the free market. They make the free market work better.

There's no question that some regulations are outdated, unnecessary, or too costly. In fact, I've approved fewer regulations in the first three years of my presidency than my Republican predecessor did in his. I've ordered every federal agency to eliminate rules that don't make sense. We've already announced over 500 reforms, and just a fraction of them will save business and citizens more than $10 billion over the next five years. We got rid of one rule from 40 years ago that could have forced some dairy farmers to spend $10,000 a year proving that they could contain a spill—because milk was somehow classified as an oil. With a rule like that, I guess it was worth crying over spilled milk.

Now, I'm confident a farmer can contain a milk spill without a federal agency looking over his shoulder. Absolutely. But I will not back down from making sure an oil company can contain the kind of oil spill we saw in the Gulf two years ago. I will not back down from protecting our kids from mercury poisoning, or making sure that our food is safe and our water is clean. I will not go back to the days when health insurance companies had unchecked power to cancel your policy, deny your coverage, or charge women differently than men.

And I will not go back to the days when Wall Street was allowed to play by its own set of rules. The new rules we passed restore what should be any financial system's core purpose: Getting funding to entrepreneurs with the best ideas, and getting loans to responsible families who want to buy a home, or start a business, or send their kids to college.

So if you are a big bank or financial institution, you're no longer allowed to make risky bets with your customers' deposits. You're required to write out a "living will" that details exactly how you'll pay the bills if you fail—because the rest of us are not bailing you out ever again. And if you're a mortgage lender or a payday lender or a credit card company, the days of signing people up for products they can't afford with confusing forms and deceptive practices–those days are over. Today, American consumers finally have a watchdog in Richard Cordray with one job: To look out for them.

We'll also establish a Financial Crimes Unit of highly trained investigators to crack down on large-scale fraud and protect people's investments. Some financial firms violate major anti-fraud laws because there's no real penalty for being a repeat offender. That's bad for consumers, and it's bad for the vast majority of bankers and financial service professionals who do the right thing. So pass legislation that makes the penalties for fraud count.

And tonight, I'm asking my Attorney General to create a special unit of federal prosecutors and leading state attorney general to expand our investigations into the abusive lending and packaging of risky mortgages that led to the housing crisis. This new unit will hold accountable those who broke the law, speed assistance to homeowners, and help turn the page on an era of recklessness that hurt so many Americans.

Now, a return to the American values of fair play and shared responsibility will help protect our people and our economy. But it should also guide us as we look to pay down our debt and invest in our future.

Right now, our most immediate priority is stopping a tax hike on 160 million working Americans while the recovery is still fragile. People cannot afford losing $40 out of each paycheck this year. There are plenty of ways to get this done. So let's agree right here, right now: No side issues. No drama. Pass the payroll tax cut without delay. Let's get it done.

When it comes to the deficit, we've already agreed to more than $2 trillion in cuts and savings. But we need to do more, and that means making choices. Right now, we're poised to spend nearly $1 trillion more on what was supposed to be a temporary tax break for the wealthiest 2 percent of Americans. Right now, because of loopholes and shelters in the tax code, a quarter of all millionaires pay lower tax rates than millions of middle-class households. Right now, Warren Buffett pays a lower tax rate than his secretary.

Do we want to keep these tax cuts for the wealthiest Americans? Or do we want to keep our investments in everything else—like education and medical research; a strong military and care for our veterans? Because if we're serious about paying down our debt, we can't do both.

The American people know what the right choice is. So do I. As I told the Speaker this summer, I'm prepared to make more reforms that rein in the long-term costs of Medicare and Medicaid, and strengthen Social Security, so long as those programs remain a guarantee of security for seniors.

But in return, we need to change our tax code so that people like me, and an awful lot of members of Congress, pay our fair share of taxes.

Tax reform should follow the Buffett Rule. If you make more than $1 million a year, you should not pay less than 30 percent in taxes. And my Republican friend Tom Coburn is right: Washington should stop subsidizing millionaires. In fact, if you're earning a million dollars a year, you shouldn't get special tax subsidies or deductions. On the other hand, if you make under $250,000 a year, like 98 percent of American families, your taxes shouldn't go up. You're the ones struggling with rising costs and stagnant wages. You're the ones who need relief.

Now, you can call this class warfare all you want. But asking a billionaire to pay at least as much as his secretary in taxes? Most Americans would call that common sense.

We don't begrudge financial success in this country. We admire it. When Americans talk about folks like me paying my fair share of taxes, it's not because they envy the rich. It's because they understand that when I get a tax break I don't need and the country can't afford, it either adds to the deficit, or somebody else has to make up the difference–like a senior on a fixed income, or a student trying to get through school, or a family trying to make ends meet. That's not right. Americans know that's not right. They know that this generation's success is only possible because past generations felt a responsibility to each other, and to the future of their country, and they know our way of life will only endure if we feel that same sense of shared responsibility. That's how we'll reduce our deficit. That's an America built to last.

Now, I recognize that people watching tonight have differing views about taxes and debt, energy and health care. But no matter what party they belong to, I bet most Americans are thinking the same thing right about now: Nothing will get done in Washington this year, or next year, or maybe even the year after that, because Washington is broken.

Can you blame them for feeling a little cynical?

The greatest blow to our confidence in our economy last year didn't come from events beyond our control. It came from a debate in Washington over whether the United States would pay its bills or not. Who benefited from that fiasco?

I've talked tonight about the deficit of trust between Main Street and Wall Street. But the divide between this city and the rest of the country is at least as bad–and it seems to get worse every year.

Some of this has to do with the corrosive influence of money in politics. So together, let's take some steps to fix that. Send me a bill that bans insider trading by members of Congress; I will sign it tomorrow. Let's limit any elected official from owning stocks in industries they impact. Let's make sure people who bundle campaign contributions for Congress can't lobby Congress, and vice versa—an idea that has bipartisan support, at least outside of Washington.

Some of what's broken has to do with the way Congress does its business these days. A simple majority is no longer enough to get anything—even routine business—passed through the Senate. Neither party has been blameless in these tactics. Now both parties should put an end to it. For starters, I ask the Senate to pass a simple rule that all judicial and public service nominations receive a simple up or down vote within 90 days.

The executive branch also needs to change. Too often, it's inefficient, outdated and remote. That's why I've asked this Congress to grant me the authority to consolidate the federal bureaucracy, so that our government is leaner, quicker, and more responsive to the needs of the American people.

Finally, none of this can happen unless we also lower the temperature in this town. We need to end the notion that the two parties must be locked in a perpetual campaign of mutual destruction; that politics is about clinging to rigid ideologies instead of building consensus around common-sense ideas.

I'm a Democrat. But I believe what Republican Abraham Lincoln believed: That government should do for people only what they cannot do better by themselves, and no more. That's why my education reform offers more competition, and more control for schools and states. That's why we're getting rid of regulations that don't work. That's why our health care law relies on a reformed private market, not a government program.

On the other hand, even my Republican friends who complain the most about government spending have supported federally financed roads, and clean energy projects, and federal offices for the folks back home.

The point is, we should all want a smarter, more effective government. And while we may not be able to bridge our biggest philosophical differences this year, we can make real progress. With or without this Congress, I will keep taking actions that help the economy grow. But I can do a whole lot more with your help. Because when we act together, there's nothing the United States of America can't achieve. That's the lesson we've learned from our actions abroad over the last few years.

Ending the Iraq war has allowed us to strike decisive blows against our enemies. From Pakistan to Yemen, the al Qaeda operatives who remain are scrambling, knowing that they can't escape the reach of the United States of America.

From this position of strength, we've begun to wind down the war in Afghanistan. Ten thousand of our troops have come home.

Twenty-three thousand more will leave by the end of this summer. This transition to Afghan lead will continue, and we will build an enduring partnership with Afghanistan, so that it is never again a source of attacks against America.

As the tide of war recedes, a wave of change has washed across the Middle East and North Africa, from Tunis to Cairo; from Sana'a to Tripoli. A year ago, Qaddafi was one of the world's longest-serving dictators—a murderer with American blood on his hands. Today, he is gone. And in Syria, I have no doubt that the Assad regime will soon discover that the forces of change cannot be reversed, and that human dignity cannot be denied.

How this incredible transformation will end remains uncertain. But we have a huge stake in the outcome. And while it's ultimately up to the people of the region to decide their fate, we will advocate for those values that have served our own country so well. We will stand against violence and intimidation. We will stand for the rights and dignity of all human beings—men and women; Christians, Muslims and Jews. We will support policies that lead to strong and stable democracies and open markets, because tyranny is no match for liberty.

And we will safeguard America's own security against those who threaten our citizens, our friends, and our interests. Look at Iran. Through the power of our diplomacy, a world that was once divided about how to deal with Iran's nuclear program now stands as one. The regime is more isolated than ever before; its leaders are faced with crippling sanctions, and as long as they shirk their responsibilities, this pressure will not relent.

Let there be no doubt: America is determined to prevent Iran from getting a nuclear weapon, and I will take no options off the table to achieve that goal.

But a peaceful resolution of this issue is still possible, and far better, and if Iran changes course and meets its obligations, it can rejoin the community of nations.

The renewal of American leadership can be felt across the globe. Our oldest alliances in Europe and Asia are stronger than ever. Our ties to the Americas are deeper. Our ironclad commitment—and I mean ironclad–to Israel's security has meant the closest military cooperation between our two countries in history.

We've made it clear that America is a Pacific power, and a new beginning in Burma has lit a new hope. From the coalitions we've built to secure nuclear materials, to the missions we've led against hunger and disease; from the blows we've dealt to our enemies, to the enduring power of our moral example, America is back.

Anyone who tells you otherwise, anyone who tells you that America is in decline or that our influence has waned, doesn't know what they're talking about.

That's not the message we get from leaders around the world who are eager to work with us. That's not how people feel from Tokyo to Berlin, from Cape Town to Rio, where opinions of America are higher than they've been in years. Yes, the world is changing. No, we can't control every event. But America remains the one indispensable nation in world affairs—and as long as I'm President, I intend to keep it that way.

That's why, working with our military leaders, I've proposed a new defense strategy that ensures we maintain the finest military in the world, while saving nearly half a trillion dollars in our budget. To stay one step ahead of our adversaries, I've already sent this Congress legislation that will secure our country from the growing dangers of cyber-threats.

Above all, our freedom endures because of the men and women in uniform who defend it. As they come home, we must serve them as well as they've served us. That includes giving them the care and the benefits they have earned—which is why we've increased annual VA spending every year I've been President. And it means enlisting our veterans in the work of rebuilding our nation.

With the bipartisan support of this Congress, we're providing new tax credits to companies that hire vets. Michelle and Jill Biden have worked with American businesses to secure a pledge of 135,000 jobs for veterans and their families. And tonight, I'm proposing a Veterans Jobs Corps that will help our communities hire veterans as cops and firefighters, so that America is as strong as those who defend her.

Which brings me back to where I began. Those of us who've been sent here to serve can learn a thing or two from the service of our troops. When you put on that uniform, it doesn't matter if you're black or white;

Asian, Latino, Native American; conservative, liberal; rich, poor; gay, straight. When you're marching into battle, you look out for the person next to you, or the mission fails. When you're in the thick of the fight, you rise or fall as one unit, serving one nation, leaving no one behind.

One of my proudest possessions is the flag that the SEAL Team took with them on the mission to get bin Laden. On it are each of their names. Some may be Democrats. Some may be Republicans. But that doesn't matter. Just like it didn't matter that day in the Situation Room, when I sat next to Bob Gates–a man who was George Bush's defense secretary–and Hillary Clinton–a woman who ran against me for president.

All that mattered that day was the mission. No one thought about politics. No one thought about themselves. One of the young men involved in the raid later told me that he didn't deserve credit for the mission. It only succeeded, he said, because every single member of that unit did their job–the pilot who landed the helicopter that spun out of control; the translator who kept others from entering the compound; the troops who separated the women and children from the fight; the SEALs who charged up the stairs. More than that, the mission only succeeded because every member of that unit trusted each other—because you can't charge up those stairs, into darkness and danger, unless you know that there's somebody behind you, watching your back.

So it is with America. Each time I look at that flag, I'm reminded that our destiny is stitched together like those 50 stars and those 13 stripes. No one built this country on their own. This nation is great because we built it together. This nation is great because we worked as a team. This nation is great because we get each other's backs. And if we hold fast to that truth, in this moment of trial, there is no challenge too great; no mission too hard. As long as we are joined in common purpose, as long as we maintain our common resolve, our journey moves forward, and our future is hopeful, and the state of our Union will always be strong.

Thank you, God bless you, and God bless the United States of America.

Barack Obama's Biographical Sketch

Barack Obama's
Biographical Sketch

Barack Obama was born to a white American mother, Ann Dunham, and a black Kenyan father, Barack Obama, Sr., who were both young college students at the University of Hawaii. When his father left for Harvard, she and Barack stayed behind, and his father ultimately returned alone to Kenya, where he worked as a government economist. Barack's mother remarried an Indonesian oil manager and moved to Jakarta when Barack was six. He later recounted Indonesia as simultaneously lush and a harrowing exposure to tropical poverty. Later, he returned to Hawaii, where he was brought up largely by his grandparents. The family lived in a small apartment—his grandfather was a furniture salesman and an unsuccessful insurance agent and his grandmother worked in a bank—but Barack managed to get into Punahou School, Hawaii's top prep academy. His father wrote to him regularly. Though he traveled around the world on official business for Kenya, he visited his son only once, when Barack was ten.

Obama attended Columbia University, but found New York's racial tension inescapable. He became a community organizer for a small Chicago church-based group for three years, helping poor South Side residents cope with a wave of plant closings. He then attended Harvard Law School, and in 1990 became the first African-American President of the Harvard Law Review. He turned down a prestigious judicial clerkship, choosing instead to practice civil-rights law back in Chicago, representing victims of housing and employment discrimination and working on voting-rights legislation. He also began teaching at the University of Chicago Law School. Eventually he ran as a Democrat for the state senate seat from his district, which included both Hyde Park and some of the poorest ghettos on the South Side, and won.

In 2004 Obama was elected to the U.S. Senate as a Democrat, representing Illinois, and gained national attention by giving a rousing and well-received keynote speech at the Democratic National Convention in Boston. In 2008 he ran for president as a democrat and won. He is set to become the 44th president of the United States and the first African-American ever elected to that position.

The Accomplishments of

Barack Obama During his Presidency

The Accomplishments of President Obama

During the term of his Presidency, Barack Obama has accrued a long list of accomplishments and successes in the economic arena, in dealing with climate change and the environment, in the areas of education and humanitarianism, and in foreign relations and military affairs, among many others. The following is a list of some specific accomplishments of President Obama dated from his first days in office in 2009 to recent days in 2012.

Banking and Financial Industry:

- In the wake of the financial and banking industry's collapse in 2008, he established the National Commission on Fiscal Responsibility,
- signed into law the Dodd-Frank Wall Street Reform and Consumer Protection Act, which is the biggest financial reform law since the Great Depression,
- signed the Pension Relief Act of 2010,
- increased transparency in the industry by demanding that derivatives be traded transparently through a clearing house,
- established the Bureau of Consumer-Financial Protection,
- signed into law the Credit Card Accountability, Responsibility and Disclosure Act, and
- established a credit card bill of rights.

Public Education and College Education:

- Created the Race to the Top Fund ($4.35 billion) to reward States that created comprehensive education reform plans,

- enacted the Children's Health Insurance Program Reauthorization Act of 2009,
- provided funding for high-speed, broadband Internet access to K-12 schools,
- provided $77 billion for reforms to strengthen Elementary and Secondary education,
- put together a $26 billion state aid package that saved 160,000 teachers' jobs in 2010,
- for college students, he enacted the largest reform of student aid in 40 years,
- signed into law the Health Care and Education Affordability Reconciliation Act of 2010, and
- expanded Pell grants for low-income students.

Economy:

- Signed into law The American Recovery and Reinvestment Act of 2009: a $789 billion economic stimulus plan, and
- approved a US auto industry rescue plan to save the auto industry from collapse.
- As a result of President Obama's actions, the economy grew 5.9% in the 4th quarter, manufacturing grew by most since 2004, and GDP (Gross Domestic Product) was up 3.2% in the 1st quarter.

Taxes:

- Approved $60 billion in spending and tax incentives for renewable and clean energy,
- approved small business tax credits for the cost of health insurance for employees starting on January 1, 2010,
- raised income tax rates for the highest earners from 35% to 39.6% as of January 1, 2010,
- raised capital gains tax for the highest earners from 15% to 20% as of January 1, 2010, and
- closed offshore tax safe havens and tax credit loopholes.
- As a result of his efforts, tax bills hit their lowest levels since 1950.

Environment:

- Established an Energy Partnership for the Americas,
- more than doubled federal spending on clean fuels,
- approved $60 billion in spending and tax incentives for renewable and clean energy,
- invested in all types of alternative energies,
- increased funding for the Environmental Protection Agency (EPA), and
- invested $2 billion in solar power which hailed new jobs.
- As a result, President Obama is the first president to create a detailed vision for a clean energy economy, and wind power growth is up 39% due to government stimulus.

Health Care Reform:

- Signed into law the Patient Protection and Affordable Care Act// Health Care and Education Reconciliation Act of 2010,
- required large employers to contribute to national health plan,
- required insurance companies to cover pre-existing conditions,
- required health plans to disclose how much of the premium goes to patient care,
- provided minimum essential health care coverage by Veteran's Affairs,
- prevented children from being refused health insurance coverage, and
- increased regulation of drug manufacturers.

Humanitarianism:

- Supported the repeal of Don't Ask, Don't Tell (DADT),
- supported the Civil Rights History Project of 2009,
- enacted the Lilly Ledbetter Fair Pay Act, which instituted equal pay for women,
- amended The Matthew Shepard and James Byrd Jr. Hate Crimes Prevention Act to include gender, sexual orientation, and disability, and
- established the White House Council on Women and Girls.
- President Obama was awarded the Nobel Peace Prize in 2009.

Immigration:

- Requested $600 million in emergency funding for Border Security, and
- deported higher numbers of illegal immigrants than his predecessor.

Military Affairs:

- Recommitted the U.S. policy of "no torture" and insisted on full compliance with the Geneva Conventions,
- increased pay and benefits for military personnel,
- in Afghanistan, he changed the failing status quo military command and reformed infrastructure, diplomacy and good government practices,
- in Iraq, he ended the combat mission,
- closed secret detention facilities in Eastern Europe and other places around the world,
- restarted nuclear proliferation talks, which again reinforced the nuclear inspection infrastructure and protocols,
- and he has caught more Taliban leaders in one month than President Bush did in six years.

Foreign Affairs:

- Re-established the United States' standing in the world,
- as a result of his efforts, 47 nations rose to President Obama's challenge at the US nuke summit and agreed to four years of non-proliferation efforts,
- encouraged the G-20 summit to produce $1 trillion deal to combat the global financial crisis,
- signed the Iran Sanctions Act into law,
- helped stabilize Somalia, and
- signed nuclear arms agreements with Australia and Russia.

Trivia on Barack Obama

Trivia on Barack Obama

- His first name comes from the word that means "blessed by God" in Arabic.

- In the Kenyan town where his father was born, the long-brewed "Senator" brand of beer has been nicknamed "Obama."

- He was a U.S. Senator representing Illinois from 3 January 2005 until November of 2008 when he resigned after winning the presidential election.

- He won a Grammy for Best Spoken Word for the CD version of his autobiography "Dreams From My Father" (2006).

- He lived in Hyde Park in Chicago prior to relocating to Washington, D.C.

- On "Late Night with Conan O'Brien" (1993), he revealed that President George W. Bush nicknamed him "Bama" and "Rock".

- The movie he saw on his first date with Michelle Obama was Do the Right Thing (1989).

- He is related to Park Overall.

- He has two daughters, Malia Obama (born in 1998) and Sasha Obama (born in 2001).

- He was the candidate for the Democratic nomination in the 2008 US presidential election.

- Several celebrities including; Halle Berry, George Clooney, Sheryl Crow, Bob Dylan, Topher Grace, Macy Gray, Bruce Springsteen, Oprah Winfrey, Tom Hanks, Scarlett Johansson,

Hayden Panettiere, Zachary Quinto, Eddie Murphy and John Cleese support his 2008 presidential campaign. Robert De Niro gave his endorsement at the same rally where Barack was endorsed by Caroline and Ted Kennedy.

- He enjoys playing basketball and poker.

- At his wife's suggestion, he quit smoking before his campaign when the Democratic nomination began.

- His paternal relatives still live in Kenya.

- He confessed to teenage drug experiences in his memoirs "Dreams from My Father".

- One of his ancestors was Mareen Duvall, also an ancestor of actor Robert Duvall.

- He shares his surname with a small city in western Japan, which means "small shore" in Japanese.

- He plays basketball.

- He was born to Barack Hussein Obama, Sr. (1936-1982) and Ann Dunham (1942-1995), married from 1960 to 1965.

- He was named one of Time magazine's "100 most influential people in the world" list in 2005 and 2007.

- He was chosen as one of "10 People Who Would Change the World" by New Statesman magazine (2005).

- He won his second Grammy Award for Best Spoken Word Album for "The Audacity of Hope" (2008).

- On June 3, 2008 he won the Montana primary election giving him enough delegates to become the first Black American presidential candidate to win a major political party's presumptive nomination for the office of President of the United States.

- He is a die-hard Chicago White Sox fan.

- More than 215,000 people attended his speech in Berlin on 24 July 2008.

- He has one half-sister, Maya, born to his mother and stepfather in 1970.

- He has his look-alike puppet in the French show "Guignols de l'info, Les" (1988).

- He is very distantly related to Lon Chaney.

- Barack Obama's grandmother, Madelyn Payne Dunham died Sunday November 2, 2008 in the early evening in Honolulu from cancer. She was 86.

- He is the first African-American man to be elected President of the United States (November 2008).

- When elected President, he won the battleground states of Florida, Virginia and Colorado—all of which had voted Republican in 2004.

- He is the first American president to be born in Hawaii.

- He was the 27th lawyer to be elected American president.

- He was elected to be the 44th president of the Unites States of America on 4 November, 2008.

- As a child growing up in Hawaii, his classmates knew him as Barry.

- His presidential campaign slogan was, "Yes we can".

"Obama Talks Back: Global Lessons

A Dialogue with America's Young Leaders"

Index of Selected Letters

"Obama Talks Back: Global Lessons—
A Dialogue with America's Young Leaders"
Index of Selected Letters

Tammy	Northwestern H.S.	Detroit, MI
Olivia	John J. Pershing Elementary	Dallas, TX
Naeez		
Rufino	Central City Value H.S.	Los Angeles, CA
Chris	New Orleans College Prep.	New Orleans, LA
Leah	Western Branch Middle School	Washington, D.C.
Rachel		New Orleans, LA
Mick	Boston Latin School	Boston, MA
Michaela	Boston Latin School	Boston, MA
Shiloh	John J. Pershing H.S.	Detroit, MI
Jabar	William J. Beckham Academy	Detroit, MI
Temi	Boston Latin School	Boston, MA
Vincent	Roosevelt SHS	Washington, D.C.
Vera	Bates Academy	Detroit, MI
Beverly	Boston Latin School	Boston, MA
Antrice	William J. Beckham Academy	Detroit, MI
Mitchell	Carmel Middle School	Charlotte, NC
Blake	Western Branch Middle School	Chesapeake, VA
Raymond	Boston Latin School	Boston, MA
Emily	Hill Campus of Arts and Science	Denver, CO
Thu	Boston Latin School	Boston, MA

"Obama Talks Back: Global Lessons

A Dialogue with America's Young Leaders"

Index of Best Letters

"Obama Talks Back: Global Lessons — A Dialogue with America's Young Leaders" Index of Best Letters

Beasley	Kelly	Davidson IB Middle School	Huntersville, NC
Beasley	Shemar	Paul Roberson Academy	Detroit, MI
Beaty	Darius L	Rutherford Academy	Detroit, MI
Beckman	Julian	Open Magnet Charter School	Los Angeles, CA
Beegle	Josephine	University Park Elementary	Denver, CO
Benion	Charles	William J. Beckham Academy	Detroit, MI
Bentley	LaTaijia	Loving Elementary School	Detroit, MI
Berardi	Emily	Boston Latin School	Boston, MA
Betancourt	Laura	Northeast Academy Charter School	Denver, CO
Blade	Dallas W.	Belle Chasse Charter School	Belle Chasse, LA
Blake	Duwaine	Ballou S.T.A.Y. High School	Washington, D.C.
Bledsoe	Annie	Loving Elementary School	Detroit, MI
Blohm	Kaitlin	Western Branch Middle School	Chesapeake, VA
Bolelho	Andrew	Davidson IB Middle School	Huntsville, NC
Bolivar	Jennifer	Boston Latin School	Boston, MA
Boone	Harrison	Boston Latin School	Boston, MA
Bostick	Miracle	Jefferson Middle School	Washington, D.C.
Bozzge	Taylor	Belle Chasse Academy	Belle Chasse, LA
Brandon	Jordan	Western Branch Middle School	Chesapeake, VA
Brehane	Solomon	Boston Latin School	Boston, MA
Briones	Armando	W.H. Gaston Middle School	Dallas, TX
Bristow	Tyonna	Charles Hart Middle School	Washington, DC
Brodney	Zac	Open Magnet Charter School	Los Angeles, CA
Bronson	Maeve	Open Magnet Charter	Los Angeles, CA
Brooks	Daja	Clara W. Rutherford Elementary	Detroit, MI
Brooks II	Wesley	Bates Academy	Detroit, MI
Brown	Drew	Northeast Academy Charter School	Denver, CO
Brown	Antonia	Beckham Academy	Detroit, MI
Brown	Johnnie	Western Branch Middle School	Chesapeake, VA
Brown	Ashley	New Orleans College Prep Charter School	New Orleans, LA
Brown	Tremele	Cooley High School	Detroit, MI
Brown III	Paul	New Orleans Prep Charter School	New Orleans, LA
Browne	Hannah	Boston Latin School	Boston, MA
Brunce	Chloe	Hill Campus of Arts and Science	Denver, CO
Buchanan	Brendan	Rutherford Academy	Detroit, MI
Bufkin	Jabar	Beckham Academy	Detroit, MI
Bullock	Deron	Cooley High School	Detroit, MI
Bullock	Lori Ann	Western Branch Middle School	Chesapeake, VA
Burkhall	Meredith	Merrill Middle School	Des Moines, IA
Burns	Emily	Boston Latin School	Boston, MA
Butts	Dheryl	Esperanza Hope Medrano Elementary School	Dallas, TX
Byes	Rachelle	Belle Chasse Academy	Belle Chasse, LA
Byrd	Anastasia	Northeast Academy Charter School	Denver, CO

Byrne	William	Boston Latin School	Boston, MA
Cabrera	Isabel	Northeast Academy Charter School	Denver, CO
Cabrera	Karen	Medrano Elementary	Dallas, TX
Cahill	Victoria	Boston Latin School	Boston, MA
Camarillo	Alexis	W.H. Gaston Middle School	Dallas, TX
Cameron	Nick	Boston Latin School	Boston, MA
Campbell	Katherine	Cora Kelly School	Alexandria, VA
Campbell Jr.	Samuel	Ballou S.T.A.Y High School	Washington, DC
Canales	Luis	W.H. Gaston Middle School	Dallas, TX
Carrillo	Julian	W.H. Gaston Middle School	Dallas, TX
Carroll	Diamond	W.H. Gaston Middle School	Dallas, TX
Carter	Danielle	Beckham Academy	Detroit, MI
Carter	Nicole	Northeast Academy Charter School	Denver, CO
Carthens	Rikia	Browne Educational Campus	Washington, D.C.
Caruso	Marcella	Boston Latin School	Boston, MA
Castro	Miguel E.	John J. Pershing Elementary School	Dallas, TX
Chace	Queniqua	W.H. Gaston Middle School	Dallas, TX
Chambliss	Deyonna	Beckham Academy	Detroit, MI
Channell	Dylan	Open Magnet Charter School	Los Angeles, CA
Chase	Tia R.	Ballou S.T.A.Y High School	Washington, DC
Chavez	Marco	Esperanza Merdrano Elementary	Dallas, TX
Chavez	Cesar	W.H. Gaston Middle School	Dallas, TX
Chavez	Jennifer	W.H. Gaston Middle School	Dallas, TX
Cheatom	Stephon	Clara W. Rutherford Elementary	Detroit, MI
Cheng	Elisa	Boston Latin School	Boston, MA
Chertov	Mick	Boston Latin School	Boston, MA
Chin	Melissa	Boston Latin School	Boston, MA
Chung	Olivia	Boston Latin School	Boston, MA
Chung	Evan	Boston Latin School	Boston, MA
Chung	Hye-Won	Western Branch Middle School	Chesapeake, VA
Chung	Evan	Boston Latin School	Boston, MA
Church	Trayvon	Thurgood Marshall ES	Chesapeake, VA
Cielak	Daniel	Open Magnet Charter	Los Angeles, CA
Clark	Shonia	Beckham Academy	Detroit, MI
Clay	Sammie	Kettering High School	Detroit, MI
Clifford	Jonathan	Boston Latin School	Boston, MA
Coats	Chanel	K. B White Elementary	Detroit, MI
Coe	Aaliyah	Clara W. Rutherford Academy	Detroit, MI
Colleran	Julia Grace	Boston Latin School	Boston, MA
Collins	Emily	Boston Latin School	Boston, MA
Concannon	Kristin	Boston Latin School	Boston, MA
Cook	Keith	Ballou S.T.A.Y High School	Washington, DC
Cooper	Wayne	North Carolina Public Schools	Charlotte, NC

Cooper	Derrick	Jefferson Middle School	Washington, DC
Cooper	Harold M.	New Orleans College Prep Charter	New Orleans, LA
Cooper	Damon'yan	New Orleans College Prep Charter	New Orleans, LA
Coplin	Randy	Boston Latin School	Boston, MA
Corvman	Khalid	The Downtown School	Des Moines, IA
Costello	Kerri Lynn	Boston Latin School	Boston, MA
Couch	Kelsey	Western Branch Middle School	Chesapeake, VA
Cousins	Liam	Cora Kelly School	Alexandria, VA
Cox	Hailey	Coonley School	Chicago, IL
Crall	Paige	The Downtown School	Des Moines, IA
Crawley	LaDamien	Belle Chasse Academy	Belle Chasse, LA
Crawley	Jasmin	Clara W. Rutherford	Detroit, MI
Crayton	James	Medrano Elementary	Dallas, TX
Creighton	Emer	Boston Latin School	Boston, MA
Crutchfield	Cleanae'	New Orleans College Prep Charter School	New Orleans, LA
Cummings	Stephanie	W.H. Gaston Middle School	Dallas, TX
Cummings	Devin	Belle Chasse Academy	Belle Chasse, LA
Cunningham	Mariah	Loving Elementary School	Detroit, MI
Curcuru	Melissa	Boston Latin School	Boston, MA
Cyres	Keith	New Orleans College Charter Prep	New Orleans, LA
D'Arcy	Declan	Boston Latin School	Boston, MA
Dales	Kevin	Cleveland Intermediate High School	Detroit, MI
Damico	Sebastian	Boston Latin School	Boston, MA
Dang	Lily	Medrano Elementary	Dallas, TX
Davenport	Lenita	Pershing High School	Detroit, MI
Davis	Aaron	Belle Chasse Academy	Belle Chasse, LA
Davis	Antoniette	Cooley High School	Detroit, MI
Davis	Gage	Western Branch Middle School	Chesapeake, VA
Defoe	Bianca	MacArthur K-8 University Academy	Southfield, MI
Delcid	Jennifer	Esperanza Merdrano Elementary	Dallas, TX
Denson	DaShawn	Beckham Academy	Detroit, MI
Desmond	Jocelyn	Davidson I.B Middle School	Huntersville, NC
Diaz	Adriana	W.H. Gaston Middle School	Dallas, TX
DiChiara	Caitlin	Western Branch Middle School	Chesapeake, VA
Dicus	Jeremy	K. B White Elementary	Detroit, MI
Diliberto	Patrick	Open Magnet Charter School	Los Angeles, CA
Dingess II	Jeffery	Harms Elementary School	Detroit, MI
Diop	Michelle	Boston Latin School	Boston, MA
Diop	Gabe	Boston Latin School	Boston, MA
Dodson	Taylor	New Ellenton Middle School	New Ellenton, SC
Dominguez	Carmen	John J. Pershing Elementary School	Dallas, TX
Donald	Armani	Clara W. Rutherford Academy	Detroit, MI
Donnelly	Jordan	Pasteur Elementary	Detroit, MI

Dooley	Adam	William J. Beckham Academy	Detroit, MI
Douglas	Trevon	K.B. White Elementary School	Detroit, MI
Dover	Josh	Belle Chasse Academy	Belle Chasse, LA
Dowdell	Precious	Clara W. Rutherford Elementary	Detroit, MI
Duffy	Katherine J.	Hill Campus of Art and Science	Denver, CO
Dunbar	Orion	Western Branch Middle School	Chesapeake, VA
Duquette	Brianna	Belle Chasse Academy	Belle Chasse, LA
Echeverria	Wendy	Esperanza Merdrano Elementary	Dallas, TX
Eisler	Henry Hall	Anthony Hyde Elementary School	Washington, DC
El-Amin	Danielle	MacArthur K-8 University Academy	Southfield, MI
Elloie	Raven	New Orleans College Prep Charter	New Orleans, LA
Emerson	Maic	Bates Academy	Detroit, MI
English	Necole	Belle Chasse Academy	Belle Chasse, VA
Enoex	Deante	Beckham Academy	Detroit, MI
Erenmark	Emma	Open Magnet Charter School	Los Angeles, CA
Ervin	Octavia	Northeast Academy Charter School	Denver, CO
Esola	Allesondra	Highline Academy	Denver, CO
Espinoza	Lorena	W.H. Gaston Middle School	Dallas, TX
Esteve	Jessica	Boston Latin School	Boston, MA
Estrada	Pablo	Esperanza Hope Medrano Elementary School	Dallas, TX
Evans	Nicholas	Western Branch Middle School	Chesapeake, VA
Falls	Lillyanna	Open Magnet Charter School	Los Angeles, CA
Feagin	Maya	Cass Technical High School	Detroit, MI
Fergus	Ravyn	Beckham Academy	Detroit, MI
Fernandez	Silas	Open Magnet Charter School	Los Angeles, CA
Flemons	Dion	Northwestern High School	Detroit, MI
Flores	Aranza	John J. Pershing Elementary	Dallas, TX
Flores	Franceli	Esperanza Hope Medrano Elementary	Dallas, TX
Floyd	Alesha	Cass Technical High School	Detroit, MI
Foreman	Jarell	New Orleans College Prep Charter School	New Orleans, LA
Fowler	Jalessa	Loving Elementary School	Detroit, MI
Fraser	Adriane	Western Branch Middle School	Chesapeake, VA
Freeman	Janesse	Belle Chasse Academy	Belle Chasse, LA
Freeman	Khali	New Orleans College Prep Charter School	New Orleans, LA
Friedman	Emily	Hill Campus Arts & Science	Denver, CO
Fu	Richard	Boston Latin School	Boston, MA
Gallagher	Emily	Boston Latin School	Boston, MA
Galofaro	Christopher	Boston Latin School	Boston, MA
Gammage	Destiny	Beckham Academy	Detroit, MI
Garcia	Laura	Harms Elementary School	Detroit, MI
Garcia	Maria	W.H. Gaston Middle School	Dallas, TX
Gardner	Timothy	Cleveland Intermediate High School	Detroit, MI
Garey	Monique	Jefferson Middle School	Washington, DC

Garner	Kayla	William J. Beckham Academy	Detroit, MI
Garoy	Esmeralda	W.H. Gaston Middle School	Dallas, TX
Gay	Jasmine	W.H. Gaston Middle School	Dallas, TX
Gaymon	Jazmine	Northwestern High School	Detroit, MI
Gerik	Morgan	Carmel Middle School	Charlotte, NC
Giles	Datrice	Loving Elementary School	Detroit, MI
Gills	Cierra	John J. Pershing Elementary School	Dallas, TX
Gipson	Dionte	Mesquite Independent School District	Mesquite, TX
Gipson	John	Beckham Academy	Detroit, MI
Givertz	Hannah	Boston Latin School	Boston, MA
Goldhabler	Arielle	Boston Latin School	Boston, MA
Gomee	Edwin	W.H. Gaston Middle School	Dallas, TX
Gonzalez	Ray	W.H. Gaston Middle School	Dallas, TX
Gore	Madison	Highline Academy	Denver, CO
Gorny	Anya	Boston Latin School	Boston, MA
Graves	Jeremy	Belle Chasse Academy	Belle Chasse, LA
Grays	Jasmine	Northeast Academy Charter School	Denver, CO
Green	Spencer C	Carmel Middle School	Charlotte, NC
Greenway	Maia	Mac Arthur K-8 University	Detroit, MI
Gregg	Christopher B	Western Branch Middle School	Chesapeake, VA
Gregory	Nina Simone	The Downtown School	Des Monies, IA
Gresham	Morgan	Western Branch Middle School	Chesapeake, VA
Grier	Frances	Beckham Academy	Detroit, MI
Griffith	John	Western Branch Middle School	Chesapeake, VA
Gu	Yu	Boston Latin School	Boston, MA
Guerra	Maria	W.H. Gaston Middle School	Dallas, TX
Guerrero	Patricia	W.H. Gaston Middle School	Dallas, TX
Gustafson	Colby	Cora Kelly School	Alexandria, VA
Gutierrez	Chassen	Open Magnet Charter School	Los Angeles, CA
Gutierrez	Juana	Esperanza Hope Medrano Elementary School	Dallas, TX
Guzman	Selena	John C. Coonley School	Chicago, IL
H	Daniela	Esperanza Hope Medrano Elementary	Dallas, TX
Hall	Cody	Western Branch Middle School	Chesapeake, VA
Hammond	Briana	Open Magnet Charter School	Los Angeles, CA
Han	Samuel	Boston Latin School	Boston, MA
Hannigan	Sarah	Boston Latin School	Boston, MA
Hanson	Janine	Boston Latin School	Boston, MA
Hardeman	Corine	Swift School	Chicago, IL
Harden	LaDawn	William J. Beckham Academy	Detroit, MI
Hardnett	Taylor	Beckham Academy	Detroit, MI
Harris	Juwan	Loving Elementary School	Detroit, MI
Harris	Nelqwita	K.B. White Elementary	Detroit, MI
Harrison	Maria	Belle Chasse Academy	Belle Chasse, LA

Harsch-Moore	NaDajahnae	Beckham Academy	Detroit, MI
Harvell	Jaylin	IB Davidson Middle School	Huntsville, NC
Haslam	Devin	Western Branch Middle School	Chesapeake, VA
Hassen	Saleh	Cora School for Science, Math, & Tech.	Alexandria, VA
Hatchett	Dominique	Cleveland Intermediate High School	Detroit, MI
Hayes	Michael	Carmel Middle School	Charlotte, NC
Haynes	Alexa	Belle Chasse Academy	Belle Chasse, LA
Heard	Bobbie	Western Branch Middle School	Chesapeake, VA
Heath	Chierra	W.H. Gaston Middle School	Dallas, TX
Heath	Arvonte'	Beckham Academy	Detroit, MI
Hemingway	Yamon	Beckham Academy	Detroit, MI
Henry	Daja	Belle Chasse Academy	Belle Chasse, LA
Hernandez	Yulissa	W.H. Gaston Middle School	Dallas, TX
Hernandez	Tyler	Belle Chasse Academy	Belle Chasse, LA
Herring	Leonus	Beckham Academy	Detroit, MI
Hill	Ravyn	Spain Elementary School	Highland Park, MI
Hill	Jayla	Loving Elementary	Detroit, MI
Hill	Zakariyah	The Downtown School	Des Monies, IA
Hilliard	Christina	Medrano Elementary	Dallas, TX
Hinton	Yasmine	Kettering High School	Detroit, MI
HlaAung	Diana	Anthony Hyde Elementary School	Washington, DC
Hogan	Trystan	Boston Latin School	Boston, MA
Holberton	Mikaela	Western Branch Middle School	Chesapeake, VA
Holden	Cole	Open Magnet Charter	Los Angeles, CA
Holguin	Samuel	Open Magnet Charter School	Los, Angeles, CA
Holloway	Yvonna	Loving Elementary	Detroit, MI
Holloway	Donisha	Clara W. Rutherford Academy	Detroit, MI
Holmes	Darrell	New Orleans College Prep Charter School	New Orleans, LA
Holmes	Akira	New Orleans College Prep Charter School	New Orleans, LA
Holmes	Darrell	New Orleans College Prep Charter School	New Orleans, LA
Hooper	Angel	William J. Beckham Academy	Detroit, MI
Hossain	Abidh	K.B. White Elementary	Detroit, MI
Houlihan	Danielle	Boston Latin School	Boston, MA
Howard	Mychal	Breithaupt Career and Technical Center	Detroit, MI
Howell	Gareyth	Boston Latin School	Boston, MA
Hudson	Justin	Bates Academy	Detroit, MI
Hughes	Ced	Boston Latin School	Boston, MA
Hughes	Cedreaouna	Beckham Academy	Detroit, MI
Hummius	Sophia Von	Boston Latin School	Boston, MA
Hunter	Tiffany	William J. Beckham Academy	Detroit, MI
Husted	Katerine	W.H. Gaston Middle School	Dallas, TX
Huynh	Bryan	Boston Latin School	Boston, MA
Irvin	Amber	Beckham Academy	Detroit, MI

Irvine	William	Hill Campus of Arts & Science	Denver, CO
Ismail	Nadine	John J. Pershing Elementary	Dallas, TX
Ivie	Thaddeus	Open Magnet Charter	Los Angeles, CA
Jing	Lydia	Boston Latin School	Boston, MA
Johns	Paul	W.H. Gaston Middle School	Dallas, TX
Johnson	Delon	Beckham Academy	Detroit, MI
Johnson	Rishonda	Beckham Academy	Detroit, MI
Jones	Markeith	Loving Elementary	Detroit, MI
Jones III	Louis M.	Beckham Academy	Detroit, MI
Juarez	Alejandro	Open Magnet Charter	Los Angeles, CA
Juarez	Ramon	W.H. Gaston Middle School	Dallas, TX
Jurado	Angelica	Harms Elementary School	Detroit, MI
Kang	Joshua	Open Magnet Charter School	Los Angeles, CA
Kapuza	Malcolm	Boston Latin School	Boston, MA
Kazi	Sharzil	Boston Latin School	Boston, MA
Kelly	Ryan	Boston Latin School	Boston, MA
Kelly	Marie	Boston Latin School	Boston, MA
Kennedy	Trayaon	Beckham Academy	Detroit, MI
Kennelly	Allie	Boston Latin School	Boston, MA
Kerman	Hannah	John J. Pershing Elementary	Dallas, TX
Kim	Hae	Western Branch Middle School	Chesapeake, VA
Kindall	Michael	Beckham Academy	Detroit, MI
Koester	Ivy	Open Magnet Charter School	Los Angeles, CA
Korn	Justin	Open Magnet Charter School	Los Angeles, CA
Ku	Andrea	Hill Campus of Arts and Sciences	Denver, CO
Kyle	Miranda	William J. Beckham Academy	Detroit, MI
Lacey	Dalentino	Beckham Academy	Detroit, MI
Lake	Ikeya	Loving Elementary	Detroit, MI
Lambert	Majorie	Western Branch Middle School	Chesapeake, VA
Lancaster	William	Open Magnet Charter School	Los Angeles, CA
Landaverde	Saul	John J. Pershing Elementary School	Dallas, TX
Langford	Lauryn	Belle Chasse Academy	Belle Chasse, LA
Lard	Isidro	Medrano Elementary	Dallas, TX
Lauer	Nicholas	Western Branch Middle School	Chesapeake, VA
Lea	Asa	Ballou S.T.A.Y High School	Washington, DC
Leal	Alfredo	John J. Pershing Elementary School	Dallas, TX
Lee	Dayshana	Beckham Academy	Detroit, MI
Lee	Kyla	Beckham Academy	Detroit, MI
Lee	Brandon	Open Magnet Charter School	Los Angeles, CA
Lee	Hyun	Open Magnet Charter School	Los Angeles, CA
LeGrand	Laney	Western branch Middle School	Chesapeake, VA
Lein	Christina	Kettering High School	Detroit, MI
Lengugen	Amy	John C. Coonley School	Chicago, IL

LeSasier	Daniel A.	Open Magnet Charter School	Los Angeles, CA
Lewis	Kayla	Belle Chasse Academy	Belle Chasse, LA
Lewis	D'marcus	MacArthur K-8 University Academy	Southfield, MI
Lewis	Lottie	K.B. White Elementary	Detroit, MI
Li	Raymond	Boston Latin School	Boston, MA
Ll	Yukun	Boston Latin School	Boston, MA
Liang	Weigang	Boston Latin School	Boston, MA
Lily	Devin	Ingham Academy	Lansing, MI
Lindsey	Darryl	Beckham Academy	Detroit, MI
Link	Carter	Merrill Middle School	Des Monies, IA
Loan	Leisa	Boston Latin School	Boston, MA
Logan	Coty D.	Cleveland Intermediate High School	Detroit, MI
Lona	José	Gertz-Ressler High School	Los Angeles, CA
Long	Mariah	Beckham Academy	Detroit, MI
Lopez	Eric	W.H. Gaston Middle School	Dallas, TX
Lopez	Jocelyn	Northeast Academy Charter School	Denver, CO
Lotton	Zakiya	Cora Kelly School	Alexandria, VA
Loudato	Joel	Belle Chasse Academy	Belle Chasse, LA
Louis	Alexis	W.H. Gaston Middle School	Dallas, TX
Love	Mickayla	The Downtown School	Des Monies, IA
Lunstord	Dalvonate	Beckham Academy	Detroit, MI
Ly	Michelle	Boston Latin School	Boston, MA
Lylecyrus	Djuka	Open Magnet Charter School	Los Angeles, CA
Machado	Luisa	W.H. Gaston Middle School	Dallas, TX
Magallon	Natasha	Cora Kelly School	Alexandria, VA
Mahoney	Brian	Boston Latin School	Boston, MA
Mahony	Elizabeth A.	Boston Latin School	Boston, MA
Maibodi	Cameron	Carmel Middle School	Charlotte, NC
Malagon	Diana	Medrano Elementary	Dallas, TX
Maldonado	Melanie	W.H. Gaston Middle School	Dallas, TX
Maldonado	Wilber	Theodore Roosevelt S.H.S.	Washington, DC
Malone	Sarah	Boston Latin School	Boston, MA
Mankins	Abby	The Downtown School	Des Moines, IA
Manley	Kenyel	Thurgood Marshall Elementary	Chesapeake, VA
Mann	Grace	Boston Latin School	Boston, MA
Mannel	Ryan	Cora Kelly School	Alexandria, VA
Mapp	Keara	Pasteur Elementary	Detroit, MI
Mar	Jennifer	Boston Latin School	Boston, MA
Marbina	Steve	Swift School	Chicago, IL
Marshall	Kimberly	Western Branch Middle School	Chesapeake, VA
Martinez	Iridian	John J. Pershing Elementary School	Dallas, TX
Martinez	Eddy L.	Gaston Middle School	Dallas, TX
Martinez	Armando	Esperanza Merdrano Elementary	Dallas, TX

Martinez	Sofia	Cora Kelly Elementary	Alexandria, VA
Martinez	Kayla	John J. Pershing Elementary School	Dallas, TX
Mary	Christiana	Open Magnet Charter	Los Angeles, CA
Massey	Kevin	Northeast Academy Charter School	Denver, CO
Mata	Michelle	W.H. Gaston Middle School	Dallas, TX
Matais	Katherine	Western Branch Middle School	Chesapeake, VA
Mathiew	Kemremteam	New Orleans College Prep Charter School	New Orleans, LA
Matthews	Keivon	Cooley High School	Detroit, MI
Maurice	Dahsaan	New Orleans College Prep Charter School	New Orleans, LA
Mayo	Ashley	Benjamin Banneker Academic High	Washington, DC
McAfee	Leif	Northeast Academy Charter School	Denver, CO
McCloud	Angelia	Thurgood Marshall ES	Chesapeake, VA
McDonnell	Christina	Boston Latin School	Boston, MA
McGarth	Bridget	Boston Latin School	Boston, MA
McGregory	Danielle	Merrill Middle School	Des Moines, IW
McKennie	Kyle	W.H. Gaston Middle School	Dallas, TX
McKinnon	Maria	Cass Technical High School	Detroit, MI
McLarnon	Finnian	Open Magnet Charter School	Los Angeles, CA
McMahon	William	Boston Latin School	Boston, MA
McNamara	Elena	Open Magnet Charter	Los Angeles, CA
McRunels	Shaiqua	Kettering High School	Detroit, MI
McTavish	Saoirse	Boston Latin School	Boston, MA
Meechan	Joyce	Boston Latin School	Boston, MA
Meehan	Joyce	Boston Latin School	Boston, MA
Melo	Michael	Boston Latin School	Boston, MA
Mendez	Nelson	W,H. Gaston Middle School	Dallas, TX
Mendez	Yanneth	Medrano Elementary	Dallas, TX
Mendoza	Amy	W.H. Gaston Middle School	Dallas, TX
Meneses	Michael	W.H. Gaston Middle School	Dallas, TX
Mengistu	Elone	Open Magnet Charter	Los Angeles, CA
Mengsteab	Jonathan	John J. Pershing Elementary School	Dallas, TX
Mercedes	Jose	Roosevelt Senior School	Washington, DC
Mercer	Jahari R.	M.V. Leckie Elementary School	Washington, DC
Mercer	Jahari	M.V. Leckie Elementary School	Washington, D.C
Miah	Fhahema	K.B. White Elementary	Detroit, MI
Michael	Jeramey	Belle Chasse Academy	Belle Chasse, LA
Michael	Paxton	Medrano Elementary	Dallas, TX
Millar	Margaret	Open Magnet Charter School	Los Angeles, CA
Mills	Zoe	Anthony Hyde Elementary School	Washington, DC
Mitchell	Nayira	Loving Elementary	Detroit, MI
Molina	Cesa	Medrano Elementary	Dallas, TX
Molina	Cesa	Medrano Elementary	Dallas, TX
Moore	Dionno	John J. Pershing High School	Detroit, MI

Moore	Sierra H.	Northeast Academy Charter	Denver, CO
Morales	Maria	Esperanza Hope Medrano Elementary	Dallas, TX
Morrell	Austin	Belle Chasse Academy	Belle Chasse, LA
Morris	Isabel	Hill Campus of Art & Science	Denver, CO
Morris	Jordan	W.H. Gaston Middle School	Dallas, TX
Morrison	David	Beckham Academy	Detroit, MI
Mosley	Anthony	K. B White Elementary	Detroit, MI
Mosley	Jada	Beckham Academy	Detroit, MI
Moyes	Lucy	Boston Latin School	Boston, MA
Mulry	Paige	Boston Latin School	Boston, MA
Munoz	Victor	W.H. Gaston Middle School	Dallas, TX
Munoz	Carlos	John J. Pershing Elementary School	Dallas, TX
Murphy	Mae	The Downtown School	Des Monies, IA
Murphy	Mikayla	Davidson IB Middle School	Huntersville, NC
Murphy	Meagan	Open Magnet Charter School	Los, Angeles, CA
Myes	Amanda	Western Branch Middle School	Chesapeake, VA
Najera	Jennifer	W.H. Gaston Middle School	Dallas, TX
Napier	Amy	Western Branch Middle School	Chesapeake, VA
Navorrette	Ishmeal	W.H. Gaston Middle School	Dallas, TX
Negel	Olivia	Highline Academy	Denver, CO
Newman	Jerwana	New Orleans College Prep Charter School	New Orleans, LA
Nguyen	Beverly	Boston Latin School	Boston, MA
Nguyen	Kevin	Medrano Elementary	Dallas, TX
Nieto	Arlene	Gertz-Ressler High School	Los Angeles, CA
Nieto	Katrisha	Belle Chasse Academy	Belle Chasse, LA
Nkanta	Justina	Merrill Middle School	Des Monies, IA
Norwood	Kamaria	William J. Beckham Academy	Detroit, MI
Nunez	David	Swift School	Chicago, IL
Okubo	Kenshin	Boston Latin School	Boston, MA
Osorio	Vanessa	Esperanza Merdrano Elementary	Dallas, TX
Ovhz	Valery	Carmel Middle School	Charlotte, NC
Owens	Jada	Belle Chasse Academy	Belle Chasse, LA
Owens	Tanazia	Davidson IB Middle School	Charlotte, NC
Palacios	Gracie	Dallas Public Schools	Dallas, TX
Palafox	Juan	Carmel Middle School	Charlotte, NC
Palmer	Hawain	Gaston Middle School	Dallas, TX
Panduranga	Pooja	Hill Campus of Arts & Science	Denver, CO
Paolucci	Alessandra	Boston Latin School	Boston, MA
Park	Rebecca	Boston Public Schools	Jamaica Plan, MA
Parker	Candace	Western Branch Middle School	Chesapeake, VA
Parks	Yvonne	Carmel Middle School	Charlotte, NC
Patterson	Bria	Beckham Academy	Detroit, MI
Patterson	Caleb	Cleveland Intermediate High School	Detroit, MI

Patterson	Darren	Theodore Roosevelt S.H.S.	Washington, DC
Paz	Alma	Esperanza Hope Medrano Elementary School	Dallas, TX
Paz	Kailen	W.H. Gaston Middle School	Dallas, TX
Pedesciaux	Adam	Belle Chasse Academy	Belle Chasse, LA
Perales	Alondra	Esperanza Hope Medrano Elementary School	Dallas, TX
Perez	Aura	Harms Elementary	Detroit, MI
Perez	Mia	John C. Coonley School	Chicago, IL
Peterson	Joshua	Rutherford Academy	Detroit, MI
Pham	Nyan	W.H. Gaston Middle School	Dallas, TX
Phillips	Romello	W.H. Gaston Middle School	Dallas, TX
Pierce	Tiffany	Harms Elementary	Detroit, MI
Pinales	Kayla	W.H. Gaston Middle School	Dallas, TX
Pineda	Nancy	Medrano Elementary	Dallas, TX
Pink	Mahlia	John J. Pershing Elementary School	Dallas, TX
Plummer	Paris	Beckham Academy	Detroit, MI
Poon	Raymond	Boston Latin School	Boston, MA
Pope	Mark	Jefferson Middle School	Washington, DC
Posada	Brandon	W.H. Gaston Middle School	Dallas, TX
Posey	Osjha	Beckham Academy	Detroit, MI
Powell	Kennitra	New Orleans College Prep Charter School	New Orleans, LA
Powell	Kennitra	New Orleans College Prep Charter School	New Orleans, LA
Pravimchandra	David	John C. Coonley School	Chicago, IL
Prescott	Jonathan	Open Magnet Charter School	Los Angeles, CA
Primas	Charles	Bates Academy	Detroit, MI
Prime	Renato	Boston Latin School	Boston, MA
Principi	Michelle	Boston Latin School	Boston, MA
Puente	Esperanza	Medrano Elementary	Dallas, TX
Purcell	Rontrez	Kelly Miller Middle School	Washington, DC
Quintana	Daniela	John J. Pershing Elementary School	Dallas, TX
Ragland-Fuller	Aryies	Loving Elementary School	Detroit, MI
Ramirez	Gerardo	Gaston Middle School	Dallas, TX
Ramirez	Pamela	W.H. Gaston Middle School	Dallas, TX
Ramirez	Angel	Esperanza Merdrano Elementary	Dallas, TX
Ramirez	Jazmin	W.H. Gaston Middle School	Dallas, TX
Ramirez	Lluvia	John J. Pershing Elementary School	Dallas, TX
Ramon	Aylin	Esperanza Merdrano Elementary	Dallas, TX
Ramos	Jesse	W.H. Gaston Middle School	Dallas, TX
Rawlings	Vincent	Roosevelt Senior School	Washington, DC
Rayas	Guadalupe	John J. Pershing Elementary School	Dallas, TX
Reyes	Ivan	W.H. Gaston Middle School	Dallas, TX
Reyes	William	W.H. Gaston Middle School	Dallas, TX
Reynolds	Gus	Hill Campus of Arts and Science	Denver, CO
Richardson	Angel	John J. Pershing High School	Detroit, MI

Richardson	Nicholas	Western Branch Middle School	Chesapeake, VA
Rico	Rocio	W.H. Gaston Middle School	Dallas, TX
Rimson	Iyona	Loving Elementary	Detroit, MI
Rivas	Helen	John J. Pershing Elementary School	Dallas, TX
Roarty	Niamh	Boston Latin School	Boston, MA
Roberts	Camden	Western Branch Middle School	Detroit, MI
Roberts	Shannon	Breithaupt Career and Technical Center	Detroit, MI
Robertson	Lanessa	William J. Beckham Academy	Detroit, MI
Robinson	Brena	Beckham Academy	Detroit, MI
Robinson	Christion	Beckham Academy	Detroit, MI
Rodriguez	Dianna	Breithaupt Career & Tech	Detroit, MI
Rodriguez	Maria Hulisa	W.H. Gaston Middle School	Dallas, TX
Rodriguez	Christopher	W.H. Gaston Middle School	Dallas, TX
Rodriguez	Tiffany	Port of Los Angeles High School	San Pedro, CA
Rodriguez	Zulema	Northeast Academy Charter School	Denver, CO
Rodrisuez	Anna	W.H. Gaston Middle School	Dallas, TX
Rosas	Angie	John J. Pershing Elementary	Dallas, TX
Ross	Anthony	Balou S.T.A.Y. High School	Washington, D.C.
Rowe	Tiara	Jefferson Middle School	Washington, D.C.
Roy	Emma	Hill Campus of Arts and Science	Denver, CO
Royster	Daniel	Western Branch Middle School	Chesapeake, VA
Ruff	Antoine	Beckham Academy	Detroit, MI
Rufus	Candance	Northeast Academy Charter School	Denver, CO
Ruiz	Vanga	Esperanza Merdrano Elementary	Dallas, TX
Ruiz	Anissa	W.H. Gaston Middle School	Dallas, TX
Russo	Lia	Harms Elementary School	Detroit, MI
Ryan	Roberson	Davidson IB Middle School	Charlotte, NC
Sahagian	Micheal	Boston Latin School	Boston, MA
Salma	Syeda	K. B White Elementary	Detroit, MI
Sam	Tenisha	Ballou S.T.A.Y High School	Washington, DC
Sams	Tenisha	Balou S.T.A.Y High School	Washington, DC
Sanchez	Rufino	Central City Value High School	Los Angeles, CA
Sanders	Taileona	Northeast Academy Charter School	Denver, CO
Sanders	Brionna	New Orleans College Prep Charter School	New Orleans, LA
Sandler	Daisha	Paul Robeson Academy School	Detroit, MI
SanJuan	Prisciliano	Esperanza Merdrano Elementary	Dallas, TX
Sankey	Shannon	Highline Academy	Denver, CO
Santos	Joanna	W.H. Gaston Middle School	Dallas, TX
Santoscoy	Nathan	Cass Technical High School	Detroit, MI
Santoyo	Leandra	W.H. Gaston Middle School	Dallas, TX
Schmitt	Noah	Iowa Public Schools	Des Monies, IA
Schulte	Lily	Merrill Middle School	Des Moines, IA
Searles	Dane	Western Branch Middle School	Chesapeake, VA

Seawood	Troie	Clara Oliver Elementary	Dallas, TX
Sellers	Andrea	Western Branch Middle School	Chesapeake, VA
Sentell	Kymberly	W.H. Gaston Middle School	Dallas, TX
Sergeant	Lucy	Boston Latin School	Boston, MA
Sergeant	Nick	Boston Latin School	Boston, MA
Serrano	Llesli	Esperanza Hope Medrano Elementary School	Dallas, TX
Shah	Rishi	The Downtown School	Des Moines, IA
Sharay	Robertson	Beckham Academy	Detroit, MI
Sharpe	Rashid D.	Cora Kelly Elementary	Alexandria, VA
Shaver	Ariana	K.B. White Elementary	Detroit, MI
Shaw	Dakhara	Beckham Academy	Detroit, MI
Shepherd	Ladonna	Brown Junior High School	Washington, DC
Sherrington	Olivia	John J. Pershing Elementary School	Dallas, TX
Shockley	Frederick	Beckham Academy	Detroit, MI
Shorter	Jahmeir	Beckham Academy	Detroit, MI
Shy	Jayla	Spain Elementary School	Detroit, MI
Simms	Tamera	Browne Educational Campus	Washington, D.C.
Simpson	Andres	Boston Latin School	Boston, MA
Sivertson	Grant	Western Branch Middle School	Chesapeake, VA
Skinner	Amanda	Western Branch Middle School	Chesapeake, VA
Sklar	Leah V.	Western Branch Middle School	Chesapeake, VA
Smiley	Lauren	Belle Chasse Academy	Belle Chasse, LA
Smith	Chaz	Ingham Academy	Lansing, MI
Smith	Juwuan	Beckham Academy	Detroit, MI
Smith	Katie	Denver Public Schools	Denver, CO
Smith	Sean	Boston Latin School	Boston, MA
Smith	Jacquelynn	Beckham Academy	Detroit, MI
Smith	LaKeena	Bates Academy	Detroit, MI
Smith	Lamarie	Paul Roberson Academy School	Detroit, MI
Smothers	Chrishana	Beckham Academy	Detroit, MI
Sogbesan	Nafisat	Swift School	Chicago, IL
Solis	Melissa	Medrano Elementary School	Dallas, TX
Speeks	LaTena	Rutherford Academy	Detroit, MI
Spencer	Candise	John J. Pershing High School	Detroit, MI
Steffen	Bridget	Western Branch Middle School	Chesapeake, VA
Stephens	Jane	University Park Elementary School	Denver, CO
Stormont	Matthew	Davidson IB Middle School	Charlotte, NC
Styklunas	Grace	Boston Latin School	Boston, MA
Sullivan	Molly	Boston Latin School	Boston, MA
Sun	Sophia	Boston Latin School	Boston, MA
Sutton	Renice	Ballou S.T.A.Y High School	Washington, DC
Swain	Keiarra	John J. Pershing High School	Detroit, MI
T'Asia	Stewart	Beckham Academy	Detroit, MI

Tabron	Elijah	Davis Elementary School	Washington, DC
Tan	Anson	Boston Latin School	Boston, MA
Tarrance	Treshawn	William J. Beckham Academy	Detroit, MI
Tate	Demond	New Orleans College Prep Charter School	New Orleans, LA
Tatnull	Tatiana	John J. Pershing Elementary School	Dallas, TX
Taylor	Turner	New Orleans College Prep Charter School	New Orleans, LA
Taylor	Tyiece	Beckham Academy	Detroit, MI
Terry	Celeste	New Ellington Middle School	
Theaphile III	Bickett	New Orleans College Prep	New Orleans, LA
Thomas	Jasmine M.	John J. Pershing High School	Detroit, MI
Thomas	Ameenah	Thomas M. Cooley High School	Detroit, MI
Thomas	TaeJuan	Breithaupt Career and Technical Center	Detroit, MI
Thompson	Ric-Kayla	Belle Chasse Academy	Belle Chasse, LA
Thompson	Mikayla	Bates Academy	Detroit, MI
Thornton	Dionna	K.B. White Elementary	Detroit, MI
Tidwell	Blake L.	Western Branch Middle School	Chesapeake, VA
Timko	James	Western Branch Middle School	Chesapeake, VA
Tobierre	Courtney	Boston Latin School	Boston, MA
Tolbert	Emani	Jefferson Junior High School	Washington, DC
Toler	Darrin	New Orleans College Prep Charter School	New Orleans, LA
Torres	Belinda	W.H. Gaston Middle School	Dallas, TX
Toster	Andrew	Beckham Academy	Detroit, MI
Tran	My-Ngan	Boston Latin School	Boston, MA
Trevino	Sammy	W.H. Gaston Middle School	Dallas, TX
Truong	Vinh	Boston Latin School	Boston, MA
Tucker	Shaw'd	Adelaide Davis Elementary	Washington, DC
Tuner	Destane	Bates Academy	Detroit, MI
Turner	John	Western Branch Middle School	Chesapeake, VA
Tyminski	Camila	Boston Latin School	Boston, MA
Tyus	Shiloh	John J. Pershing High School	Detroit, MI
Uddyback	Lauren	Bates Academy	Detroit, MI
Ude	Sandra	Cooley high School	Detroit, MI
Underwood	Cassy	Western Branch Middle School	Chesapeake, VA
Valadez	Topazio	W.H. Gaston Middle School	Dallas, TX
Valdez	Jacquelyn	Pola High School	Los Angeles, CA
Vandi	Aminata D.	Northland High School	Columbus, OH
Vasquez	Alexandra	W.H. Gaston Middle School	Dallas, TX
Vass	Gabriella	Northeast Academy Charter School	Denver, CO
Vaughan	Morgan	Cora Kelly School	Alexandria, VA
Vaughn	Aubrey	Northeast Academy Charter School	Denver, CO
Velasquez	Margarita	Esperanza Hope Medrano Elementary School	Dallas, TX
Velazquez	Guadalupe	John J. Pershing Elementary School	Dallas, TX
Vien	Thomas	Boston Latin School	Boston, MA

Vilarruel	Gloria	W.H. Gaston Middle School	Dallas, TX
Villegas	Javier	Esperanza Hope Medrano Elementary School	Dallas, TX
Vitagliano	Michaela	Boston Latin School	Boston, MA
Vivas	Silvana	Boston Latin School	Boston, MA
Vo	Andy	Boston Latin School	Boston, MA
Vo	Long	Carmel Middle School	Alexandria, VA
Vu	Don Nguyen	Boston Latin School	Boston, MA
Walker	Brianna	Clara W. Rutherford Academy	Detroit, MI
Walker	LaShea'	Theodore Roosevelt High School	Washington, DC
Walker	Chuckie	Breithaupt Career and Technical Center	Detroit, MI
Walker	Talia	Northeast Academy Charter School	Denver, CO
Wallace	John	Western Branch Middle School	Chesapeake, VA
Wallace	Jeremiah	New Orleans College Prep Charter School	New Orleans, LA
Walter	Chris	New Orleans College Prep	Chesapeake, VA
Walters	Arjanae	Adelaide Davis Elementary School	Washington, D.C.
Ward	Darian	Bates Academy	Detroit, MI
Ward	Owen	Boston Latin School	Boston, MA
Ward	Owen	Boston Latin School	Boston, MA
Washington	Shaneika	Beckham Academy	Detroit, MI
Watson	Drew	Open Magnet Charter	Los Angeles, CA
Watson	Donavon	Beckham Academy	Detroit, MI
Watson	Justin	Jefferson Middle School	Washington, D.C.
Weathers	Michael	Bates Academy	Detroit, MI
Wei	Frank	Boston Latin School	Boston, MA
Weise	Nicolas	Open Magnet Charter	Los Angeles, CA
Weitzner	Leah	Hill Campus of Arts and Science	Denver, CO
West	Maurice	Ballou S.T.A.YHigh School	Washington, DC
West	Mercedes	Loving Elementary	Detroit, MI
Westberry	Akela	William J. Beckham Academy	Detroit, MI
Wheeler	Tiara	William J. Beckham Academy	Detroit, MI
White	Charna	New Orleans Prep Charter School	New Orleans, LA
White	Kerria	Beckham Academy	Detroit, MI
White	Jason	Balou S.T.A.Y High School	Washington, DC
White	Ka'Bria	William J. Beckham Academy	Detroit, MI
Whitehurst	Travis	Thurgood Marshall	Chesapeake, VA
Whitelock	Daniel	Boston Latin School	Boston, MA
Whitson	Miranda	New Ellenton Middle School	New Ellenton, SC
Wiley	Quiana	K.B. White Elementary	Detroit, MI
Wilks	Vincent	Loving Elementary	Detroit, MI
Williams	Deon	Cleveland Intermediate High School	Detroit, MI
Williams	Maurice	Adelaide Davis Elementary	Washington, DC
Williams	Sky	Belle Chasse Academy	Belle Chasse, LA
Williams	Bria	Belle Chasse Academy	Belle Chasse, LA

Williams	Fredqueshia	New Orleans College Prep Charter	New Orleans, LA
Williams	Jamar	W.H. Gaston Middle School	Dallas, TX
Williams	Jaron	Beckham Academy	Detroit, MI
Williams	Michael	Mac Arthur K-8 University Academy	Southfield, MI
Williams	Chase	Open Magnet Charter School	Los Angeles, CA
Williams	Jada	K.B. White Elementary	Detroit, MI
Williams	Justin	John J. Pershing Elementary	Dallas, TX
Wilson	Xavier	Belle Chasse Academy	Belle Chasse, LA
Wilson	De Shawn	Cleveland Intermediate High School	Detroit, MI
Wilson	James Parker	Boston Latin School	Boston, MA
Wilson	Jazmyne C.	Beckham Academy	Detroit, MI
Wilson	Rashad	Beckham Academy	Detroit, MI
Woerner	Brian	Northland High School	Columbus, OH
Woldeghiorgis	Sara	Boston Latin School	Boston, MA
Wood	Jeffery	Theodore Roosevelt High School	Washington, DC
Woods	Maxwayle	Loving Elementary	Detroit, MI
Wright	Tivon	William J. Beckham Academy	Detroit, MI
Wynn	Joshua	Western Branch Middle School	Chesapeake, VA
Yarbrough	Sarah	Belle Chasse Academy	Belle Chasse, LA
Yen	Lauren	Boston Latin School	Boston, MA
Yenter	Henry	John C. Coonley School	Chicago, IL
Young	Shatonia	New Orleans College Prep Charter School	New Orleans, LA
Yu	Dazhi	Jefferson Middle School	Washington, DC
Zach	Luke	Downtown School	Des Moines, IA
Zadrazil	Juliette	Western Branch Middle School	Chesapeake, VA
Zeiler	Ella	Hill Campus of Arts and Sciences	Denver, CO
Zhao	Quianqian	Boston Latin School	Boston, MA
Zuhiri	Alejandro	W.H. Gaston Middle School	Dallas, TX
Zuluaga	Alexandra	Boston Latin School	Boston, MA
Zuniga	Keith	John J. Pershing Elementary	Dallas, TX
Zuniga	Xilonen	W.H. Gaston Middle School	Dallas, TX
Zuniga	Christian	Medrano Elementary	Dallas, TX

If you would like to submit your own letter to President Barack Obama, send your letter to:

> The Keeper of the Word Foundation
> 1201 Bagley
> Detroit MI 48226

or email your letter to:

> The Keeper of the Word Foundation
> gjrassoc@aol.com

Gregory J. Reed

Bio-Sketch

Gregory J. Reed, Esq. has been an active practitioner in the legal profession for twenty plus years. His clients are preeminent in their fields; his professional and civic contributions carry national and international significance.

Mr. Reed's fields of specialty in the legal profession include entertainment, intellectual properties, corporate, and tax laws. He is the author of sixteen books, many of which are award winners, (NAACP Image Award, American Book Award, etc.) best sellers, and used extensively throughout professional and educational communities. In 2007, Mr. Reed was instrumental in drafting the proposal to establish Detroit's

Entertainment Commission Advisory Body to promote entertainment, culture, education and provide an economic stimulus and employment base for the city on various levels. Detroit City Council, in 2009, voted unanimously for Reed to be Detroit's first commission chairman. The Commission launched the city's Walk of Fame project as a tourist destination for the city.

In 2008, Mr. Reed and his foundation, Keeper of the Word, were designated to be the guest curator with the Michigan State University Museum and the Nelson Mandela Museum in South Africa to present an exhibit in South Africa entitled, "Dear Mr. Mandela...Dear Mrs. Parks: Children's Letters, Global Lessons," the first international collaborative exhibit between America and South Africa. Reed was selected as Nelson Mandela's personal escort for the exhibit premiere.

Mr. Reed is actively involved in diverse professional organizations and civic foundations. He has served as a professor of taxation at a major university, has lectured widely at universities throughout the United States and abroad, and has appeared on major television networks, cable outlets, and radio talk shows in the United States. Reed has been presented with numerous civic and professional awards, he has been included in the BESLA Hall of Fame for distinguished entertainment lawyers, and has been honored by the city of Windsor, Ontario as an International Humanitarian.

William Alexander Haley

Bio-Sketch

William Alexander Haley, Phd., son of the late Alex Haley, Pulitzer Prize author for "Roots" and "The Autobiography of Malcolm X," both cited as the top books of the 20th century, continues his legacy. Haley is a frequent keynote speaker and panelist before educational institutions and civil organizations. Haley has three upcoming book publications: "The Omitted Chapters of Malcolm X's Autobiography," "The Pro-Racist," and "Black Legacy, Lost, Stolen or Strayed."

    Haley urges people to collect, document, and preserve their family history. Haley's message is aimed at people of all ages. He is particularly concerned that young families understand the importance of tracking their roots for the medical, psychological, and social benefits. Through strategic relationships, Haley empowers people to discover their roots. Haley partnered with McDonalds and Coca-Cola and took hundreds of people to the African continent in search of their roots. Also, Haley joined with the Latter-day Saints Family History Center in Salt Lake City to present Freeman's Bank Records. In addition, Haley joined the Pinnacle Studios to develop programs that allow independent filmmakers to tell stories that impact on the moral compass and human values that resonate in our daily lives.

Mr. Haley is the CEO of the Alex Haley Foundation and the Founder and President of the Alex Haley Center for Cultural Values, the Alex Haley Museum and the Roots Foundation. The center aids in the design and implementation of cultural competent service delivery programs for the public and private sectors. The museum is dedicated to preserving the legacy of Alex Haley and produces traveling exhibits that recently includes the works of Rosa Parks, "Mother of the Civil Rights Movement" in association with the Keeper of the Word Foundation.

Caitlin Buchanan

Bio-Sketch

Caitlin Buchanan is an intern of Gregory J. Reed in his Detroit, Michigan office. She worked as researcher, editor, and contributor for *Obama Talks Back: Global Lessons from Young People in America.*

Ms. Buchanan is a graduate of Michigan State University and has a Bachelor of Arts in International Studies. She has traveled extensively to Europe, West Africa, and parts of North America. She is currently enrolled at Wayne State University and will be attending law school in the fall of 2013 to study International Law.

Obama Talks Back: Global—A Dialogue with America's Young Leaders is her first book project as a contributor.

Bibliography

- ABC News. 2012. ABC News Network. "Michelle Obama: Let's Move Initiative." 9 February 2010. abcnews.com. 1 August 2012. http://www.abcnews.com/.

- Best Speeches of Barack Obama Through his 2009 Inauguration.

- Bio. 1996. A&E Television Networks, LLC. "Barack Obama-Biography."2012. Bio.com. 2 August 2012. http://www. biography.com/

- DemocracyNow!. Goodman, Amy. 2002. democracynow.org. 1 August 2012. http://democracynow.org/.

- Govtrack.com. 2001.NA Media. 10 July 2012. http://www. govtrack.com/.

  a. H.R. 3630: Middle Class Tax Relief and Job Creation Act of 2012

  b. H.R. 2845: Pipeline Safety, Regulatory Certainty, and Job Creation Act of 2011

- IRS. 2011. Internal Revenue Service. 10 July 2012. http://www. irs.gov/.

  a. Payroll Tax Cut 2012

- Obama, Barack. The Audacity of Hope: Thoughts on Reclaiming the American Dream. New York. Three Rivers Press. 2006.

- "Obama's Speech on Climate Change." The New York Times. 22 September 2009. www.nytimes.com. 3 July 2012. http://www.nytimes.com/.

- Open Congress. Conor Kenny. Participatory Politics Foundation. Opencongress.org. 10 July 2012. http://www.opencongress.org/.

  a. Serve America Act of 2009

- The American Presidency Project.Gerhard Peters. 1999. University of California, Santa Barbara. 3 July 2012. http://www.presidency.ucsb.edu/.

  a. Address Accepting the Presidential Nomination at the National Democratic Convention in Denver: "The American Promise." (8/28/09)

  b. Inaugural Address (1/20/09)

  c. State of the Union 2012

  d. State of the Union 2011

  e. Weekly Address (1/22/11, 2/2/11, 2/19/11, 3/26/11, 4/23/11, 5/21/11, 7/2/11, 7/16/11, 7/23/11, 9/24/11, 11/11/11, 11/22/11, 12/17/11, 1/7/12, 2/18/12, 3/10/12, 3/24/12, 4/14/12, 4/21/12, 4/28/12, 5/26/12, 6/2/12)

  f. Presidential Proclamation (1/13/12, 4/3/12, 4/9/12, 6/1/12)

  g. Executive Order (1/22/09)

  h. President's News Conference (3-6-12)

- The Atlanta-Journal Constitution. 2012. Cox Media Group. "Q: How Many Letters Does the President Receive Daily?". Smith, Steven. 30 December 2009. ajc.com. 2 August 2012. http://www.ajc.com/.

- The Los Angeles Sentinel. 2012. Brooks, Brandon. "President Obama's Favorites." 22 January 2009. lasentinal.net. 2 August 2012. http://www.lasentinel.net/

- Recovery.Gov: Track the Money. 2009. United States Government. 10 July 2012. http://www.recovery.gov/.

    a.   American Recovery and Reinvestment Act of 2009

- The Whitehouse-President Barack Obama. The White House, Washington D.C. whitehouse.gov. 28 June 2012. http://www. whitehouse.gov/.

    a.   "Obama's 1ˢᵗ Speech on Iraq" 2/27/09

    b.   "Remarks by the President on Comprehensive Immigration Reform" 5/10/11

    c.   "Obama's End of Combat Mission in Iraq Speech" 8/31/10

    d.   "Remarks by the President at the University of Maryland Townhall" 7/22/11

    e.   "Obama on Innovation and Technology" 9/16/11

    f.   "Obama's All Troops are Withdrawn from Iraq Speech" 10/21/11

    g.   "Obama at Fort Bragg" 12/21/11

    h.   "Obama Speaks at National Museum of African American History and Culture Groundbreaking" 2/22/12

    i.   "Obama on Food Security at G8 Meeting" 5/8/12

    j.   "Obama Speaks at Barnard College Commencement" 5/14/12

    k.   "Obama on Investing in Clean Energy" 5/24/12

    l.   "LGBT Pride Month Reception" 6/15/12

    m. Support for Troops Legislation 2009

    n.   American Jobs Act 2011

- Wikipedia. 2012. "Maya Soetoro-Ng." wikipedia.org. 2 August 2012. en.wikipedia.org/

- Youtube. 2005. 28 June 2012. http://youtube.com/.

    a.   "Barack Obama's Presidential Announcement" 2/10/07

    b.   "C-SPAN: Barack Obama Speech at 2004 DNC Convention" 7/27/04

c. "C-SPAN: President-Elect Barak Obama Victory Speech" 11/4/08

d. "Obama on Katrina and Racism" 9/17/05

e. "Obama's Closing Story About Racial Progress" 10/30/08

f. "Obama on Racism"-Chris Matthews-Hardball 9/19/09

g. "Obama Press Conference on Gulf Oil Spill" 5/27/10

h. "President Obama-Gay Marriage" 5/9/12

ORDER FORM

FOR THIS HISTORIC COLLECTION OF LETTERS AND RESPONSES FROM PRESIDENT BARACK OBAMA

OBAMA TALKS BACK: GLOBAL LESSONS— A DIALOGUE WITH AMERICA'S YOUNG LEADERS

(ISBN #: 978-1-937269-38-8 / 314 pages / $19.95)

Please Mail Checks or Money Orders to:
   Amber Communications Group, Inc.
   1334 East Chandler Boulevard – Suite 5-D67
   Phoenix, AZ 85048

Please send ____ copy(ies) of *Obama Talks Back: Global Lessons — A Dialogue with America's Young Leaders*

Name:_____

Address:_____

City: State: Zip:_____

Telephone: (___)_____ / (___)_____

Email:_____

I have enclosed $19.95, plus $6.00 shipping per book for a total of
$_____.
To pay by Credit Card or PayPal, call: 602-743-7211
or email Amberbk@aol.com.
For Bulk or Wholesale Rates, Call: 602-743-7211
Or email: Amberbk@aol.com

Please visit: WWW.AMBERBOOKS.COM